LAN Troubleshooting Handbook

M&T BOOKS

M&T Publishing, Inc.
Redwood City, California

LAN Troubleshooting
Handbook

Mark A. Miller

M&T BOOKS

M&T Publishing, Inc.
Redwood City, California

M&T Books
A Division of M&T Publishing, Inc.
501 Galveston Drive
Redwood City, CA 94063

© 1989 by M&T Publishing, Inc.

Printed in the United States of America
First Edition published 1989

Library of Congress Cataloging in Publication Data

Miller, Mark, 1955–
    LAN troubleshooting handbook / Mark Miller.
        p.   cm.
    ISBN 1-55851-056-7   (book/disk) $39.95
    ISBN 1-55851-054-0   (book) $29.95
    ISBN 1-55851-055-9   (disk) $20.00
    1. Local area networks (Computer networks)--Maintenance and
repair.   I. Title.
TK5105.7.M55 1989
621.39'81--dc20   89-13988
                                                              CIP

93 92 91   5   4

ARCNET is a registered trademark of Datapoint Corp. Cable Sender, Cable Tracer, and Cable Checker are registered trademarks of MicroTest, Inc. Datatracker and Micropatch are registered trademarks of Datatran Corp. DECnet is a registered trademark of DEC. Digital TDR is a registered trademark of Lanca Instruments, Inc. Ethernet is a registered trademark of Xerox. FELINE is a registered trademark of Frederick Engineering, Inc. LANalyzer is a registered trademark of Novell. NetBIOS and SNA are registered trademarks of IBM. NetWare is a registered trademark of Novell, Inc. ONEVIEW and ONEGRAPH are registered trademarks of Oneac Corp. PC-Technician is a registered trademark of Windsor Technologies, Inc. Smart Cable is a registered trademark of IQ Technologies, Inc. Sniffer is a registered trademark of Network General Corp. System Sleuth is a registered trademark of DTG, Inc.

Project Editor: David Rosenthal

How to Order
the Accompanying Disk

Collected are a number of practical programs for troubleshooting and monitoring data communications systems. Included are files that allow the user to change the baud rate of a program, display the RS-232 signals of the COM1 or COM2 ports, provide CPU information, turn a PC into a data scope or data line monitor, perform a LAN read/write performance test and CPU speed and relative performance tests, and much more.

The disk is $20, plus sales tax if you are a California resident. Order by sending a check, or credit card numbert and expiration date, to:

LAN Troubleshooting Handbook Disk
M&T Books
501 Galveston Drive
Redwood City, CA 94063

Or, you may order by calling our toll-free number between 8 A.M. and 5:00 P.M. Pacific Standard Time: 800/533-4372 (800/356-2002 in California). Ask for Item #055-9.

Contents

Illustrations

Chapter 4

Chapter 8

Preface

This book has a very fundamental thesis: how to keep your local area network alive. There are three parts to that goal. First, you must understand how the LAN *should* operate if you are to properly define when it is *not* operating. Secondly, you must have the proper hardware and software tools readily available to troubleshoot problems. Third, you must take preventative measures to keep those failures from recurring in the future.

To accomplish this goal, the book is divided into "network generic" and "network-specific" chapters. Chapters 1, 2, 3, and 4 address the generic issues of LAN Standards, Documentation, Test Equipment, and Cabling. Chapters 5, 6, 7, and 8 address specific issues associated with popular LAN architectures: ARCNET, Token Ring, Ethernet, and StarLAN, respectively. Also included in the network-specific chapters are examples of protocol analysis of Novell's NetWare, IBM's NetBIOS, DEC's DECnet, and TCP/IP. Chapter 9 concludes with a dose of preventative medicine. Each topic is relatively self-contained. Pick and choose those that are relevant to your network.

Today's technology is changing too rapidly for any one person to have intimate knowledge of all available LAN hardware and software products. As a result, I relied upon the following experts on specific networks to provide comments on the manuscript. In alphabetical order, they are: Bill Aranguren, James Baker, Ernesto Bautista, Dan Beougher, David Bolles, Linda Collins-Hedegard, Billy Cox, Charles Dillon, Michael Fischer, Rich Geasey, Mike Harrison, Kathy Hoswell, Geof Karlin, Gary Kessler, Mark Kulper, Ike Mustafa, Margaret Rimmler, Bob Ryan, Carl Shinn, Jr., Mike Willett, and Scott Zumbahlen.

Recognition is due the companies that provided LAN test equipment for evaluation. Those products are mentioned throughout the book, but principally in Chapter 3.

No consulting engineer could exist without an expert secretary. Krystal Valdez took many pages of manuscript (most of which was written on airplanes) and made it readable. Thank you, Krys, for all the hard work.

The staff at M&T Books worked very diligently (despite an earthquake!) to make this book a reality. Special thanks are due to Ellen Ablow, Brenda McLaughlin, Michelle Hudun, David Rosenthal, and Kurt Rosenthal.

Finally, I owe a great deal to my family. Holly, Nicholas, and Nathan have provided much encouragement and support. Your love makes it all worthwhile.

— *Mark A. Miller*

CHAPTER ONE

LAN Standards and the OSI Model

As a veteran of many, many computer seminars (with experience as both student and teacher), one common thread emerges: the Open Systems Interconnection (OSI) Reference Model is always present, regardless of the seminar subject, title, or duration. We can only conclude that many people consider OSI to be important! Given that as a thesis, let's take a brief look at the OSI model, and apply it to troubleshooting and maintaining local area networks (LANs) (see reference [1-1]).

1.1 A Historical Perspective

In the 1970s, computer networks were largely defined by each manufacturer to take advantage of specific mainframe features. IBM's System Network Architecture (SNA) was first published in 1974, followed in 1976 by Digital Equipment Corporation's Digital Network Architecture (DNA). Other major manufacturers soon followed and before long, Burrough's Burroughs Network Architecture (BNA), Honeywell's Distributed Systems Architecture (DSA), and others were all vying for their portion of the market. Each of these networks, however, had one principle theme: a proprietary architecture, different protocols, and a variety of interfaces. Some of these network specifications met industry standards such as EIA-232, and some remained proprietary.

From this basis emerged a variety of standards organizations, all addressing the computer network and/or communications arena from a slightly different perspective. From an international point of view, the

International Telecommunication Union (ITU), a United Nations agency, coordinates various communication standards, including radio, telephone, and computer communication. One committee of the ITU is the International Telegraph and Telephone Consultative Committee (CCITT). The State Department is the United States' representative to the CCITT, and standards such as V.32, a recommendation for dial-up, full duplex, synchronous or asynchronous communication at 9.6 KBPS over the public switched telephone network (PSTN); X.25, the interface standard to packet switched public data networks (PSPDNs); and I.431, 441, and 451 for access to an Integrated Services Digital Network (ISDN) are all results of CCITT work.

International standards on a variety of subjects are defined by the International Organization for Standardization (ISO). The American National Standards Institute (ANSI) represents the ISO in the United States. The most notable contribution of ISO in the data communication world is the OSI Reference Model.

In the area of LAN standards, the principle player has been the Institute of Electrical and Electronics Engineers (IEEE), 802 committee. We will specifically address those standards in Section 1.4.

Finally, a variety of other organizations, both private and government, address specific areas. Examples are the Electronic Industries Association (EIA), European Computer Manufacturers Association (ECMA), U.S. Department of Defense Military Standards (MIL-STD), Federal Information Processing Standards (FIPS), and common carriers such as AT&T. Appendix 1 gives the mailing addresses of the various standards organizations.

1.2   The OSI Reference Model

Given the proprietary network environment that existed during the mid-1970s, ISO undertook development of a model for computer communication protocols in 1978, and published the OSI Reference Model in 1984 (see references [1-2] and [1-3]). Figure 1-1 shows the familiar, seven-layer model. Each of the seven layers will be considered separately.

Figure 1-1
The Open Systems Interconnection (OSI)
reference model

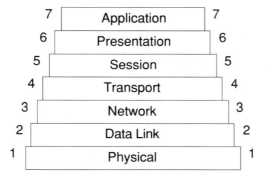

1.2.1   Physical Layer

The Physical Layer is responsible for the physical, electrical, and procedural specifications required to transmit the actual data across the physical medium or cables. In addition, connectors, pinouts, and voltage or current levels must be defined. The Physical Layer deals in units of bits.

1.2.2   Data Link Layer

The Data Link Layer must maintain a reliable connection between adjacent nodes, assuming an error-prone (or noisy) physical channel. As such, it must package the bits accordingly into frames, provide some mechanism for addressing between multiple nodes or workstations, and provide for error-free node-to-node connections. The Data Link Layer deals in units of frames.

1.2.3 │ Network Layer

The Network Layer is responsible for routing, switching, and controlling the flow of information between two hosts. For LANs, this problem may be trivial—if there is only one transmission path (that is, only one route), little Network Layer responsibility exists. For wide area networks, or internetworks, the Network Layer becomes much more important. Layers 1 through 3, taken collectively, are referred to as the communications subnetwork or subnet, a collection of switching nodes that provide a path for the data packet. The Network Layer deals in units of packets.

1.2.5 │ Transport Layer

The Transport Layer assures an error-free host-to-host connection. Said differently, the source-to-destination (or end-to-end) reliability is assured. In many cases, the communications subnet requires smaller data units than the length of the Transport Layer message. Another function of Transport is to break up the arbitrary length message into smaller units, manage their transmission through the communications subnet, and assure the correct reassembly of the message at the distant end. The Transport Layer (and higher layers) deals in units of messages.

1.2.6 │ Session Layer

The Session Layer provides for the establishment and termination of communication sessions between host processes. In addition, the Session Layer provides for management of that session, such as synchronization and translation between name and address databases.

1.2.7 Presentation Layer

The Presentation Layer provides a mechanism to translate the data format of the sender to/from the data format of the receiver. Instead of concerning itself with communication functions, Presentation provides user services, such as code conversion, data compression, or file encryption.

1.2.8 Application Layer

The Application Layer provides protocols for common end-user functions or applications. Example protocols include file transfer, electronic mail, or remote database access.

1.2.9 Wide Area Networks

Figure 1-2 extends the OSI reference Model to include a wide area network (WAN) connection between hosts. Note that Layers 1 through 3 are implemented only in the communication subnet nodes, while Layers 1 through 7 are implemented in the hosts. In addition, the Transport Layer is seen as the first end-to-end layer, assuring reliable host-to-host message delivery.

As noted earlier, considerable literature exists on the OSI model, all based upon the ISO standard (reference [1-2]) and identical CCITT standard (reference [1-3]). Excellent texts include Tanenbaum (reference [1-4]) and Stallings (reference [1-5]).

Figure 1-2
The wide area network model

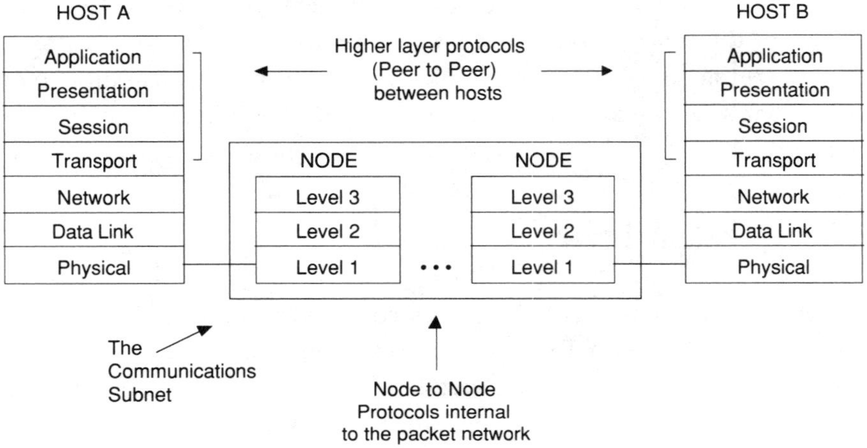

HOST A				HOST B
Application		Higher layer protocols (Peer to Peer) between hosts		Application
Presentation				Presentation
Session				Session
Transport	NODE		NODE	Transport
Network	Level 3		Level 3	Network
Data Link	Level 2		Level 2	Data Link
Physical	Level 1	•••	Level 1	Physical

The Communications Subnet

Node to Node Protocols internal to the packet network

1.3   Applying the OSI Model to LANs

Computer architecture theory can be interesting, but only to the extent that it can be realized in practice. Therefore, to add the practical element, the first question that we must address is, "Which of the layers are implemented in software and which are implemented in hardware?" Figure 1-3 shows a possible explanation. The Physical Layer (cables, connectors, etc.) is clearly hardware. The end-user layers (Transport through Application) are clearly software. The Data Link Layer could be either hardware and firmware, such as protocol handler and memory ICs, which implement software functions, or some other combination of hardware and software. The Network Layer, when required for wide area networks, will usually be implemented in software. The exception would be older electro-mechanical switching systems, which are generally being replaced with all-electronic devices within the Public Switched Telephone Network (PSTN).

The second question gets more specific—"Where on the LAN (or the LAN components) can these functions be found?" Figure 1-4 provides further elaboration. The Physical and Data Link Layers is defined by the cables, connectors, transceivers, etc., and the Network Interface Card (NIC) or network adapter, is defined in the Host or PC. The Network and Transport layers will be software drivers specific to the network, such as Novell's SPX/IPX or TCP/IP (more on these in chapters 5 and 8, respectively). The Session Layer is usually implemented by NetBIOS, the Network Basic Input/Output System (see Chapter 6). Presentation and Application Layer functions fall to the combination of DOS, the Network Operating System (NetWare, OS/2 LAN Manager, Banyan VINES, etc.) and the application protocols for file transfer, electronic mail, etc.

Figure 1-3
Implementing the OSI model in hardware and software

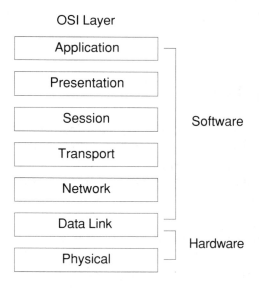

The third question might be, "Why do we care?" That answer is the easiest. Troubleshooting involves making our best (educated!) guess as to the nature of the network failure, and proceeding with failure analysis. By understanding the functional layers of the OSI model, plus the hardware/software implementations, we are in a better position to make our first troubleshooting attempt also our last.

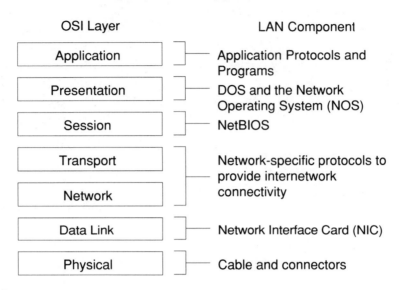

Figure 1-4
The OSI model applied to LANs

1.4 IEEE Project 802

The Institute of Electrical and Electronics Engineers (IEEE) responded to the challenges of the single-vendor, closed-architecture networking environment by starting Project 802 in February 1980, with the first standard published in 1985. The IEEE family of LAN standards is summarized below:

- 802.1 Higher Layers and Internetworking
- 802.2 Logical Link Control (LLC)
- 802.3 Carrier Sense Multiple Access with Collision Detection (CSMA/CD)
- 802.4 Token Passing Bus
- 802.5 Token Passing Ring
- 802.6 Metropolitan Area Network (MAN)
- 802.7 Broadband Technology Advisory Group
- 802.8 Optical Fiber Technology Advisory Group

- • 802.9   Voice/Data Integration on LANs
- • 802.10   Standard for Interoperable LAN Security

In our study of baseband (digital transmission without modulation) LANs, we will concentrate on 802.3 and 802.5, but we'll also consider the 802.4 architecture and the 802.2 protocol.

1.4.1 IEEE 802 vs. OSI

Figure 1-5 and 1-6 show how the IEEE LAN standards compare with the OSI Reference Model. Note that 802.1 is more global in nature, while the other standards specifically address only the Physical and Data Link Layers. As we discussed previously, Layers 1 and 2 of OSI handle the reliable transmission of data between adjacent network nodes.

Figure 1-5
Comparing the IEEE 802 model with OSI

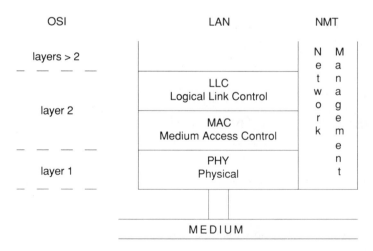

Note in Figure 1-5 that the Physical and Data Link Layer functions of OSI are implemented in three layers of IEEE 802: the Physical Layer, the Medium Access Control (MAC) Layer, and the Logical Link Control (LLC) Layer. The Physical and MAC Layers are further specified by

802.3, 802.4, 802.5, and 802.6; the LLC protocol is global across all 802 networks. The functions of each layer are summarized in the following section.

Figure 1-6
The IEEE LAN model standards

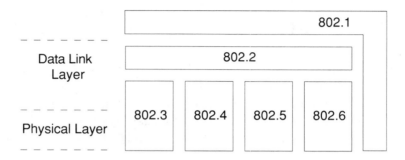

1.4.1.1   Physical (PHY) Layer

- Physical topology
- Cable and connector types
- Transmission rate(s)
- Signal encoding
- Synchronization

1.4.1.2   Medium Access Control (MAC) Layer

- Logical topology
- Access to the transmission media
- Frame format definition
- Node addressing
- Reliability or Frame Check Sequence

| 1.4.1.3 | ## Logical Link Control (LLC) Layer |

- Managing the data link communication
- Link addressing
- Definitions of Service Access Points (SAPs), a logical interface between the LLC and higher layers
- Sequencing (as required)

Since LLC is common to all of the MAC implementations, we will consider it first.

| 1.4.2 | ## IEEE 802.2—Logical Link Control |

Logical Link Control provides a common way for the upper layers to deal with any type of MAC Layer. The LLC Protocol Data Unit (PDU) is transmitted within the Data field of the MAC frames and is shown in Figure 1-7a (see reference [1-6]).

Figure 1-7a
The Logical Link Control protocol data unit

DSAP Address	SSAP Address	Control	Information
8 bits	8 bits	y bits	8*M* bits

y = 8 or 16
M = number of octets of higher layer information

The Destination and Source Service Access Point Addresses (DSAP and SSAP, respectively) are each one octet (8 bits) in length, and provide a means of identifying a higher layer protocol destined to receive the PDU. In this way, LLC provides multiplexing over the data link.

The Control Field, one or two octets in length, defines three types of PDUs: Information (I), for the transmission of user data; Supervisory (S), responsible for acknowledgements and flow control of the I frames; and Unnumbered (U), frames which control the data link and allow the exchange of unsequenced data. Figure 1-7b further details the LLC PDU Control Field.

Figure 1-7b
The LLC PDU control field bits

	1	2	3	4	5	6	7	8	9	10-16
Information Transfer command/response (I - format PDU)	0				N(S)				P/F	N(R)
Supervisory command/responses (S - format PDUs)	1	0	S	S	X	X	X	X	P/F	N(R)
Unnumbered command/response (U - format PDUs)	1	1	M	M	P/F	M	M	M		

where:

N(S)	=	Transmitter send sequence number (Bit 2 = low-order bit)
N(R)	=	Transmitter receive sequence number (Bit 10 = low-order bit)
S	=	Supervisory function bit
M	=	Modifier function bit
X	=	Reserved and set to zero
P/F	=	Poll bit - command LLC PDU transmissions Final Bit - response LLC PDU transmissions (1 = Poll/Final)

LLC, which is modeled after the ISO High-Level Data Link Control (HDLC) protocol, allows three types of operation: Type 1 (unacknowledged connectionless), a datagram service without acknowledgements, flow control, or error control; Type 2 (connection-oriented), a virtual circuit service; and Type 3 (acknowledged connectionless), a datagram service with acknowledgements.

The Information field contains the higher layer information, down-loaded to the NIC from its software driver. Any user information would reside in this field.

1.4.4 IEEE 802.3—Carrier Sense Multiple Access with Collision Detection (CSMA/CD)

The CSMA/CD standard for bus topology networks (see reference [1-7]) is modeled after the original Ethernet network standard developed by DEC, Intel, and Xerox. Figure 1-8a shows the configuration for a single segment network. Figure 1-8b shows the Media Access Control (MAC) format for bit transmission of 802.3 frames. A variety of Physical Layer options exist. The nomenclature used specifies the transmission rate in MBPS, baseband or broadband signaling, and the length of a segment in hundreds of meters. These options include:

- Type 10BASE5: 10 MBPS transmission, baseband signaling, 500 meters per coax segment
- Type 10BASE2: 10 MBPS transmission, baseband signaling, 185 meters per thin (RG-58A/U) coax segment
- Type 10BASE-T: 10 MBPS transmission over twisted pairs
- Type 1BASE5: 1 MBPS transmission, baseband signaling, 500 meters per twisted pair segment
- Type 10BROAD36: 10 MBPS broadband transmission, 3600 meters per coax segment
- Type 10BASE-F: 10 MBPS transmission over fiber optic segments

Further details on IEEE 802.3 will be given in chapters 7 and 8.

Figure 1-8a
IEEE 802.3 (10BASE5) minimal network configuration

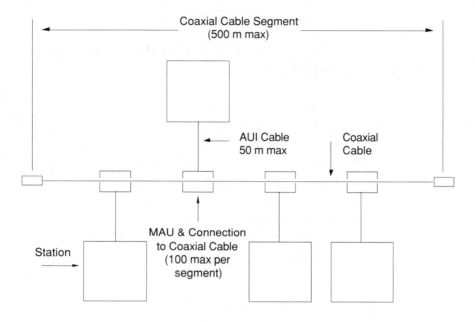

Figure 1-8b
IEEE 802.3 MAC frame format

Preamble	SFD	Destination	Source	Len	Data Unit	Pad	FCS

Preamble (7 octets)
SFD - Start Frame Delimiter (1 octet)
Destination Address (2 or 6 octets)
Source Address (2 or 6 octets)
Len - Length of LLC Data Unit (2 octets)

Data Unit - LLC PDU
Pad - fill if Data Unit is too short
Data + Pad = 46-1500 octets total
FCS - Frame Check Sequence (4 octets)

1.4.5   IEEE 802.4—Token Passing Bus

The 802.4 standard, (see reference [1-8]) also a bus topology, provides for a broadband, deterministic network for applications where a probabalistic (that is, CSMA/CD) bus architecture is unsuitable, such as factory automation. The token bus configuration, shown in Figure 1-9a, results in a *physical* bus, but a *logical* ring—that is, the permission to transmit the token follows a logical ring progression between workstations (designated A, B, C... in Figure 1-9a), irrespective of their physical location on the bus cable.

Figure 1-9a
IEEE 802.4 network configuration

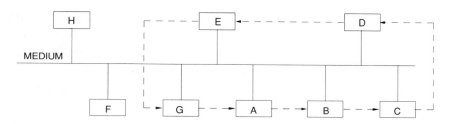

Note: stations F and H can receive but not transmit frames

Figure 1-9b
IEEE 802.4 MAC frame format

Preamble	SD	FC	DA	SA	Data_Unit •••	FCS	ED

where:

Preamble = Pattern sent to set receiver's modem clock and level (1 or more octets)
SD = Start delimiter (1 octet)
FC = Frame control (1 octet)
DA = Destination address (2 or 6 octets)
SA = Source address (2 or 6 octets)
Data_Unit = Information (0 or more octets)
FSC = Frame check sequence (4 octets)
ED = End delimiter (1 octet)

The number of octets between SD and ED, exclusive, shall be 8191 or fewer.

The 802.4 MAC frame format is shown in Figure 1-9b. The Physical Layer standard includes both single and dual cable broadband systems; transmission rates of 1, 5, and 10 MBPS; and phase continuous or phase coherent Frequency Shift Keying (FSK), or multilevel duobinary amplitude modulated Phase Shift Keying (PSK) signaling schemes.

1.4.6 IEEE 802.5—Token Passing Ring

The 802.5 standard (see reference [1-9]) provides for a ring topology configuration (that is, a closed set of active taps connected by point-to-point links). Access to the ring is granted when a token is received and passed in a logical (and physical) ring sequence between the workstations. (The physical topology is electrically a ring but is wired as a star). As seen in Figure 1-10a, when a workstation is not active on the ring, it is in bypass mode, thus maintaining the electrical continuity of the ring. Figure 1-10b shows the 802.5 MAC frame format; other formats will be discussed in Chapter 6.

Figure 1-10a
IEEE 802.5 network configuration

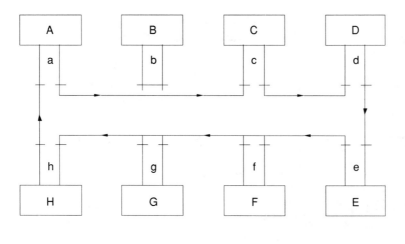

Physical Medium

A, B, C, D, E, F, G, H - Ring Stations
a, b, c, d, e, f, g, h - Bypass Function

All stations are active except B (b illustrated in bypass mode)

Figure 1-10b
IEEE 802.5 MAC frame format

SFS		FCS Coverage					EFS	
SD	AC	FC	DA	SA	INFO	FCS	ED	FS

SFS = Start-of-Frame Sequence
SD = Starting Delimiter (1 octet)
AC = Access Control (1 octet)
FC = Frame Control (1 octet)
DA = Destination Address (2 or 6 octets)
SA = Source Address (2 or 6 octets)
INFO = Information (0 or more octets)
FCS = Frame-Check Sequence (4 octets)
EFS = End-of-Frame Sequence
ED = Ending Delimiter (1 octet)
FS = Frame Status (1 octet)

1.5 | ARCNET

ARCNET, which stands for Attached Resource Computer Network, was developed by Datapoint Corporation and released in 1977 (see reference [1-10]). It is considered a proprietary architecture and does not adhere to the IEEE family of standards, although topologically it has many similarities to IEEE 802.4. Chapter 5 is devoted to ARCNET.

1.6 | LAN Software Standards

Volumes could be written about the need (and lack of) software standards for LANs. The IEEE LAN model only considers this issue within the 802.2 Logical Link Control Standard, leaving the higher layers (3 through 7) open for standard 802.1 or others.

Two standards emerged in the earlier days of LANs—MS-DOS 3.1 and NetBIOS. These two are fairly consistent among the various manufactures today. The DOS standard from Microsoft, added functions required for multi-user file access, and NetBIOS from IBM and Sytek, Inc., provided a means of establishing communications links between workstations. As these are considered Layer 6 (DOS) and Layer 5 (NetBIOS) functions, other protocols, such as TCP/IP have been used at Layers 4 and 3, respectively. Layer 7 is still very user-dependent, although ISO standards under development may some day fill this gap. See reference [1-11] for further details on DOS and NetBIOS. Chapter 6 will discuss the various NetBIOS functions, and Chapter 8 will discuss TCP/IP.

1.7   References

[1-1]   Some of the material in this chapter first appeared in "Troubleshooting Local Area Networks with the OSI Model" by Mark A. Miller, *Micro/Systems Journal*, Volume 4, Number 10, October 1988.

[1-2]   International Organization for Standardization, Information Processing Systems—Open Systems Interconnection—Basic Reference Model, ISO 7498—1984.

[1-3]   The International Telegraph and Telephone Consultative Committee, Red Book Volume VIII, Fascicle VIII.5—Recommendation X.200, 1985.

[1-4]   Andrew S. Tanenbaum, *Computer Networks, Second Edition*, Prentice-Hall, 1988.

[1-5]   William Stallings, *Local Networks, Second Edition*, Macmillan, 1988.

[1-6]   Institute of Electrical and Electronics Engineers, Logical Link Control, ISO 8802-2, IEEE Std 802.2—1989.

[1-7] Institute of Electrical and Electronics Engineers, Carrier Sense Multiple Access with Collision Detection (CSMA/CD) Access Method and Physical Layer Specifications, ISO 8802/3, ANSI/IEEE Std 802.3.—1988.

[1-8] Institute of Electrical and Electronics Engineers, Token Passing Bus Access Method, ISO/DIS 8802/4, ANSI/IEEE Std 802.4—1985.

[1-9] Institute of Electrical and Electronics Engineers, Token Ring Access Method, IEEE Std 802.5—1989.

[1-10] ARCNET Designer's Handbook, Document 61610, Datapoint Corporation, 2nd Edition, 1988.

[1-11] LAN Operating System Report, Novell, Inc., 1986.

Addresses of Standards Organizations

CCITT RECOMMENDATIONS AND FEDERAL INFORMATION
PROCESSING STANDARDS (FIPS)—U.S.A

> United States Department of Commerce
> National Technical Information Service
> 5285 Port Royal Road
> Springfield, VA 22161   Telephone (703) 487-4650

ISO AND ANSI STANDARDS

> American National Standards Institute
> 1430 Broadway
> New York, NY 10018   Telephone (212) 354-3300

ECMA STANDARDS

> European Computer Manufacturers Association
> 114, Rue de Rhone
> CH-1204 Geneva, Switzerland   Telephone 41 22 35-36-34

EIA STANDARDS

> Electronic Industries Association
> Standards Sales
> 2001 Eye Street, NW
> Washington, D.C. 20006   Telephone (202) 457-4966

FEDERAL TELECOMMUNICATION STANDARDS—U.S.A.

General Services Administration
Specification Distribution Branch
Building 197, Washington Navy Yard
Washington, D.C. 20407

IEEE

Institute of Electrical and Electronics Engineers
445 Hoes Lane
P.O. Box 1331
Piscataway, NJ 08855   Telephone (201) 562-3800

AT&T PUBLICATIONS

AT&T Technologies Commercial Sales
P.O. Box 19901
Indianapolis, IN 46219   Telephone (800) 432-6600

CHAPTER TWO

Documenting Your Network

There's an old saying among project managers that goes something like "A project reaches the point of 95% completion and remains at that point forever." That can certainly be true of tying up the loose ends associated with a network installation—it's very easy to put off documenting the network until later. Unfortunately for most of us, later equates to never.

2.1 | The Network Library

Network failures always occur at the most inopportune times: the VP is coming for a visit or the month-end reports are due. The speed with which you can define the problem, isolate the failure, and repair, replace, or re-initialize the faulty component is directly proportional to your intimate knowledge of the network hardware and software. There are three sections to a network library that should be addressed: technical resource material specific to that network, a listing of human resources (that is, who to call when a problem surfaces), and specific drawings regarding the network topology, cable plant, and details of the individual workstations. We'll look at each area separately.

2.1.1 | Technical Resources

All network hardware and software components come with some sort of installation guide. Most of these do a very adequate job in guiding the reader through the installation, administration, and maintenance of the network, but are often short on technical details of specific network operation. For that reason, it is often useful to go to the level of technical detail that the network designers did for further information.

Each NIC includes controller chips that implement the access protocol. An example would be a CSMA/CD controller for Ethernet or StarLAN functions, and the Intel 82586 LAN coprocessor. For hardware specifics, the manufacturers of these protocol handler ICs can be most helpful. While this is by no means an exhaustive list, here are some firms to contact and request data sheets on their respective devices:

ARCNET: Standard Microsystems Corporation
                           (516) 273-3100
                    and
                           NCR Microelectronics, Inc.
                           (303) 226-9500

Token Ring: Texas Instruments, Inc.
                           (713) 274-2380

Ethernet: Intel Corporation
                           (800) 548-4725
                    and
                           National Semiconductor Corporation
                           (408) 721-5000

StarLAN and
Twisted Pair Ethernet: AT&T Microelectronics
                           (800) 372-2447
                           NCR Microelectronics, Inc.
                           (303) 226-9500
                    and
                           Intel Corporation
                           (800) 548-4725

References to specific devices and documents will be given in chapters 5 through 8.

Software developers, including Novell, Inc., Banyan Systems, and others also have technical documentation on their protocols. Become familiar with these resources and add them to your technical library as well.

If your LAN is part of a wide area network, other reference material, such as EIA or CCITT standards or AT&T Publications (PUBs) on communication lines should also be considered. See Appendix 1 for addresses of the various standards organizations.

2.1.2 Human Resources

When a network failure occurs, a phone call to someone who may have faced (and solved) a similar problem can greatly reduce the time involved.

Three areas should be considered. First, maintain a telephone directory of all people that have had direct responsibility for any previous installation and maintenance of the network. This list would include personnel from your own company, electrical contractors, hardware and software vendors, and network designers or consultants. In compiling your directory, consider anyone that has had a direct involvement with the technical details of your network, and add that person to your directory.

Secondly, consider other users of networks similar to yours. These might be your counterparts managing networks in other company locations, or contacts made through user groups, trade associations, etc.

Third, consider technical resources that are made available from the various network vendors. Most vendors have a technical assistance hotline. The charge for these services is very nominal, or sometimes free. Make sure that you become familiar with these services before a network failure makes them necessary. In addition, a wealth of information is available through CompuServe Information Service. In the Computers and Technology Section, both hardware and software forums are available, plus on-line services from Novell, Inc., (NetWire), and 3Com Corporation (Ask 3Com). Contact CompuServe at (800) 848-8990 or (614) 457-8650 (within Ohio) for further information.

Finally, a wealth of information can be obtained in a very short amount of time by attending seminars, trade shows and conferences that address the LAN and networking industries. Examples include the Communications Networks Conference (ComNet) and Network Management Solutions Conference, both sponsored by IDG Conference Management Group, (508) 879-6700; Interface, sponsored by The Interface Group, Inc. (617) 449-6600; and Networld, sponsored by H.A. Bruno, Inc., (800) 444-3976.

2.2 | Cable System Documentation

When a cable fault is suspected, accurate documentation is critical; a crisis is not a good time to wonder which wire pair goes to Nathan's workstation. We'll look at twisted pair cable documentation first.

Figure 2-1 shows an example of an as-built twisted pair cable layout in a large facility. Again using telephone industry nomenclature, the cables are labeled first by number, then by the pair count. Thus the notation 1, 301-400 indicates cable number 1, pairs 301 through 400. Each unique feeder cable has its own number. Distribution cables that branch off from the feeder cables have unique pair counts. The color codes for these pair counts will be discussed in Chapter 4. Wiring closets should also be noted, along with their room numbers and any access restrictions such as cipher locks on the doors.

Figure 2-2 goes into further cable details, showing specific documentation for each wire pair. Dial-up, intra-building, inter-building, and LAN circuits can all be documented in a similar manner.

Figure 2-1
As-built twisted pair cable layout

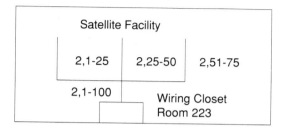

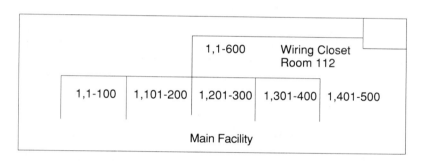

Coaxial and fiber optic cables are most easily identified with a drawing similar to Figure 2-1, or by a separate notation on a copy of the building's blueprints. A second requirement exists, however, because the coaxial cables are not color-coded, and may be resident in a common cable tray. Figure 2-3 shows one convenient solution to this problem, the Mini-Tags from Almetek Industries, Inc., in Hackettstown, NJ (telephone 201-850-9700). The tags come in two parts. The first part is a black polyethylene holder that the cable can easily be threaded through. Into the holder are placed letters and numbers that uniquely identify that cable. The tags should be used at both ends of the cable, along with any splices, junctions, or transceiver taps that may be accessed in the future. As a minimum, identify the origin and destination ("To" and "From") for each cable, plus any additional information such as workstation or server locations that is required. These tags are highly superior to adhesive tape labels, which have a tendency to unwrap and fall off with age.

Figure 2-2
Twisted pair wiring documentation

Dial-up Circuits

Telephone Number	Station Location	Wire Closet	Wire Block	Cable Pair
555-1212	30K15	22	17	2,224

Intra-Building Circuits

Circuit Number	Modem Location	Pair	Origin			Destination		
			Wire Closet	Wire Block	Cable Pair	Wire Closet	Wire Block	Cable Pair
675-2233	2B07	TX	26	12	1,103	19	7	6,451
		RX	26	12	1,104	19	7	6,452

Inter-Building Circuits

Circuit Number	Modem Location	Pair	Origin			Destination
			Wire Closet	Wire Block	Cable Pair	
AEDG1255	AE13	TX	32	21	5,507	Colorado Springs
		RX	32	21	5,508	

LAN Circuits

Originating Node	Pair	Origin			Destination			Connecting Node
		Wire Closet	Wire Block	Cable Pair	Wire Closet	Wire Block	Cable Pair	
PC1	TX	26	12	1,103	26	7	2,201	Server1
	RX	26	12	1,104	26	7	2,202	

Figure 2-3
Minitags from Almetek Industries, Inc.

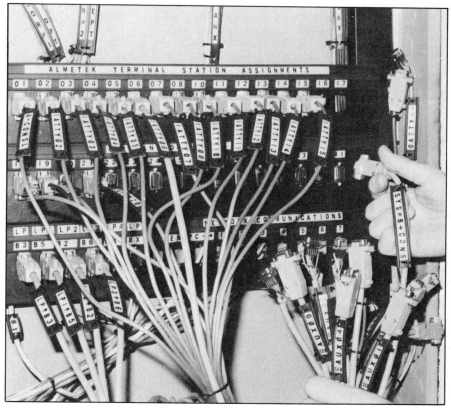

(photo courtesy of Almetek Industries, Inc.)

2.3 Network Topology Documentation

Documentation on the network topology can be divided into two distinct parts. The first is the physical topology: where the various workstations are located within the building, which cables go inside which walls, where the cross-connect fields or wire closets are located, etc. Figure 2-4 shows an example document of a telephone and equipment room layout, plus a small Ethernet network in the adjacent room.

Figure 2-4
Physical network topology

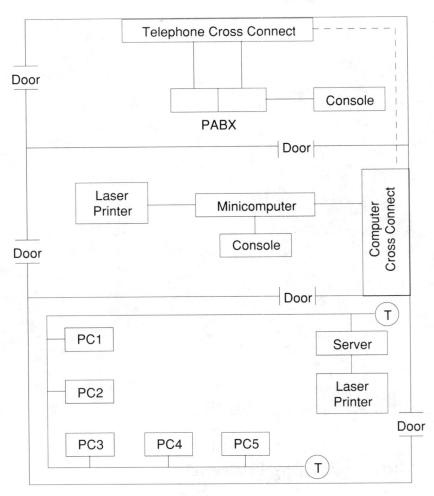

The second documentation requirement is for the logical topology, indicating which users are attached to which server, plus the associated user group assignments. If Nicholas calls with a network problem, a drawing similar to Figure 2-5 will pinpoint which server he is attached to.

Knowing both the physical and logical connections to the network are invaluable when a user on one part of the network is unable to access the server. You must first determine where the user is physically located, and then determine to which server the user is logically attached. Having these details readily available can be a real time saver.

Figure 2-5
Logical network topology

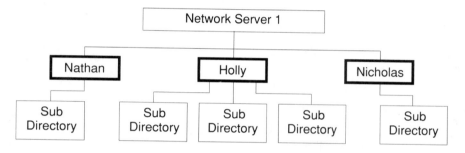

2.4 Workstation Documentation

Each user on the network has unique requirements, and with these requirements comes an individual set of hardware and software parameters. The workstation documentation should include both hardware and software components. As shown in Figure 2-6, the hardware section would show the type of workstation or PC, plus all internal peripherals, such as communication ports or video adapters.

Specific attention should be given to the LAN adapter or NIC to note the Interrupt Request (IRQ) Line, RAM Buffer memory location, I/O Port address and Node address. For ARCNET networks, the node address is set manually with DIP switches. For Token Ring, Ethernet, and StarLAN networks, the address is burned into a ROM on the board and must be read with the diagnostic disk that accompanies the board or with a protocol analyzer. More on the use of these two particular tools is in Chapter 3.

The user software, including any configuration (CONFIG.SYS), batch
(AUTOEXEC.BAT) or login script files should be documented either on
paper, backed up on a floppy disk, or stored in the user's subdirectory
on the server.

Figure 2-6
Workstation documentation

User Hardware

PC Type	Peripherals	Port	IRQ	RAM buffer	I/O Port Address	Node ID
Compaq Port II	Floppy Drive	A	6	—	—	—
	Hard Disk	C	14	—	—	—
	Serial Port	COM1	4	—	—	—
	Serial Port	COM2	3	—	—	—
	Printer Port	LPT1	7	—	—	—
	LAN Adapter	—	2	D0000H	2E0H	7 (dec)

User Software

CONFIG.SYS: device=ansi.sys
device=c:\tops\atalk.sys /dma=none
device=netdrvr.sys vector=5b
files=99
buffers=20

AUTOEXEC.BAT: path=c:\;c:\dos;c:\tops;
clck
ncsmall

Login Script: map d:=sys:public/dos
map e:=sys:public/cross
map m:=sys:public/maxhead
map u:=sys:public/utility

2.5 | Trouble Reports

Network problems tend to repeat themselves. As a result, any history that can be used from previous network difficulties may be valuable to solve the current problems. Figure 2-7 shows a sample network maintenance report. Entries are made for the problem, diagnosis, and any hardware or software components that require replacement. These reports should be kept in a notebook for future reference, or when a change in network administrators occurs.

Figure 2-7
Network maintenance report

Failure Date _____

Network User _____ Telephone _____

Network Address _____ Location _____

Briefly summarize the maintenance problem

_____

_____

_____

Hardware or software replaced

_____

Hardware or software updated

_____

Is the problem now completely resolved? _____

Is the network user satisfied? _____

Any other comments?

_____

_____

_____

Person completing this form _____

Date _____ Telephone _____

2.6 | Documentation Tools

Unfortunately, not many tools are available to assist with network documentation. ConnectManage, from Davcom, Inc., Midland Park, NJ (telephone 201-444-2177), is one tool. ConnectManage is a PC-based cable management system for both voice and data communication networks. It includes several modules for cable, cross-connect field, and terminal management. Support for the IBM cabling system is included.

Another tool is the Ethernet Cable AutoCAD Template (ECAT), available from Cable Technology Group, Inc., of Newton, MA (telephone 617-969-8552). As seen in Figure 2-8, ECAT produces physical network documentation that can be easily stored and modified at a later time. Contact Cable Technology Group for further information.

A database of different LAN parameters are included in the NETmanager software from Brightwork Software, Inc. (Red Bank, NJ). In addition, a variety of reports, including trouble ticket, user information, and server information can be produced.

Two other software tools may prove useful: the Formworx software from Formworx Corporation, Waltham, MA, for creating network documentation and maintenance forms, and the Micro Resource Manager database for PC tracking from Computer Associates International, Inc., San Jose, CA (telephone 800-531-5236 or 408-432-1727).

Many vendors assist the administrator in providing forms specific to that type of network. For example, the forms shown in appendixes 2A, 2B, and 2C were taken from references [2-1], [2-2], and [2-3], respectively, and were provided by IBM and AT&T for their customers' use. Ask the vendor of your network hardware or cabling system if they provide similar resources.

Figure 2-8
Ethernet Cable AutoCAD Template (ECAT)

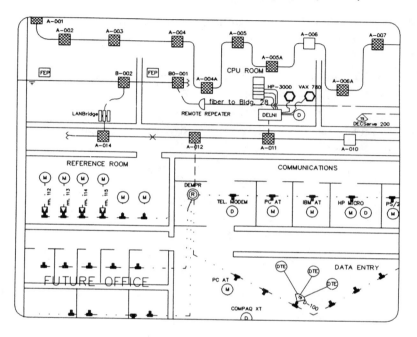

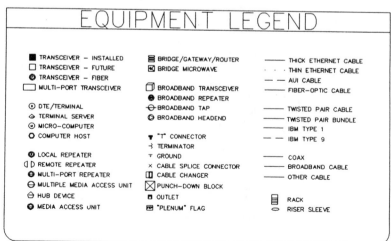

(courtesy of Cable Technology Group, Inc.)

2.7 References

[2-1] IBM Cabling System Planning and Installation Guide, document GA27-3361-6, June 1986.

[2-2] IBM Token-Ring Network Introduction and Planning Guide, document GA27-3677-1, April 1986.

[2-3] AT&T StarLAN 10 Network Hardware Design Guide, document 999-120-002, 1989.

APPENDIX 2A

IBM Cabling System
Worksheets and Forms

| Building _____ | Cable Schedule | Wiring Closet Location _____ |
| Floor _____ | | Date of Last Update _____ |

| Cable Number | Cable Routing Information | | Cable Length | Distribution Panel Jumpers | Additional Information |
	Cable Runs From	Cable Runs To			

Note: When you update this cable schedule you should also update the System Configuration Worksheet found in *Using the IBM Cabling System with Communication Products*.

Work Area Worksheet

Worksheet Number _____

Cable Requirements

Wiring Closet Location Number	Work Area Location	Faceplates/Devices						Cable Drop Length	1	Plenum 1	2	Plenum 2	8	9
		1S	1W	2	2S	UM	WB							
	1													
	2													
	3													
	4													
	5													
	6													
	7													
	8													
	9													
	10													
	11													
	12													
	13													
	14													
	15													
	16													
	17													
	18													
	19													
	Totals													

Total drops on this worksheet

Wiring Closet Worksheet

Worksheet Number _____

Totals from Work Area Worksheet

Wiring Closet Location Number	Faceplates/Devices						Total Drops	Cable Requirements							
Work sheet Number	1	1S	1W	2	2S*	UM**	WB		1 Plenum	1	2	2 Plenum	5	8	9
1															
2															
3															
4															
5															
6															
7															
8															
9															
10															
11															
12															
13															
14															
15															
16															
17															
Totals for this Wiring Closet															

Data Connectors — Standard / Underscript

Telephone Jack Connectors

Cables from Wiring Closet/ Controller Room Worksheet

Total Drops for this Wiring Closet

Optical Fiber Connector

Dual Socket Clips

Two data connectors are required for each faceplate (any type).

One telephone jack connector is required for each type 2 and 2S faceplate.
* Record the port number for the type 2 and 2S faceplates.

** Record the port number for the Wall box used.

Distribution Panels

Equipment Racks

Rack Grounding Kits

Cable Label Packages

57

Wiring Closet/Controller Room Worksheet

Building _____
Floor _____
Worksheet _____

Cable Routes Within a Single Building

	Wiring Closet Location/ Floor	Wiring Closet or Controller Room Location/ Floor	Number of Cables	Cable Length	Cable Requirements					
					Type 1	Type 1 P	Type 5	Faceplate Devices 1 1S 1W		
1										
2										
3										
4										
5										
6										
7										
8										
9										
10										
11										
12										
13										
14										
15										
		Totals								

Cable Routes Between Buildings

	Wiring Closet Location/ Floor	Surge Suppressor Location/ Floor	Wiring Closet or Controller Room Location/ Floor/ Building	Length of Indoor Cable in this Building	Cable Requirements							
					Type 1		Type 1 P		Length of Outdoor Cable	Type 1 Outdoor		Surge Suppressors
					No.	Total Feet	No.	Total Feet		No.	Total Feet	
1												
2												
3												
4												
		Totals										

Data Connectors _____

Distribution Panels _____

Distribution Racks _____

Rack Grounding Kit _____

Cable Label Packages _____

IBM Token Ring Network Planning Forms

Rack Inventory Chart

Wiring closet number ————————
Rack number ————————
Date ————————
Planner's initials ————————

Instructions

Fill out a Rack Inventory Chart for each equipment rack.

1. Enter the wiring closet location number, the equipment rack identification number, and the planner's initials.

2. Using the template for the Rack Inventory Chart that came with this manual, draw an outline of each component that will be installed in the rack.

3. The slots at the bottom of the distribution panel tempate are used only for the lowermost distribution panel in a rack. The slots indicate that there are 38.1 mm (1-1/2 in.) between that panel and the next unit in the rack.

4. Write the unit identification number on each component on the chart.

Example:

| 21 |
| 22 |
| 0010 |
| 0011 |
| 0012 |

IBM 8228 Cabling Chart

Date _____ _____

Section 1 Identification

| Unit Number _____ | Building _____ Location _____ | Rack-mounted ☐ Wall-mounted ☐ | Ring _____ |

Section 2 Receptacle Connections

Receptacle	1	2	3	4	5	6	7	8
Connect to:								

Device								

Section 3 Ring Connections

A. Connect RI of this 8228 to: _____

B. Connect RO of this 8228 to: _____

IBM 8218 Cabling Chart

Section 1

Date _____

Ring _____

_____ Unit Number _____

Building _____

Location _____

Rack-Mounted ☐

Wall-Mounted ☐

Section 2

RI

RI

Connect to:

Connect to:

_____

_____

RO

RO

Yellow
Crossover
Cable

Yellow
Crossover
Cable

IBM 8219 Cabling Chart

Section 1 Date _____

Ring _____

_____ Unit Number _____

_____ Building _____

_____ Location _____

☐ Rack-Mounted ☐

Section 2 ☐ Wall-Mounted ☐

O-O _____ DP or MB Connections O-O

B-B _____ B-B

Receive Receive

O B

B O

Transmit Transmit

Connect to: Connect to:

_____

☐ Yellow Crossover Cable Yellow Crossover Cable
or
☐ Patch Cable

B = Black
O = Orange
MB = Optical Fiber Cable Mounting Bracket
DP = Distribution Panel

Ring Sequence Chart

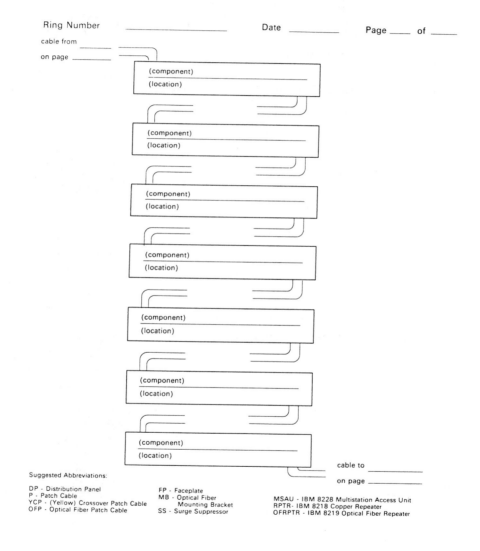

Ring Number _____   Date _____   Page ____ of ____

cable from _____

on page _____

(component) _____

(location) _____

(component) _____

(location) _____

(component) _____

(location) _____

(component) _____

(location) _____

(component) _____

(location) _____

(component) _____

(location) _____

(component) _____

(location) _____

cable to _____

on page _____

Suggested Abbreviations:

DP - Distribution Panel
P - Patch Cable
YCP - (Yellow) Crossover Patch Cable
OFP - Optical Fiber Patch Cable

FP - Faceplate
MB - Optical Fiber
    Mounting Bracket
SS - Surge Suppressor

MSAU - IBM 8228 Multistation Access Unit
RPTR - IBM 8218 Copper Repeater
OFRPTR - IBM 8219 Optical Fiber Repeater

Bridge Planning Chart

Date _____

Bridge Identification _____

Section 1- Bridge Configuration Parameters

Bridge Number (default = 1) _____

Dump on Error (default = 0) _____

Restart on Error (default = 1) _____

Primary Adapter   **Alternate Adapter**

_____ (001) Ring Number (002) _____
                   (Default)   (Default)

_____ Hop Count Limit (Default = 7) _____

_____ Limited Broadcast (Default = 1) _____

_____ (D800) Shared RAM (D400) _____
                  (Default)   (Default)

_____ Locally Administered Address _____

Section 2 - Physical Connections

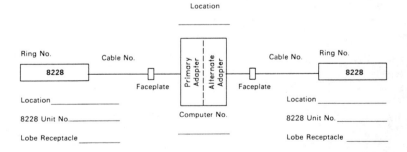

Physical Location to Adapter Address Locator Chart

Physical Location	Adapter Address	Device Identification	Ring Number	IBM 8228 Unit No.

Adapter Address to Physical Location
Locator Chart

Adapter Address	Physical Location	Device Identification	Ring Number	IBM 8228 Unit No.

AT&T StarLAN 10 Network Forms

StarLAN 10 Network Wiring Closet Design Form

Organization: _____   Date: _____
Building:_____   Sheet _____ of _____
Network Designer: _____
Building Wiring: _____

Location: _____
Number of Hubs: _____
Number of Nodes: ____

Cable Length	Cable No.		Cable Length	Cable No.		Cable Length	Cable No.
_____	_____		_____	_____		_____	___ __

SATELLITE CLOSET

Location: _____
Number of Hubs: _____
Number of Nodes: ____

SATELLITE CLOSET

Location: _____
Number of Hubs: _____
Number of Nodes: ____

SATELLITE CLOSET

Location: _____
Number of Hubs: _____
Number of Nodes: ____

Cable Length	Cable No.	Cable Length	Cable No.
_____	_____	_____	_____

SATELLITE CLOSET

Location: _____
Number of Hubs: _____
Number of Nodes: ____

SATELLITE CLOSET

Location: _____
Number of Hubs: _____
Number of Nodes: ____

Cable Length	Cable No.		Cable Length	Cable No.		Cable Length	Cable No.
_____	_____		_____	_____		_____	_____

SATELLITE CLOSET

Location: _____
Number of Hubs: _____
Number of Nodes: ____

SATELLITE CLOSET

Location: _____
Number of Hubs: _____
Number of Nodes: ____

SATELLITE CLOSET

Location: _____
Number of Hubs: _____
Number of Nodes: ____

Cable Length	Cable No.	Cable Length	Cable No.
_____	_____	_____	_____

SATELLITE CLOSET

Location: _____
Number of Hubs: _____
Number of Nodes: ____

SATELLITE CLOSET

Location: _____
Number of Hubs: _____
Number of Nodes: ____

StarLAN 10 Network Hub Unit Design Form

Organization: _____ Date: _____

Hub Location: _____ Hub ID: _____

Network Designer: _____ Building: _____

Hub Serial Number: _____ Hub Purchase Date: _____

IN or OUT JACK 1:
Node Name or Hub ID: _____
User: _____
Location: _____ Cord Length: ____

JACK 2:
Node Name: _____
User: _____
Location: _____ Cord Length: ____

JACK 3:
Node Name: _____
User: _____
Location: _____ Cord Length: ____

JACK 4:
Node Name: _____
User: _____
Location: _____ Cord Length: ____

JACK 5:
Node Name: _____
User: _____
Location: _____ Cord Length: ____

JACK 6:
Node Name: _____
User: _____
Location: _____ Cord Length: ____

JACK 7:
Node Name: _____
User: _____
Location: _____ Cord Length: ____

JACK 8:
Node Name: _____
User: _____
Location: _____ Cord Length: ____

JACK 9:
Node Name: _____
User: _____
Location: _____ Cord Length: ____

JACK 10:
Node Name: _____
User: _____
Location: _____ Cord Length: ____

JACK 11:
Node Name: _____
User: _____
Location: _____ Cord Length: ____

AUI PORT:
Node Name: _____
User: _____
Location: _____ Cable Length: ____

NOTES:
_____
_____
_____
_____

StarLAN 10 Network Fiber Hub Unit Design Form

Organization: _____   Date: _____

Fiber Hub Location: _____   Fiber Hub ID: _____

Network Designer: _____   Building: _____

Fiber Hub Serial Number: _____   Fiber Hub Purchase Date: _____

IN or OUT JACK:
Node Name or Hub ID: _____

User: _____

Location: _____   Cord Length: _____

OPTICAL FIBER PORT 1:
Node Name: _____

User: _____

Location: _____   Fiber Length: _____

OPTICAL FIBER PORT 2:
Node Name: _____

User: _____

Location: _____   Fiber Length: _____

OPTICAL FIBER PORT 3:
Node Name: _____

User: _____

Location: _____   Fiber Length: _____

OPTICAL FIBER PORT 4:
Node Name: _____

User: _____

Location: _____   Fiber Length: _____

OPTICAL FIBER PORT 5:
Node Name: _____

User: _____

Location: _____   Fiber Length: _____

OPTICAL FIBER PORT 6:
Node Name: _____

User: _____

Location: _____   Fiber Length: _____

AUI PORT:
Node Name: _____

User: _____

Location: _____   Cable Length: _____

NOTES:
_____

_____

_____

_____

StarLAN 10 Network Node Record Form

Name and Location

User: _____

Primary Server: _____ Login: _____

Office Location: _____

Phone Number: _____ Node Type: _____

Node Function: _____ Node Name: _____

NAU Type: _____

NAU Network Physical Address: _____

NAU Serial Number: _____ NAU Purchase Date: _____

NAU Diskette Serial Number: _____

Computer

Operating System and Version/Release: _____

Network Software Package(s): _____

_____

Software Serial Number(s): _____

Purchase Date(s) _____

NOTES: _____

_____

_____

_____

_____

CHAPTER THREE

Test Equipment for Your LAN

In Chapter 1, we saw how the OSI Reference Model could be applied to a LAN, and specifically, how the various elements of the model are implemented within the various LAN components.

In this chapter, we will look at various example of tools that might be contained in a network troubleshooter's tool kit. A variety of devices, including cabling system testers, power line monitors, and analog and digital interface diagnosis equipment will be discussed. This is by no means an exhaustive list. Each network, because of its uniqueness, will require additions and deletions to this smorgasbord. Use it only as a guide—a starting point for assembling your own tool kit.

3.1 Cable Testing Tools

LANs employ both copper (twisted pair and coaxial) and fiber optic transmission media. Because of the vast difference in technologies, we will discuss the tools for testing copper-based transmission media first.

3.1.1 Tone Generator and Detector

Figures 3-1 and 3-2 show the Model 77M tone generator and Model 200B inductive amplifier from Progressive Electronics, Inc., of Mesa, AZ. Both of these instruments have been used extensively in the telephone industry to trace twisted pair cabling between cross-connect fields (usually 66-type wiring blocks) in telephone equipment rooms.

Figure 3-1
Model 77M tone generator

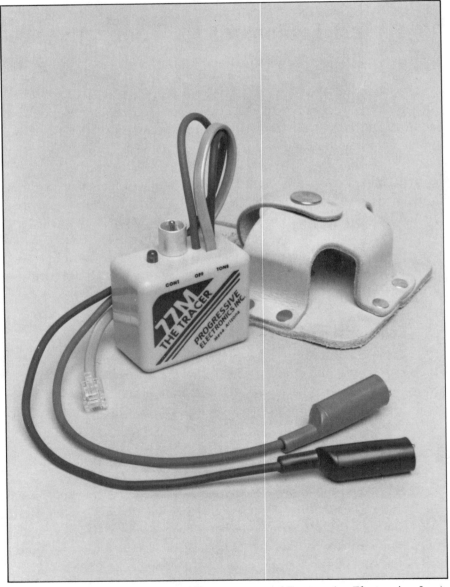

(photo courtesy of Progressive Electronics, Inc.)

To correctly identify a cable pair, the tone generator is connected to one end of a twisted pair. At the other end, the inductive amplifier receives the audible signal when in the immediate vicinity of the correct pair. These tools are most useful to verify the continuity of a cable pair, or to identify an individual cable pair.

Figure 3-2
Model 200B inductive amplifier

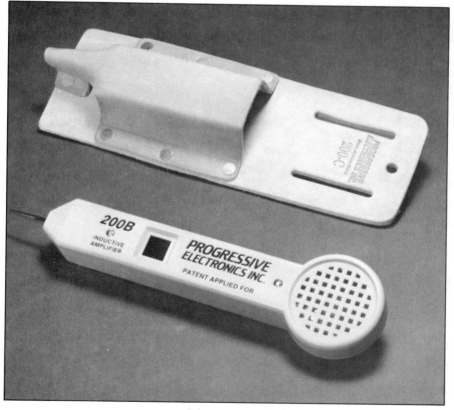

(photo courtesy of Progressive Electronics, Inc.)

3.1.2 Cable Tracers

One major issue surrounding the re-use of twisted pair wiring in many buildings is locating where the wire actually goes. The Cable Sender and Cable Tracer from MicroTest, Inc., of Phoenix, AZ, in Figure 3-3 provide a solution to that problem. The Cable Sender transmits a signal that can be received by the Cable Tracer along a cable up to 1,000 feet in length. The hidden cable can be located inside any floor, ceiling wall, or patch panel and still be identified if the Cable Tracer is placed within one foot of that cable.

Figure 3-3
Cable Sender and Cable Tracer

(photo courtesy of MicroTest, Inc.)

3.1.3 Cable Continuity Testers

Figure 3-4 shows two other MicroTest, Inc., instruments, called Cable Checkers. These devices provide a simple "go/no-go" test for cable shorts (a connection between conductors), cable opens (a break in a single conductor), or a complete break of all conductors. Testing procedures for Ethernet, Token Ring, ARCNET, and StarLAN cabling are included in the operation manual.

Figure 3-4
Cable Checkers

(photo courtesy of MicroTest, Inc.)

3.1.4 | Time Domain Reflectometer (TDR)

A TDR operates by transmitting a short pulse of known amplitude and duration down a cable, and measuring the corresponding amplitude and time delay associated with any resultant signal reflection. Open and short circuits, impedance mismatches, crimps, kinks, and sharp bends in the cable all create unique reflections, which are then measured and analyzed by the TDR. We'll look in more detail at cable testing procedures in Chapter 4.

Figure 3-5 shows one TDR, the Cable Scanner by MicroTest, Inc. In addition to testing for open and short cables, the Cable Scanner can measure cable and terminator resistance, noise level or interference into the LAN cable, and rudimentary network traffic. Outputs to an oscilloscope and printer are also provided.

Figure 3-5
The Cable Scanner

(photo courtesy of MicroTest, Inc.)

The Lanca Instruments, Inc., (Round Rock, TX) Digital TDR, shown in Figure 3-6, is designed to test all types of coaxial and twisted pair cables having characteristic impedances between 50 and 150 ohms. These ranges cover all LAN applications. The device also has an analog test mode which permits a direct output to a dual channel, 60 MHz oscilloscope.

A more complex TDR is shown in Figure 3-7, the Tektronix, Inc., (Redmond, OR) Model 1503B. In addition to the standard TDR functions, this device includes a graphical display on the front panel, plus a strip chart recorder. The recorder is useful for taking benchmark measurements of the cable plant when it is first installed, and then having a hard copy reference when network failures occur.

Figure 3-6
Lanca Instruments Digital TDR

(photo courtesy of Lanca Instruments, Inc.)

Figure 3-7
Tektronix Model 1503B TDR

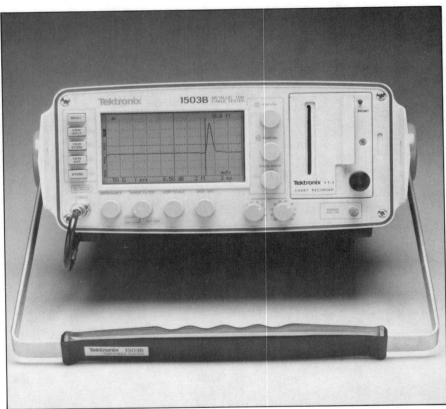

(photo courtesy of Tektronix, Inc.)

3.1.5   Optical Power Source and Meter

Fiber optic cables experience problems similar to copper media, however, because of the optical (rather than electrical) signaling, the test
equipment is necessarily more complex. Optical TDRs are available,
but with price ranges between $10,000 and $50,000, most LAN administrators look for less expensive equipment. A more cost-effective
solution is an optical power source and optical power meter. Wilcom
Products, Inc., of Laconia, NH, makes the optical test kit shown in

Figure 3-8. It is operated in a similar manner to the tone generators and detectors discussed earlier, with the optical power source connected to one end of the cable, and the resultant optical power measured at the other end. We will discuss fiber optic testing in greater detail in Chapter 4.

Figure 3-8
An optical test kit

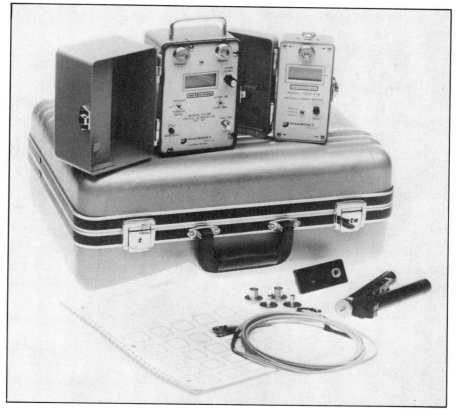

(photo courtesy of Wilcom Products, Inc.)

3.2 | Power Line Testing Tools

Volumes have been written regarding the damage that electrical transients, surges, and improper grounding techniques can cause to sensitive computer equipment. Instead of providing details on the subject of power protection per se, we will concentrate on test equipment that a typical LAN administrator might use. If a power problem does exist, it may be solved with power conditioning equipment, or may require corrections to the building's power distribution by an electrical contractor.

Figure 3-9 shows an easy-to-use device, the AC monitor from Tasco, Ltd. of Englewood, CO. When plugged into an electrical outlet, the AC Monitor indicates the magnitude of the AC line voltage, and records spikes, high and low voltage conditions, and power failures. An audible alarm sounds anytime that a potentially damaging condition exists.

A more complex device, the Computer Power Diagnostic Instrument from TLC S.E., Inc. (Santa Clara, CA) is shown in Figure 3-10. More extensive tests are available, such as the magnitude of line to neutral and neutral to ground noise, and a test of the electrical wiring at that outlet. Diagnostic LEDs indicate what corrective action should be taken.

Figure 3-9
AC monitor

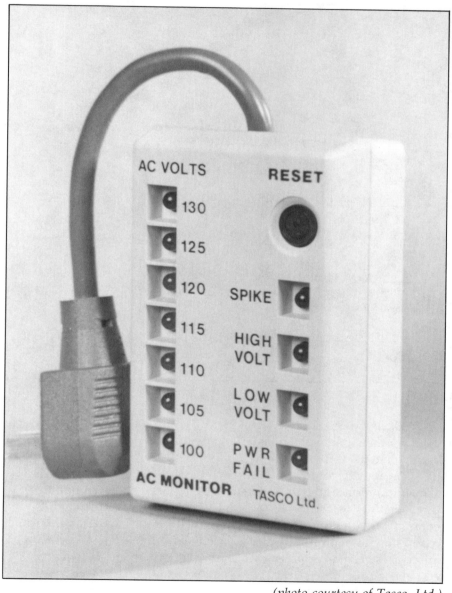

(photo courtesy of Tasco, Ltd.)

Figure 3-10
The Computer Power Diagnostic Instrument

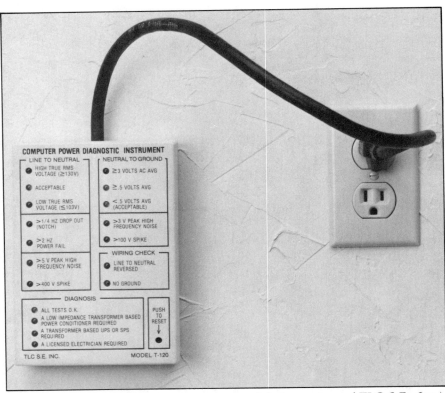

(photo courtesy of TLC S.E., Inc.)

To track down the sources of electrical noise, an oscilloscope, which displays the signal voltage as a function of time, is often required. A very convenient interface between the AC line and the oscilloscope is the Oneac Corporation (Libertyville, IL) ONEVIEW Line Noise Viewing Interface, shown in Figure 3-11. When connected to a two- or three-channel oscilloscope, the ONEVIEW allows the display of both common mode (line or neutral conductor to ground) and normal mode (line to neutral) noise. By selectively turning on and off various appliances such as printers, coffee pots, light dimmers, radiant heaters, etc., the sources of electrical noise can be identified. Power conditioning equipment could then be added to prevent harm to the LAN equipment.

Figure 3-11
ONEVIEW Line Noise Viewing Interface

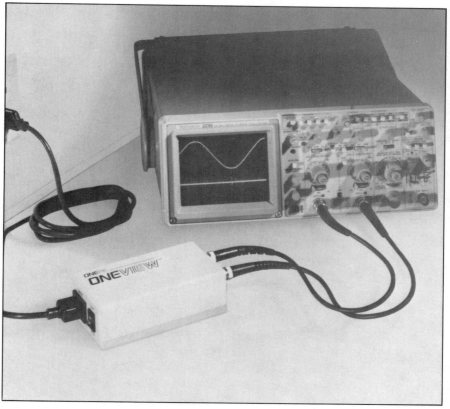

(photo courtesy of Oneac Corporation)

For long-term monitoring with tabulated results, a strip chart recorder is necessary. Figure 3-12 shows the Oneac Corporation ONEGRAPH Evaluation Power Monitor. This device monitors both Normal Mode noise (line to neutral) and Common Mode noise (line to ground) over either an 8-hour or 6-day duration, and produces a strip chart recording for further analysis.

Figure 3-12
ONEGRAPH Evaluation Power Monitor

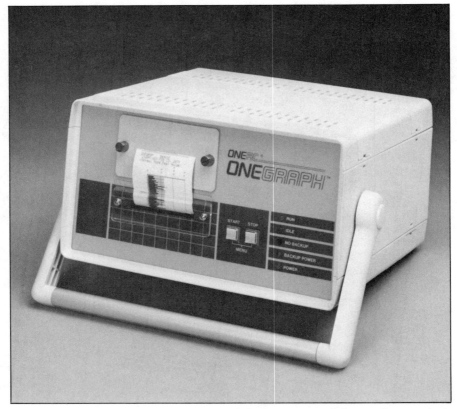

(photo courtesy of Oneac Corporation)

3.3 Analog Interface Testing Tools

Given the digital transmission nature of baseband LANs, one might easily overlook the need for analog test equipment. Three devices are valuable additions to the tool kit: the volt-ohm-milliameter (VOM), the oscilloscope, and the transmission impairment measurement system (TIMS). Figure 3-13 shows the test points used by analog and power line test equipment.

The TIMS is used at the interface between the LAN and an analog leased telephone line, the oscilloscope is used to measure noise at the power feed to the network server or on the network cable itself, and the VOM is good for many purposes, such as measuring the resistance of a cable terminator or the output voltage of the PC's internal power supply. We'll look at each device individually.

Figure 3-13
Test points for analog and power line test equipment

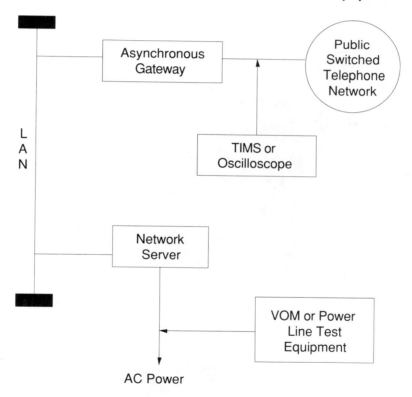

3.3.1 Volt-Ohm-Milliameter (VOM)

As the name implies, this instrument measures potential (voltage), resistance (ohms), and current (milliamperes). Typically packaged in a calculator-sized box, the VOM has a liquid crystal display (LCD) and measures the following ranges:

DC Voltage:	200 millivolts to 1000 volts
AC Voltage:	2000 millivolts to 750 volts
Resistance:	0.1 ohms to 20 megohms
DC Current:	200 milliamps to 10 Amps
AC Current:	200 milliamps to 10 Amps

Figure 3-14
Model 3350 Digital Multimeter

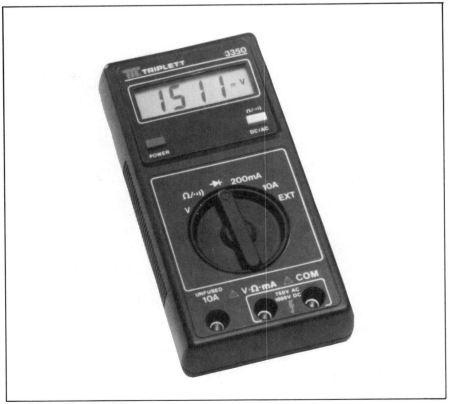

(photo courtesy of Triplett Corp.)

Figure 3-14 shows the Triplett Corporation's (Bluffton, OH) Model 3350 Digital Multimeter. The "digital" in the VOM's name implies an LCD digital display on the front panel. Older devices have an analog display.

Figure 3-15
Model 5 Loop Tester

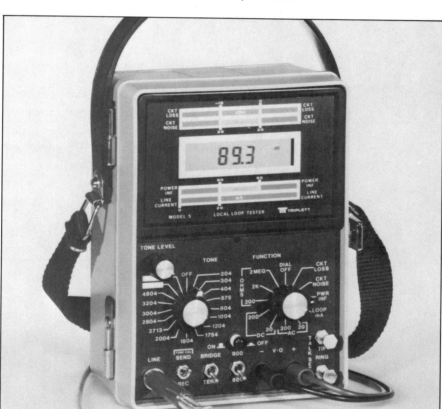

(photo courtesy of Triplett Corp.)

3.3.2 | Transmission Impairment Measurement System (TIMS)

This device is used to measure the analog impairments that may disrupt data communication on telephone lines. Parameters that may be measured by TIMS include signal-to-noise ratios, line loss, impulse noise, envelope delay, phase jitter, and so on. As seen in Figure 3-13, the TIMS is attached to the output (telephone line) side of an Asynchronous Gateway or Communications Server in wide area network (WAN) configurations.

The Tripplett Model 5 Loop Tester in Figure 3-15 is a portable unit featuring an LCD display.

3.3.3 Oscilloscope

This graphic device displays the signal voltage (vertical axis) per unit time (horizontal axis), and as such, provides a true representation of analog or digital signals. It can be used to measure the voltage output of EIA-232 or EIA-422 interfaces, and to analyze the noise component of commercial power sources. Figure 3-16 shows the Tektronix, Inc. (Beaverton, OR) Model 2235 oscilloscope.

Figure 3-16
Model 2235 Oscilloscope

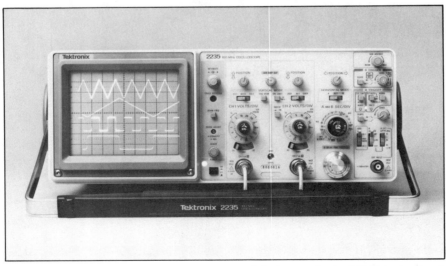

(photo courtesy of Tektronix, Inc.)

3.4 | Digital Interface Testing Tools

The digital (or discrete) signal levels present at the LAN interfaces to PCs, printers, modems and other peripherals are the test points most familiar to network managers. Figure 3-17 shows a variety of these points, and where the different tools might be connected. Appendix 3A shows pinouts for many of the common interfaces that are commonly found with LAN peripherals.

Figure 3-17
Test points for digital equipment

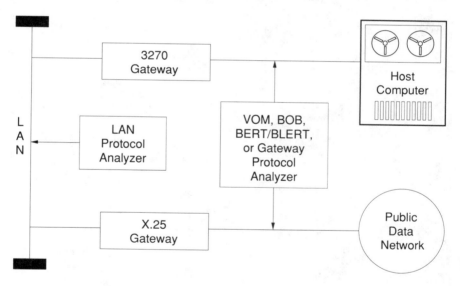

3.4.1 | Breakout Box (BOB)

This box allows the status of the EIA-232-D interface leads between Data Terminal Equipment (DTE) and Data Circuit-Terminating Equipment (DCE) to be displayed and monitored. Its greatest importance is its ability to reconfigure the interface by opening a path between corresponding pins of the interface connectors and rearranging that path. In this manner, a BOB can be used to quickly configure a null modem cable. The Datatran Corporation (Denver, CO) Datatracker Model DT-4 is shown in Figure 3-18, and is an example of a full-featured BOB that allows monitoring and reconfiguration of all leads on the EIA-232-D interface.

Figure 3-18
Datatracker Model DT-4

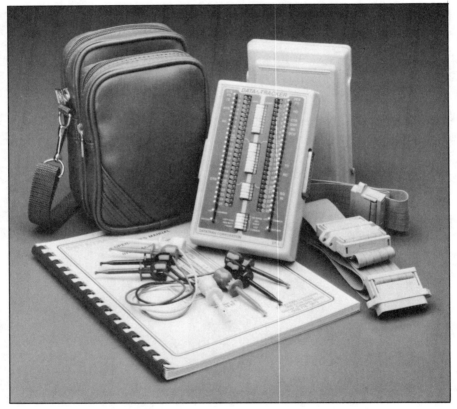

(photo courtesy of Datatran Corp.)

3.4.2 Pulse Trap

Similar in connection to a BOB, the pulse trap monitors selected leads of an interface and visually records any activity (high-to-low or low-to-high transitions) that occurs on those leads. This can be useful in recording extremely fast pulse activity that may be impossible to visibly recognize on a BOB. Figure 3-19 is the Datatran Corporation Pulse-Tracker Model PT-1, which can be used with or without a BOB.

Figure 3-19
Pulse Tracker Model PT-1

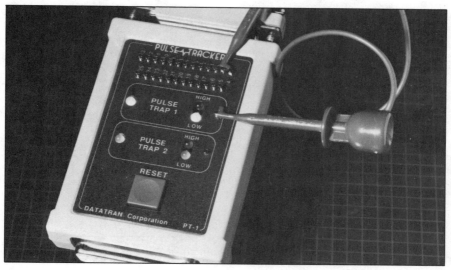

(photo courtesy of Datatran Corp.)

3.4.3 Smart Cable 821 Plus

IQ Technologies, Inc., of Bellevue, WA, has three products that can be real time savers for the network administrator. The Smart Cable 821 Plus, shown in Figure 3-20, will automatically configure an EIA-232-D connection between two asynchronous devices. Three switches, configured using LED indicators, control the internal connections of the SC821. The first switch selects the data leads for either straight through or crossover, the second switch configures the control lines, and the third switch sets the handshaking leads. An additional bank of DIP switches sets other leads required for specific applications. A null modem cable can thus be configured in less than a minute without using a soldering iron.

Figure 3-20
Smart Cable 821 Plus

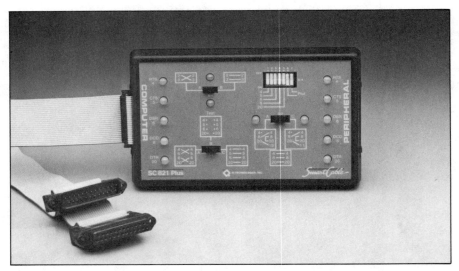

(photo courtesy of IQ Technologies, Inc.)

3.4.4 | Smart Data Meter 931

The IQ Technologies Smart Data Meter 931, seen in Figure 3-21 provides a low-cost tool to determine the data transmission parameters. Any EIA-232 compatible device can transmit some data to the Data Meter, and the display will give the bit rate, number of data bits, parity, and number of stop bits. The device can also determine the proper transmission settings for a receive-only device, such as a printer, by sending all possible combinations of parameters until the correct setting is matched. In this manner, it is relatively painless to determine the proper settings for a server-to-printer interface.

Figure 3-21
Smart Data Meter 931

(photo courtesy of IQ Technologies, Inc.)

3.4.5 | Smart Asynchronous Data Meter

Figure 3-22 shows the IQ Technologies' Smart Asynchronous Data Meter, Model SAM2000. It includes the capabilities of the Smart Cable Maker and Smart Data Meter, plus a Breakout Box and a Bit or Block Error Rate Tester (BERT/BLERT). The BERT/BLERT is a digital interface testing device that compares a received signal with a known transmitted signal to determine if any bit or block errors have occurred. A typical BERT/BLERT will operate at various data rates, and will have several canned test messages (such as "The quick brown fox..."). It may also include application packages (in ROM) for various Layer 2 and 3 protocols, such as asynchronous, SDLC, X.25, and so on.

Figure 3-22
Smart Asynchronous Data Meter

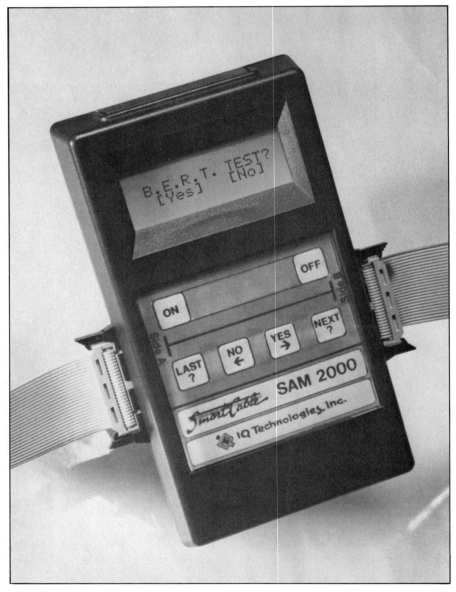

(photo courtesy of IQ Technologies, Inc.)

3.4.6 Datatran Micropatch

Another very useful tool is the Datatran Micropatch, in Figure 3-23, which can be used to wire a custom null modem in a very compact device. Once the null modem configuration has been verified with a BOB or Smart Cable Maker, it can be wired inside the small (1-1/2" x 2-1/2" x 1/2") Micropatch for direct connection between DTE and DCE using a minimum of space and clutter. The unit is then closed to avoid any accidental disconnections.

Figure 3-23
Datatran Micropatch

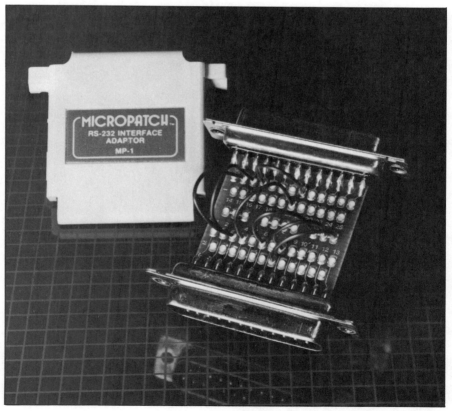

(photo courtesy of Datatran Corp.)

3.4.7 Interface Converters

Similar in size to the Micropatch, the Interface Converters from B & B Electronics Manufacturing Company (Oak Brook, IL) provide an economical way of permitting the use of a piece of test equipment, such as an RS-232-C Breakout Box, to be used for testing other interfaces, such as RS-422, RS-485, or RS-530. Figure 3-24 shows the RS-232 to RS-422 model converter.

Figure 3-24
Interface converter

(photo courtesy of B&B Electronics Manufacturing Co.)

3.5 Protocol Analyzers

The previous tools that we have discussed have all been used for hardware testing: cables, the power system, and various interfaces. We now turn our attention to tools that can assist in solving software problems.

Two different types of protocol analyzers, shown in Figure 3-25, can be used with LANs. A LAN protocol analyzer, such as Sniffer (Network General Corporation, Mountain View, CA), LANalyzer (Excelan, Inc., San Jose, CA), and 4972A (Hewlett-Packard, Colorado Springs, CO), attach as a workstation on the LAN. A second protocol analyzer attaches to a digital interface on the output (that is, non—LAN) side of an X.25, 3270, or Asynchronous gateway.

Figure 3-25
Using protocol analyzers on a LAN

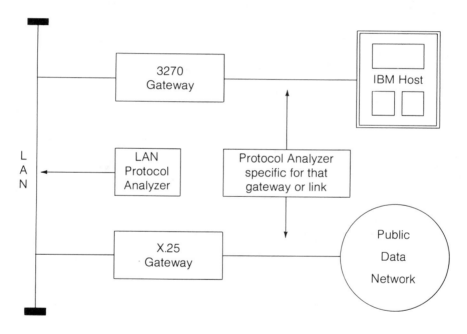

The LAN protocol analyzer can capture, record, and analyze frames that have been transmitted on the LAN. They must therefore contain a NIC for that particular LAN, and will attach to the backbone cable in the same way that any workstation would connect. LAN protocol analyzers are used to selectively eavesdrop on all LAN transmission, thus capturing, monitoring, and digesting frames of information. A representative LAN protocol analyzer, the Network General Corporation Sniffer Model 500, is shown in Figure 3-26. In chapters 5, 6, 7, and 8, we will show examples of frames that have been captured and analyzed with the Sniffer.

Figure 3-26
Sniffer Model 500

(photo courtesy of Network General Corporation)

Analyzers on the gateway side perform a function distinct from the LAN analyzers. Data going from the LAN into the gateway can be captured by a LAN analyzer, but this does not assure proper operation of the gateway. Only an analysis at the output from the gateway can do that. For a definitive confirmation of the gateway's operation, the information into and out of the device can be captured by both analyzers and then compared.

One example of this type of analyzer is the FELINE protocol analyzer from Frederick Engineering, Inc., of Columbia, MD. In Figure 3-27, the three elements of the device are visible: a half-size card for the PC, an interface pod for EIA-232 devices, plus the analysis software. The FELINE can decode the Physical and Data Link layers of the OSI model, with capabilities for HDLC, SDLC, X.25, Bisync, and other protocols.

Figure 3-27
Three elements of the FELINE protocol analyzer

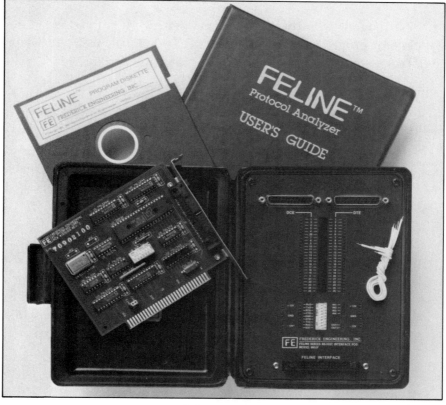

(photo courtesy of Frederick Engineering, Inc.)

3.6 | Other Useful Tools

Other additions to the network tool kit might include the following:

- **Walkie-Talkies**: easily obtained from Radio Shack stores, these can prove invaluable when tracing cable faults.

- **PC Diagnostic Software**: since many network failures are PC-related, programs such as the PC-Technician from Windsor Technologies, Inc. (San Rafael, CA), and the System Sleuth from DTG, Inc. (El Toro, CA), can be very useful.

- **Technical Database Software**: keeping up to date with all the latest hardware and software options, compatibilities, and potential conflicts can be a real challenge. The Technical Encyclopedia of Computer Hardware and Software (TECHS) from Techs International, Inc. (Anaheim, CA), is a subscription database that can assist in solving many of these configuration problems.

- **Network Specific Test Equipment**: several devices to test specific network interfaces are available. Among these are the Standard Microsystems Corporation (Hauppauge, NY) ARCNET Network Tester, shown in Figure 3-28, and the Black Box Corp. (Pittsburgh, PA) Ethernet Line Monitor in Figure 3-29. These devices, while useful on only one type of network, can quickly verify operation of a specific hardware component.

- **NIC Diagnostic Software**: many NIC manufacturers provide a diagnostic disk with the board. Make sure that you become familiar with the loop-around tests, internal diagnostic tests, and other built-in exercises available on these disks. It is one of the most valuable and timesaving tools.

- **Public Domain Utilities**: a variety of useful programs are available from public domain and shareware sources for diagnosing data communications problems. Those programs included with this handbook are listed in Appendix 3B.

Figure 3-28
ARCNET network tester

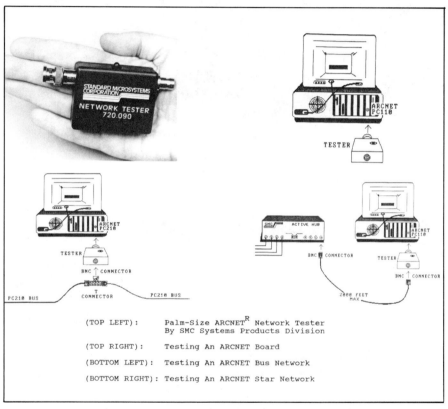

(TOP LEFT):   Palm-Size ARCNET^R Network Tester
                 By SMC Systems Products Division

(TOP RIGHT):   Testing An ARCNET Board

(BOTTOM LEFT):   Testing An ARCNET Bus Network

(BOTTOM RIGHT): Testing An ARCNET Star Network

(photo courtesy of Standard Microsystems Corp.)

Figure 3-29
Ethernet Line Monitor

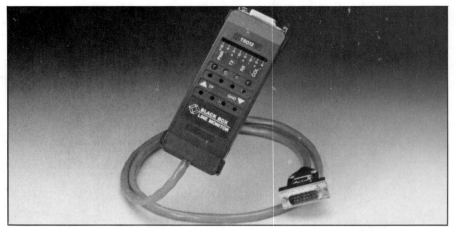

(photo courtesy of Black Box Corp.)

3.7 Assembling a Toolkit for Your LAN

After seeing this smorgasbord of equipment, the next logical question is, "Which tools should I purchase for my network?" Here are some guidelines:

1. Obtain any network-specific tools such as the NIC diagnostic disk from the manufacturer. These tools are the least expensive, and provide a great amount of diagnostic power at a very nominal cost.

2. Prepare for cable failures. Surveys indicate that a high percentage of network failures are related to the network wiring. Therefore, have the tools required to test your twisted pair, coax or fiber optic cables.

3. Be able to test the network interfaces. Compile a list of all the various interfaces (EIA-232, EIA-422, Centronics, etc.) on your LAN, and purchase test equipment that can test these points.

4. Consider software analyzers if either multiple LAN protocols or gateways are part of your network. If the network is relatively large (100 or more workstations) or heavily utilized, a LAN protocol analyzer can also assist with network optimization.

Data Communication and LAN Interfaces

Figure 3A-1
Interface Connectors

If your equipment has this connector type	For this interface
DB25 (4-, 12-, or 24-pin)	RS-232(V.24), RS-530 IBM® Parallel
DB37	RS-449, 442, 423 Bernoulli®
DB50	Dataproducts® Datapoint®, UNIVAC®, and others
DB15 / High Density DB15	Texas Instruments®, NCR® POS Ethernet IBM PS/2™ (High Density)
DB9	449 Secondary, ATARI® DAA, and Video Interfaces
5-Pin Din / Mini 6-Pin Din	IBM PC Keyboard (5-Pin) PS/2 Keyboard (Mini 6-Pin)
Mini 8-Pin Din	Apple® Macintosh®
36-Pin	Parallel printers: Centronics®, EPSON®, Gemini®, and others
Mate-N-Lok®	Current Loop, Telephone

If your equipment has this connector type	For this interface
IEEE-488	GPIB, HPIB
M/34	V.35
M/50	Dataproducts, UNIVAC, DEC™, and others
BNC / BNC and TNC	Coaxial (BNC or TNC), WANG®, Dual Coaxial (BNC and TNC)
Twinaxial	IBM AS/400™, Systems 34, 36, 38, 5520, and others
Telco	Telephone (Voice and data)
RJ-11 / RJ-45	Voice Telephone (RJ-11) Data Telephone (RJ-45)
Modified Modular Jack (MMJ)	DEC423 DECconnect™ System
Barrier Block	Utility current loop, and other 2- or 4-wires

Figure 3A-2
RS-449 and RS-232 Interface

RS-449 Interface

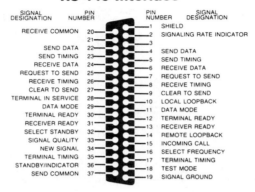

SIGNAL DESIGNATION	PIN NUMBER		PIN NUMBER	SIGNAL DESIGNATION
			1	SHIELD
RECEIVE COMMON	20		2	SIGNALING RATE INDICATOR
	21		3	
SEND DATA	22		4	SEND DATA
SEND TIMING	23		5	SEND TIMING
RECEIVE DATA	24		6	RECEIVE DATA
REQUEST TO SEND	25		7	REQUEST TO SEND
RECEIVE TIMING	26		8	RECEIVE TIMING
CLEAR TO SEND	27		9	CLEAR TO SEND
TERMINAL IN SERVICE	28		10	LOCAL LOOPBACK
DATA MODE	29		11	DATA MODE
TERMINAL READY	30		12	TERMINAL READY
RECEIVER READY	31		13	RECEIVER READY
SELECT STANDBY	32		14	REMOTE LOOPBACK
SIGNAL QUALITY	33		15	INCOMING CALL
NEW SIGNAL	34		16	SELECT FREQUENCY
TERMINAL TIMING	35		17	TERMINAL TIMING
STANDBY/INDICATOR	36		18	TEST MODE
SEND COMMON	37		19	SIGNAL GROUND

RS-232 Interface

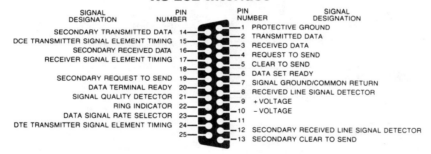

SIGNAL DESIGNATION	PIN NUMBER		PIN NUMBER	SIGNAL DESIGNATION
SECONDARY TRANSMITTED DATA	14		1	PROTECTIVE GROUND
DCE TRANSMITTER SIGNAL ELEMENT TIMING	15		2	TRANSMITTED DATA
SECONDARY RECEIVED DATA	16		3	RECEIVED DATA
RECEIVER SIGNAL ELEMENT TIMING	17		4	REQUEST TO SEND
	18		5	CLEAR TO SEND
SECONDARY REQUEST TO SEND	19		6	DATA SET READY
DATA TERMINAL READY	20		7	SIGNAL GROUND/COMMON RETURN
SIGNAL QUALITY DETECTOR	21		8	RECEIVED LINE SIGNAL DETECTOR
RING INDICATOR	22		9	+ VOLTAGE
DATA SIGNAL RATE SELECTOR	23		10	– VOLTAGE
DTE TRANSMITTER SIGNAL ELEMENT TIMING	24		11	
	25		12	SECONDARY RECEIVED LINE SIGNAL DETECTOR
			13	SECONDARY CLEAR TO SEND

Figure 3A-2 *(continued)*
Pinout Table for EIA RS-449, EIA RS-232/CCITT V.24

9 PIN AUX	37 PIN A	37 PIN B	RS-449 CIRCUIT	RS-449 DESCRIPTION	25 PIN	EIA-RS-232C CIRCUIT	CCITT-V.24 CIRCUIT	RS-232 DESCRIPTION	GND	DATA From DCE	DATA To DCE	CONTROL From DCE	CONTROL To DCE	TIMING From DCE	TIMING To DCE
1	1			Shield	1	AA	101	Protective Ground	X						
5	19		SG	Signal Ground	7	AB	102	Signal Ground/Common Return	X						
9	37		SC	Send Common			102a	DTE Common	X						
6	20		RC	Receive Common			102b	DCE Common	X						
	4	22	SD	Send Data	2	BA	103	Transmitted Data			X				
	6	24	RD	Receive Data	3	BB	104	Received Data		X					
	7	25	RS	Request to Send	4	CA	105	Request to Send					X		
	9	27	CS	Clear to Send	5	CB	106	Clear to Send				X			
	11	29	DM	Data Mode	6	CC	107	Data Set Ready				X			
	12	30	TR	Terminal Ready	20	CD	108.2	Data Terminal Ready					X		
	15		IC	Incoming Call	22	CE	125	Ring Indicator				X			
	13	31	RR	Receiver Ready	8	CF	109	Received Line Signal Detector				X			
	33		SQ	Signal Quality	21	CG	110	Signal Quality Detector				X			
	16		SR	Signaling Rate Selector	23	CH	111	Data Signal Rate Selector (DTE)					X		
	2		SI	Signaling Rate Indicator	23	CI	112	Data Signal Rate Selector (DCE)				X			
	17	35	TT	Terminal Timing	24	DA	113	Transmitter Signal Element Timing (DTE)							X
	5	23	ST	Send Timing	15	DB	114	Transmitter Signal Element Timing (DCE)						X	
	8	26	RT	Receive Timing	17	DD	115	Receiver Signal Element Timing (DCE)						X	
3			SSD	Secondary Send Data	14	SBA	118	Secondary Transmitted Data			X				
4			SRD	Secondary Receive Data	16	SBB	119	Secondary Received Data		X					
7			SRS	Secondary Request to Send	19	SCA	120	Secondary Request to Send					X		
8			SCS	Secondary Clear to Send	13	SCB	121	Secondary Clear to Send				X			
2			SRR	Secondary Received Ready	12	SCF	122	Secondary Received Line Signal Detector				X			
	10		LL	Local Loopback			141	Local Loopback					X		
	14		RL	Remote Loopback			140	Remote Loopback					X		
	18		TM	Test Mode			142	Test Indicator				X			
	32		SS	Select Standby			116	Select Standby					X		
	36		SB	Standby Indicator			117	Standby Indicator				X			
	16		SF	Select Frequency			126	Select Transmit Frequency					X		
	28		IS	Terminal in Service								X			
	34		NS	New Signal								X			

(Reprinted by permission, Black Box Corporation, Pittsburgh, PA
© Copyright, 1989. All rights reserved.)

Figure 3A-3
V.35 Interface

V.35 Interface

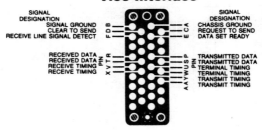

PIN	NAME	To DTE	To DCE	FUNCTION
A	FG			Frame (or protective) ground
B	SG			Signal (or reference) ground
C	RTS		→	Request to send
D	CTS	←		Clear to send
E	DSR	←		Data set ready
F	RLSD	←		Received line signal
H	DTR		→	Data terminal ready
J	RI	←		Ring indicator
K	LT		→	Local test
R				Received data (Sig. A)
	RD	←		
T				Received data (Sig. B)
V				Serial clock receive (Sig. A)
	SCR	←		
X				Serial clock receive (Sig. B)
P				Send data (Sig. A)
	SD		→	
S				Send data (Sig. B)
U				Serial clock xmit ext. (Sig. A)
	SCTE		→	
W				Serial clock xmit ext. (Sig. B)
Y				Serial clock transmit (Sig. A)
	SCT	←		
a				Serial clock transmit (Sig. B)
h, i, j, k, m, n				Unused
L, M, N, Z, b, c, d, f, g				Unused

(Reprinted by permission, Black Box Corporation, Pittsburgh, PA
© Copyright, 1989. All rights reserved.)

Figure 3A-4
Centronics Parallel Interface

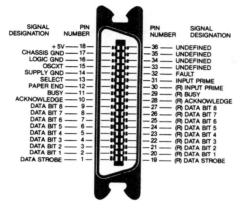

(R) INDICATES SIGNAL GROUND RETURN

SIGNAL PIN NO.	RETURN PIN NO.	SIGNAL	DIRECTION (with ref. to printer)	DESCRIPTION
1	19	STROBE	In	STROBE pulse (negative going) enables reading data.
2	20	DATA 1	In	1st to 8th bits of parallel data.
3	21	DATA 2	In	Each signal is at "HIGH" level when data is logical
4	22	DATA 3	In	"1" and "LOW" when
5	23	DATA 4	In	logical "0".
6	24	DATA 5	In	
7	25	DATA 6	In	
8	26	DATA 7	In	
9	27	DATA 8	In	
10	28	ACKNLG	Out	"LOW" indicates that data has been received and that the printer is ready to accept other data.
11	29	BUSY	Out	"HIGH" indicates that the printer cannot receive data.

NOTE: Pins 12, 13, 14, 15, 18, 31, 32, 34, 35, and 36 vary in function depending upon application; they are commonly used for printer auxiliary controls, and error handling and indication.

Pins 16 and 17 are commonly used for logic ground and chassis ground, respectively.

(Reprinted by permission, Black Box Corporation, Pittsburgh, PA
© Copyright, 1989. All rights reserved.)

Data Communications, PC, and LAN Diagnostic Software

We have collected a number of programs for your use in diagnosing PC and LAN faults. Please understand that these programs are public-domain or shareware—we DO NOT offer any license or guarantee regarding any program's performance. Please use these programs with some caution.

Some programs use on-screen documentation, others have documentation files with a .DOC or .TXT extension. You should not attempt to use any program without first printing out and reading the documentation.

The files on the disk are:

ARCDIAG:	ARCNET diagnostic program.
BAUDCHG:	Allows user to change baud rate of a program.
BRKBOX:	Displays the RS-232 signals of the COM1 or COM2 ports.
CHIPS:	Benchmark program for CPU MIPS and performance.
CI:	Provides CPU information.

D'SCOPE: Turns a PC into a data scope or data line monitor.

DIAGS: Serial port, parallel port, video and memory diagnostics. Allows the currently used IRQ lines to be determined.

IRQR: Reports status of 8259 hardware interrupt channels.

EQUIP: Displays the current equipment configuration for the PC.

RS232:   Displays status of COM1 or COM2 signals on the CRT.

SETUP: Sets up printer, CRT, and serial port parameters, will also redirect printer to a serial port.

SPEED99:   Performs CPU speed and relative performance tests.

SWAPCOM: Swaps between COM1 and COM2 ports; executing a second time will swap the ports back.

SWAPPRT: Swaps between LPT1 and LPT2 ports; executing a second time will swap the ports back.

VSI: Visual display of the PC's current configuration.

CHAPTER FOUR

Troubleshooting Cabling Systems

4.1 Transmission Line Fundamentals

Figure 4-1 shows the basic model for a transmission line, along with the line parameters known as primary constants. These constants are usually expressed on a per distance basis, and include DC resistance (R), inductance (L), mutual capacitance (C) and conductance (G). The DC resistance is measured in ohms; the inductance is measured in millihenries; the capacitance is measured in picofarads, and the conductance is measured in micromhos.

From these primary constants is derived the characteristic impedance, Zo, of the cable:

$$Z_O = \sqrt{\frac{R + j\omega L}{G + j\omega C}} \quad \text{ohms}$$

Note that both resistance and impedance are measured in units of ohms. There is a major difference, however. Resistance measures the opposition to Direct Current (DC), while impedance measures the opposition to Alternating Current (AC). For copper transmission media, three of the above parameters are commonly specified: R, C, and Z_O. See Chapter 5 of reference [4-1] for further details.

Figure 4-1
The transmission line model

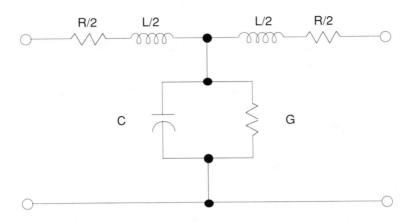

R = Resistance per unit length
L = Inductance per unit length
C = Capacitance per unit length
G = Conductance per unit length

4.1.1   Balanced and Unbalanced Transmission

The terms "balanced" and "unbalanced" are often used in describing transmission lines. A balanced line is shown in Figure 4-2a, where the unbalanced case is shown in Figure 4-2b.

In a balanced design (also called differential mode), the currents flowing between generator and receiver in each of the wires are equal in magnitude, but opposite in direction. The voltages in these conductors, with respect to ground, are also equal in magnitude and opposite in polarity. A ground potential difference (shown as Vg in Figure 4-2a) may exist between generator and receiver. Twisted pair and twinax cables are examples of balanced transmission lines.

Figure 4-2a
Balanced digital interface circuit

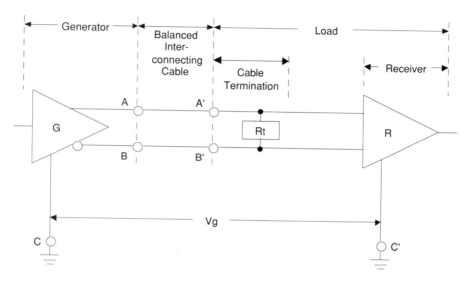

Legend

Rt = Optional Cable Termination Resistance
Vg = Ground Potential Difference
A, B = Generator Interface Points
A', B' = Load Interface Points
C = Generator Circuit Ground
C' = Load Circuit Ground

Coaxial cable is an unbalanced transmission line. The current flowing in the signal conductor returns via a ground connection that may be shared with other circuits. Both the current and voltage in the signal conductor is measured with respect to this signal return conductor.

Figure 4-2b
Unbalanced digital interface circuit

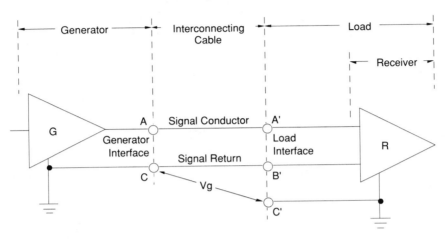

Legend

A, C = Generator Interface
A', B' = Load Interface
   C' = Load Circuit Ground
   C = Generator Circuit Ground
  Vg = Ground Potential Difference

To convert between a balanced and unbalanced transmission line, a balun transformer (short for balanced to unbalanced) is used. To eliminate a length of coaxial cable, a pair of baluns (one on each end of the twisted pair transmission line) can provide the necessary conversions from coax to twisted pair and then back to coax. Baluns are becoming more popular with Ethernet and ARCNET networks, since they provide a very economical replacement for coaxial cables. If baluns are used, make sure that they are certified by the manufacturer for use on that particular type of LAN.

4.1.2 | Crosstalk

Crosstalk is caused by the inductive (or magnetic field) coupling from one line into another line. It is most pronounced in cables having bidirectional transmission in the same sheath, such as twisted pair. Crosstalk is depicted in Figure 4-3, taken from reference [4-2].

Figure 4-3
Crosstalk

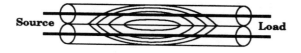

Source ... Load

(courtesy of Trompeter Electronics, Inc.)

Crosstalk is measured in decibels (dB), as follows:

$$dB = 10 \log_{10} \frac{Pout}{Pin} = 20 \log_{10} \frac{Vout}{Vin}$$

where Pout/Pin and Vout/Vin are the power and voltage measurements, respectively, of the interfered-with and interfering signals. The "log" designates the base 10 logarithm of the power or voltage ratio. For example, a power ratio of 10:1 yields 10 dB, 100:1 yields 20 dB, etc. When Pout is less than Pin, a loss (rather than a gain) results. This measurement yields a negative value. As an example, if the input power was 10 watts, and the output power measured 7 watts, the loss would be:

$$Loss = 10 \log_{10} \frac{7}{10} = 10 \, (-0.15) = -1.5 \, dB$$

In many cases, a reference power of 1 milliwatt or a reference voltage of 1 millivolt is used for the denominator of the equation:

$$dBm = 10 \log_{10} \frac{Power}{1 \, mW} \quad or \quad dBmV = 20 \log_{10} \frac{Voltage}{1 \, mV}$$

This yields the values decibel milliwatts (dBm) and decibel milli-volts (dBmV), respectively. The interfering (or crosstalk) signal disrupts normal communication from generator to receiver. It thus behooves us to keep the crosstalk signal as low as possible, and signal-to-noise ratios as high as possible. The easiest way to accomplish this is to keep the LAN cables as far away as possible from sources of interference, known as noise.

4.1.3 Noise

Noise is defined as any unwanted signal that enters the transmission line from another source and also impairs communication signals. Noise is generally classified in two ways: radio frequency interference (RFI) from radio and television transmitters; and electromagnetic interference (EMI) from fluorescent lights, arc welders, fan motors, light dimmers, etc. Figure 4-4a and 4-4b illustrate the effects of RF and electromagnetic interference on a transmission line.

Figure 4-4a
RF interference

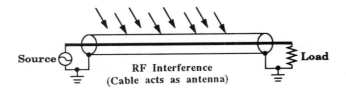

(courtesy of Trompeter Electronics, Inc.)

Figure 4-4b
Electromagnetic Interference

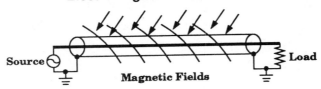

(courtesy of Trompeter Electronics, Inc.)

To measure the effects of noise, a ratio (again given in decibels or dB) between the signal and noise powers is calculated as follows:

$$dB = 10 \log_{10} \frac{S}{N}$$

where S and N are signal and noise powers, measured in watts or milliwatts.

See reference [4-1] for further information on noise measurement.

4.1.4   Effects of Crosstalk and Noise

In order for all of the above mathematics to be meaningful, we must somehow relate them to practical LAN applications. The question then boils down to "how much interference (crosstalk and/or noise) can the LAN cable tolerate before data errors occur?" This question becomes even more significant if the issue is raised of reusing existing building wiring.

Because of the intermittent nature of noise, measurements (either as a signal to noise ratio or in terms of noise amplitude in millivolts) can be very misleading. Nevertheless, let us make some generalizations.

The ARCNET receiver contains an extremely sensitive filter that passes only the frequency of interest (5 MHz), and severely attenuates other frequencies. As a result, ARCNET cabling is extremely tolerant of induced noise, and testimonials of ARCNET cables running next to sources of great EMI (such as arc welders) have been told. The IEEE 802.3 and 802.5 standards specify the receiver characteristics, and with that, a minimum receive signal level (measured in millivolts) or crosstalk (measured in millivolts or dB of attenuation). Depending on the particular standard, the maximum noise amplitudes range from 50–300 millivolts. Any interfering signal that exceeds these values could cause data corruption. One tool which will measure these noise amplitudes is the Cable Scanner shown in Figure 3-5.

The safest approach, however, is prevention. Keep your LAN cables away from potential noise sources such as AC power, analog telephones, etc. Doing so will minimize network maintenance in the long run.

4.2 National Electric Code Considerations

While it may not directly affect network troubleshooting, the type of LAN cable installed can certainly affect the network cost, building code compliance, fire insurance premiums, etc. In the United States, the National Electric Code (NEC), published by the National Fire Protection Association (NFPA), governs many safety regulations concerning the placement of cable in buildings (see reference [4-3]). The NEC is concerned with many different types of cable, including twisted pair, coaxial, and optical fiber, used for both horizontal and vertical distribution of signals. Underwriters Laboratories (UL) has devised tests to rate specific types of cables as being certified for plenum, nonplenum, or other uses.

The plenum is the space (usually about two feet) between the false ceiling and the floor above. It is used for circulating warm and cold air throughout the building. Because of this purpose, fire codes are quite explicit as to requirements for any wire that is placed in the plenum. Plenum cable is certified to be fire resistant, and also to produce a minimum of smoke. It can be installed in air handling spaces without conduit, and must pass the UL910 Modified Steiner Tunnel Test. Riser cables must not carry the fire from one floor to the next, and must pass the UL1666 Riser Cable Flame Test. It can be installed in vertical runs without conduit. Other types of cable are defined for specific uses or short distances, and are also tested to prevent the spread of fire, as described in reference [4-4].

4.2.1 Cable Categories

The NEC contains five different articles relating to building cables:

- NEC Article 725: for remote control signaling and power limited circuits, such as LANS.

- NEC Article 760: for fire protection signaling systems, operating at 600 volts or less, such as smoke detectors.

- NEC Article 770: for fiber optic cables used for data processing.

- NEC Article 800: for communication cables for telephone, telegraph, burglar alarms, and PBXs.

- NEC Article 820: for coaxial cables for radio frequency (RF) signals, such as those used with CATV or broadband systems.

Of the above cable types, Article 725 and Article 800 cables are most frequently used with LANs.

Article 725 cables are divided into two classes: Class 2, rated up to 150 volts, and Class 3, rated up to 300 volts. Each category is further specified for either riser or plenum cable:

CL2R:	Class 2 Riser Cable
CL2P:	Class 2 Plenum Cable
CL3R:	Class 3 Riser Cable
CL3P:	Class 3 Plenum cable
PLTC:	Power Limited Tray Cable

Ethernet transceiver and trunk cables are examples of Article 725 type cables.

Article 800 cables are what used to be strictly telephone cable, but have now been expanded to include both shielded and unshielded twisted pair cable, plus coax. Cable markings are as follows:

CM: Communications Cable
CMR: Communications Riser Cable
CMP: Communications Plenum Cable
CMX: Communications Cable, Limited Use

Examples of Article 800 type cables include the IBM Type 1 (shielded twisted pair), IBM Type 3 (unshielded twisted pair), and typical telephone cable that can be used with StarLAN and IEEE 10BASE-T networks.

A gradual combining of Article 725 and Article 800 cables into a new category of low-voltage communication cables is anticipated by some cable manufacturers. Check the latest building codes before planning any network cabling jobs to assure compliance with any new regulations.

4.2.2 | Cable Installation

In most cases, installing Poly Vinyl Chloride (or PVC) cable inside conduit greatly exceeds the cost of installing plenum-rated (Teflon or TFE) cable without conduit. An excellent cost comparison is given in reference [4-5], which would be worth considering before any additional cable is added to your network. Information on the techniques and procedures for proper wire installation is given in reference [4-6].

4.3 | Twisted Pair Cable

Twisted pair cable, the most popular media for voice and data transmission within the office environment is shown in Figure 4-5. Twisted pairs are so named because the two wires (or one pair) are twisted longitudinally to minimize crosstalk between the pairs. The tightness of the twisting is referred to as the "pitch" and varies from two to twelve twists per foot. Telephone cables make a lower pitch, while special-purpose data cables have a higher pitch.

Data grade, or shielded twisted pairs, are also used with LANs, principally token ring networks. The shield, shown in Figure 4-6, reduces electrical interference, similar to the shield of a coaxial cable.

Figure 4-5
Twisted pair cable

(Courtesy of Mohawk Wire and Cable)

Figure 4-6
Shielded twisted pair cable

(Courtesy of Mohawk Wire and Cable)

4.3.1 | Electrical Characteristics

Twisted pairs have four principle electrical characteristics: the gauge of the conductors, which determines the DC resistance in ohms per kilofoot (Ω/Kft); the mutual capacitance between the two conductors in picofarads per foot (pF/ft); the characteristic impedance, Zo, measured in ohms at a given reference frequency such as 1 MHz; and the attenuation in decibels (dB) as we saw above. Optimum transmission is achieved when the resistance, mutual capacitance, and attenuation of the cable are minimized. The characteristic impedance is determined by the geometry and materials such as insulation that is used in manufacturing the cable, and is a constant for a given type of cable.

4.3.2 | Twisted Pair Color Codes

Most twisted pair cable follows the telephone industry standard color code, which is based upon cluster of a twenty-five pairs, known as a binder group. Smaller cables are certainly allowed, however larger cables simply add additional binder groups inside the sheath, thus yielding 50 pair, 100 pair, 300 pair or larger cables.

The color code is based upon five primary and five secondary colors, which yield twenty-five color combinations when the primary and secondary colors are paired:

Primary Color	Secondary Color
White	Blue
Red	Orange
Black	Green
Yellow	Brown
Violet	Slate

Pair number 1 thus consists of a white wire with blue tracer plus a blue wire with white tracer. Pair seven is red/orange, pair 18 is yellow/green, etc. See reference [4-6] for further explanation on the color codes.

It is imperative that the wire pairings are consistent—that is, the two white/blue wires make a pair, one white/blue wire plus one white/green wire does not.

Figure 4-7
The 66-type punch-down block

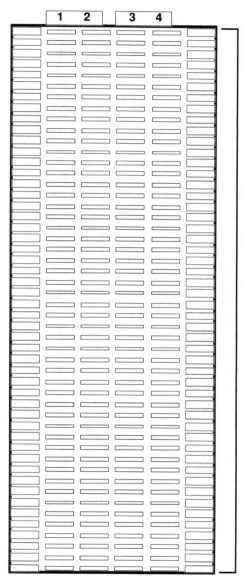

25 pairs

50 rows of insulation displacement contacts

4 columns of insulation displacement contacts

Columns 1 and 2 are electrically connected

Columns 3 and 4 are electrically connected

4.3.3 | The 66-Type Punch-Down Block

Most twisted pair cables are terminated on a 66-type block, shown in Figure 4-7. The block consists of four columns of fifty pins each, onto which the fifty wires of the twenty-five pair binder group are placed. Each wire is placed in a pin, and then "punched" into place, stripping the insulation in the process. Again looking at Figure 4-7, note that the pins in columns 1 and 2 are shorted together, plus the pins in columns 3 and 4 are shorted together. This creates an input and output side of the block. To connect the two halves, bridging (or shorting) clips are used between pins 2 and 3 of any particular row. The 66-type blocks are becoming more popular with LANs, because they allow easy access to each wire of the twenty-five pair binder group.

4.3.4 | Measuring Twisted Pair Lengths

At some point during the installation, the distance between two points via twisted pairs may need to be determined. The easiest way to determine the length of a twisted pair is to measure its DC resistance with a volt-ohm-milliameter (VOM). To do so, connect the VOM leads to one pair, and short the far end wires of the same pair together, as shown in Figure 4-8. This measurement can either be made with the cable on the reel, or with the cable already installed. If the cable pair is in place, however, make sure that it does not contain a live circuit. The DC resistance constraints can be obtained from Table 4-1.

Table 4-1
DC Resistance of Twisted Pair Cable

Wire Gauge	DC Resistance (Ohms/Km)	DC Resistance (Ohms/Kft)
22	53	16
24	84	26
26	134	41

Record the resistance as measured by the VOM, and then divide by the appropriate factor—for example, 26 ohms/Kft for 24 gauge cable. This measurement will be the round-trip distance from your end of the twisted pair cable to the short and then back again. Divide that distance in half for the end-to-end measurement. For example, if a 24-gauge twisted pair cable showed a resistance reading of approximately 19 ohms when the far end wires were shorted together, that reading would convert to 730 feet of wire. Since this is a round trip distance, the cable is actually 365 feet in length.

Figure 4-8
Measuring twisted pair cable lengths

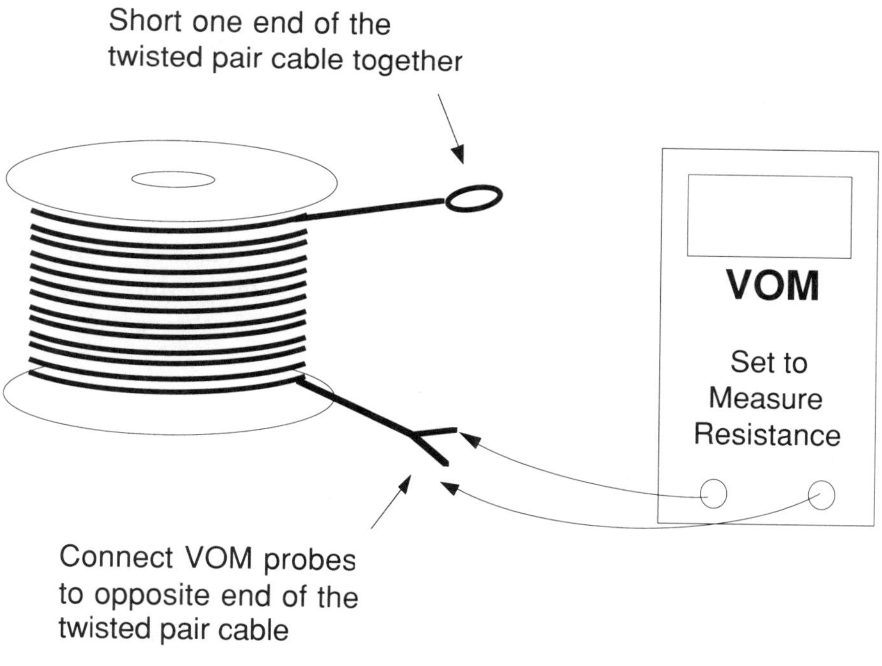

Short one end of the
twisted pair cable together

VOM

Set to
Measure
Resistance

Connect VOM probes
to opposite end of the
twisted pair cable

4.3.5 Using Modular Cords

Many ARCNET, StarLAN, and IEEE 10BASE-T networks use modular cords for connections between NICs, transceivers, hubs, etc. Most networks specify that the cables must have pin-to-pin continuity—that is, pins 1, 2, 3, and 4 are wired to pins 1, 2, 3, and 4, respectively, on the other end. Some modular cords are not wired straight through, but instead invert the pins. In other words, pins 1, 2, 3, and 4 are wired to pins 4, 3, 2, and 1, respectively. Make sure that you know what wiring your modular cord has. If in doubt, use a VOM or cable continuity tester to verify. If you assemble your own modular cords, make sure that the modular connector crimp is making a good connection to each wire.

4.4 Coaxial Cable

Coaxial cable gets its name from the center or common axis that both the center conductor, shields or braids, and insulating materials share, as shown in Figure 4-9. The purpose of the shield is to prevent any extraneous signal (or noise) from entering the center conductor, and to prevent that center conductor from radiating into another cable.

Figure 4-9
Coaxial cable

(Courtesy of Mohawk Wire and Cable)

4.4.1 Electrical Characteristics

Coaxial cables have five principle electrical characteristics: the DC resistance of the center conductor and shield, measured in ohms per kilofoot (Ω/Kft); the characteristic impedance, Zo, at a given frequency such as 1 MHz, measured in ohms; the attenuation, measured in decibels (dB); the capacitance between the center conductor and shield, measured in picofarads per foot (pF/ft); the nominal velocity of propagation (NPV) or speed of transmission relative to the speed of light in a vacuum (C, equal to 300,000 meters/second); and finally the propagation delay, measured in nanoseconds per foot (ns/ft). As with twisted pairs, optimum transmission is obtained when the attenuation and capacitance are minimized. The characteristic impedance, velocity of propagation and propagation delay are usually fixed parameters that the system engineers have used to design the transmitter and receiver circuitry. These parameters may also define protocol parameters such as response timeouts, maximum end-to-end signal propagation delays, etc.

4.4.2 | Coaxial Cable Used for LANs and Data Communication

Four types of coax are used with LANs, as shown in Table 4-2:

Table 4-2
Coaxial cables used with LANs

Cable Type	Application	Diameter	Zo (@ 1 MHz)
Ethernet	IEEE 10BASE5	0.40 inch	50 ohms
RG-58A/U	IEEE 10BASE2	0.18 inch	50 ohms
RG-59/U	CATV, ARCNET	0.25 inch	75 ohms
RG-62/U	ARCNET, IBM Terminals	0.25 inch	93 ohms

Note the very similar diameters of RG-58A/U, RG-59/U, and RG-62/U (they're all about 1/4 inch). Care should be taken not to mix these up during the installation process.

4.5 | Troubleshooting Metallic Cable

Because of the similarities in both cable failures and the corresponding solutions, both twisted pair and coaxial cable fault isolation will be considered together.

All cable problems come in two general categories: those caused by the connectors, splices, punch-down blocks, terminators or other mechanical devices; and those faults caused by the cable itself, such as opens, shorts, crimps, and kinks. In most cases, failures caused by the connectors are more prevalent than those caused by the cable itself. We'll look at two methods for identifying these faults

4.5.1 | Continuity or DC Resistance Tests

A continuity test simply measures the ability of a DC signal to follow a continuous path, or circuit within the cable. An example test was shown in Figure 4-8, determining the length of a twisted pair cable. This test can also be used to verify the length of a reel of either twisted pair or coaxial cable when it is received from the vendor. Return any defective spools to the vendor when significant differences between the spool length (usually stamped on the reel) and your measured length exist. Remember that your measurement (when shorting the far ends together) will result in a distance calculation of double the actual length.

Cables used with token ring networks will also measure twice the actual distance, if a hermaphroditic (genderless) data connector is at one end. Shorting bars inside the connector connect the Transmit + and Receive +, and Transmit - and Receive - conductors together when the connector is separated from its mate. More about the token ring wiring in section 6.3.

Terminator resistors can be easily checked with a VOM. For terminators in a BNC or N-type connector, measure between the center conductor of the connector and its outer shell. For terminators in modular (RJ-11 or RJ-45) plugs, measure between the appropriate pins, usually the two pins in the center. Consult your NIC installation manual for the proper terminator wiring. Table 4-3 lists the results that should be obtained.

Table 4-3
Terminator Values for LAN Cable

Cable Type	Terminator Resistance
Ethernet	50 ohms
RG-58A/U	50 ohms
RG-59/U	75 ohms
RG-62/U	93 ohms
Unshielded twisted pair	100-120 ohms
Shielded twisted pair	150 ohms

Figure 4-10a shows an Ethernet cable with the 50 ohm terminators attached, and an access point (either transceiver tap or BNC "T" connector) identified. If a resistance measurement is made at the access point, a value close to 25 ohms should result. Remember that this is DC ohms (resistance), not AC ohms (impedance). If the DC resistance is much different from 25 ohms (e.g. 60 ohms), one end of the cable is not properly terminated. The reason is evident from the equivalent circuit in Figure 4-10b. The two terminators when properly installed in parallel will result in an approximate 25 ohm measurement.

Figure 4-10a
Measuring Ethernet terminators

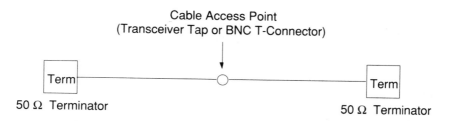

Cable Access Point
(Transceiver Tap or BNC T-Connector)

Term   Term

50 Ω Terminator   50 Ω Terminator

Figure 4-10b
Ethernet cable equivalent circuit

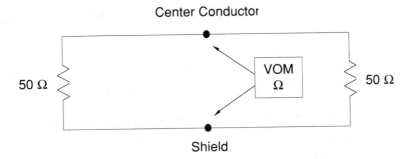

Center Conductor

50 Ω   VOM Ω   50 Ω

Shield

4.5.2 Time Domain Reflectometer Tests

A time domain reflectometer (TDR) is built as a combination of a pulse generator, a voltage sampler, and an output amplifier, supplying either a display or an oscilloscope.

Because of their distributed-star topologies, ARCNET, token ring, StarLAN, and IEEE 10BASE-T networks are easiest to test when a specific cable segment is isolated and inactive. A TDR can be used on a live Ethernet, however, if a very short pulse (less than 10 nanosecond duration) is used, and if that pulse is of a negative polarity. Don't use positive pulse TDRs, since they can affect transceiver operation.

The TDR's operation is similar to radar. A electrical pulse of known amplitude and duration is transmitted from one end of the cable. Any changes in the cable's characteristic impedance will cause reflections of the transmitted pulse. If no cable faults exist, and the cable is terminated at the far end in its characteristic impedance (Zo), no pulse reflection will occur.

A variety of cable problems, such as shorts, opens, faulty, or improper terminations, kinks, bends, crimps, shorted taps, or impedance mismatches (from mixing different types of coaxial cable) produce a unique signal reflection, known as a TDR fault signature. References [4-7] and [4-8] go into these technical details in greater depth, and illustrate various cable faults that can be diagnosed using the Tektronix, Inc., metallic TDRs. Figure 4-11 shows some representative cable faults and the associated TDR outputs.

Figure 4-11
TDR signatures for various cable faults

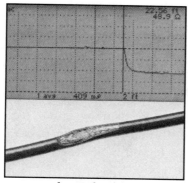

shorted cable

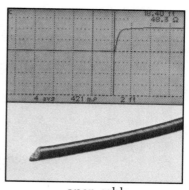

open cable

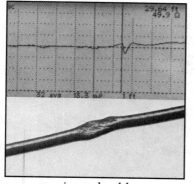

crimped cable

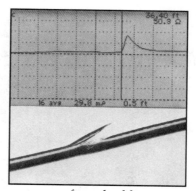

frayed cable

(photos courtesy of Tektronix, Inc.)

Another TDR, the Cable Scanner from MicroTest, Inc., which was discussed in Chapter 3, is a microprocessor-based unit that includes several additional features for cable testing that can be very helpful. Measurements of the ambient noise induced onto the cable allow the user to determine if crosstalk or noise problems are likely to exist. Secondly, a cable tracing function is available which will trace the location of existing cable within walls, floors, or ceilings. Third, measurements of network activity are available. See section 3.1 for further details.

4.6 | Fiber Optic Cable

The last decade has seen a major growth in two complementary technologies: fiber optic communication and LANs. The marriage of these two technologies has resulted in many advantages to the end user. Because optical fibers do not emit any radiation, they are immune to the typical electromagnetic interference (EMI) and radio frequency interference (RFI) that plague many LAN installations.

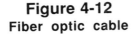

Figure 4-12
Fiber optic cable

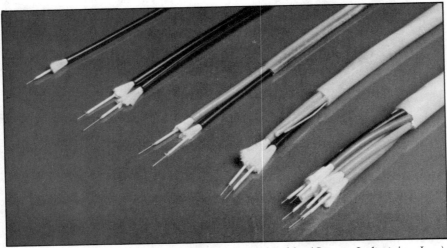

(photo courtesy of Belden/Cooper Industries, Inc.)

Secondly, ground isolation between buildings is possible, since the fiber cable itself is a non-conductor, typically silica. Third, the small size and light weight of fiber facilitates many installations. Finally, the high bandwidth, easily in the 100s of MBPS range, provide a guarantee against cable system obsolescence. Examples of fiber optic cables are shown in Figure 4-12. We'll begin by investigating the physical characteristics of fiber optic transmission.

4.6.1 | Fiber Optic Transmission Characteristics

A simple fiber optic link, described in greater detail in reference [4-9], is shown in Figure 4-13. At the transmitter, the input signal drives a light source, either a laser diode or an LED. The optical source operates in the infrared spectrum, emitting light in one of three wavelength ranges: 800-900 nanometers (nm), 1100-1300 nm, and around 1500 nm. The optical source and cable are designed for optimum transmission in one of these three ranges.

Figure 4-13
Simple fiber optic link

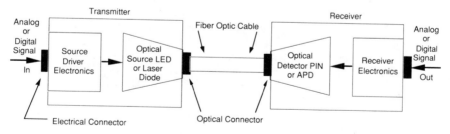

(courtesy of Belden/Cooper Industries, Inc.)

At the receiver, an optical detector consisting of either a positive-intrinsic-negative (PIN) diode or an avalanche photodiode (APD) captures the light pulses and hands them off to the electronic receiver circuitry. The optical transmission link in-between is of a point-to-point nature.

It is the transmission link that concerns us, not so much the optical drivers and receivers (we'll leave that job for the system designers). A model of the three types of fiber optic transmission, also from reference [4-9], is shown in Figure 4-14. In the single mode (or mono mode) applications, the light travels along a single path. Monomode cables are used for extremely high data rate applications, such as long distance telephone transmission. Multimode cables contain many different light rays, and can be either step index or graded index in manufacture. In step index cable, a dramatic change occurs between the core and cladding's index of refraction. In graded index, a more gradual change occurs. The step index cable yields a resulting light pattern that is a more zigzag effect, while the graded index provides a more gradual bending of the light.

Figure 4-14
Fiber optic transmission

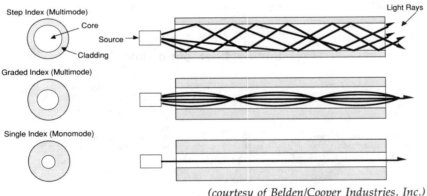

(courtesy of Belden/Cooper Industries, Inc.)

For both of these multimode cables, a phenomenon known as modal dispersion or spreading of the received light pulse occurs. When this pulse spreading occurs, the receiver has difficulty distinguishing one pulse from another. The effect of this dispersion is to limit the effective upper frequency limit of the cable. It is measured in nanoseconds per kilometer (ns/km) or alternatively in megahertz-kilometers (MHz-km). The product of the highest frequency (in MHz) and cable distance (in km) yield this model dispersion (or bandwidth) parameter.

The core of the cable is the cylinder that provides a conduit for the light, while the cladding surrounding the core provides a surface that causes reflection of the light. The diameter of the cable, measured in microns (micrometers) is usually given as two separate numbers. For example, a 62.5/125 micron cable has a core diameter of 62.5 microns, and a cladding diameter of 125 microns.

The attenuation (or loss) of the optical power is measured in decibels per kilometer (dB/km), in a similar fashion to copper media measurements, where:

$$dB = 10 \log_{10} \frac{\text{Power Out}}{\text{Power In}}$$

The typical optical source (power in) is in the milliwatt (mW) range, and a typical total power loss would be 30 dB over the range of the transmission link.

These are two sources of optical power loss, the cable itself, plus the splices and connectors associated with the link. Splices have a loss of approximately 0.15–0.5 dB, while connectors are somewhat higher, 0.5–2.0 dB. Fiber optic cable used with LANs has a typical loss of around 5 dB/km at 850 nm wavelength. Note that the loss for fiber is specified at a particular wavelength, where the attenuation of copper media is specified at a particular frequency. This attenuation is a constant for a particular type of cable. See references [4-10] and [4-11] for additional information.

4.6.2 Fiber Optic Cable Used with LANs

The four network architectures that we are studying in this book—ARCNET, token ring, Ethernet and StarLAN—have options for fiber optic cabling. When the transmission system is designed, a total loss budget (in dB) will be specified for the optical link between source and detector. In addition, the source wavelength, cable diameter, and cable transmission parameters, such as bandwidth (model dispersion), attenuation, etc. are given.

Two major standards have emerged, one from AT&T and the other from IBM. The AT&T Premises Distribution System (PDS) specifies 62.5/125 micron cable, while the IBM cabling system uses 100/140 micron cable. Each system has its own type of fiber optic connectors as well. References [4-12] and [4-13] provide further information.

4.7 | Troubleshooting Fiber

As we discussed in Chapter 3, either an optical time domain reflectometer (OTDR), or an optical source and optical power meter can be used for testing fiber transmission links with LANs. Because of the high cost ($10,000 to $50,000) associated with OTDRs, the second alternative is most commonly used.

Making optical power measurements is a very straightforward process. IBM outlines these procedures for their token ring network in reference [4-13]. Other vendor's products operate similarly.

The optical power source is first verified for proper operation using a short piece of fiber that is supplied with the unit. These results are recorded on the form shown in Figure 4-15.

The second step is to measure the attenuation (loss) of the fiber under consideration. As seen in Figure 4-16, the optical is attached to one end of the cable, and the optical power meter at the opposite end. (This is a good example of using a pair of walkie-talkies, because it certainly speeds up the process.) The optical measurements are made and recorded on the form shown in Figure 4-17. For the IBM Token-Ring Network, any optical power loss on a fiber link that exceeds 13.0 dB indicates a cable fault. A broken cable, or improperly seated or dirty connectors are possible problems. Chapter 4 of reference [4-13] goes into specific details on IBM Token-Ring problem isolation. Refer to other vendor's network specifications for similar guidance.

Figure 4-15
IBM fiber optic test equipment worksheet

Test Equipment Worksheet

Checking the Optical Power Equipment

Power Source Orange-1 Reading _____ **Power Source Black-1 Reading** _____

Power Meter Orange-1 Reading (-) _____ **Power Meter Black-1 Reading** (-) _____

Orange-1 Comparison Difference (=) _____ **Black-1 Comparison Difference** (=) _____

If both Power Source readings are not in the range from -12.0 dBm to -15.0 dBm, the optical power source does not qualify.

Optical Power Source Good ☐   Optical Power Source Bad ☐

If either Comparison Difference is greater than ±1.0 dB, the optical power meter does not qualify.

Optical Power Meter Good ☐   Optical Power Meter Bad ☐

Checking the Test Cables

Power Meter Orange-1 Reading _____   **Power Meter Black-1 Reading** _____

Orange-1 Orange-2 Reading (-) _____   **Black-1 Black-2 Reading** (-) _____

Orange-2 Loss (=) _____   **Black-1 Loss** (=) _____

Power Meter Orange-1 Reading _____   **Power Meter Black-1 Reading** _____

Orange-1 Black-2 Reading (-) _____   **Black-1 Orange-2 Reading** (-) _____

Black-2 Loss (=) _____   **Orange-1 Loss** (=) _____

If any Loss is less than or equal to 1.5 dB, test cable 1 and test cable 2 are good.
If any Losses are greater than 1.5 dB, neither test cable qualifies.

Test Cable 1 Good ☐   Test Cable 1 Bad ☐   Test Cable 2 good ☐   Test Cable 2 Bad ☐

Figure 4-16
Making optical power measurements

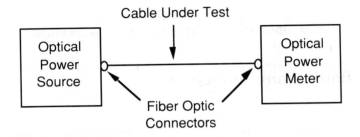

Figure 4-17
IBM fiber optic cable testing chart

Cable Testing Chart

	FROM	TO	Length
Cable Location (First Leg)	_____	_____	_____

Power Reference 1	_____	Power Reference 2	_____
Power Test 1 (-)	_____	Power Test 2 (-)	_____
Power Loss 1 (=)	_____	Power Loss 2 (=)	_____

If either Power Loss 1 or Power Loss 2 is greater than 13.0 dB, the cable does not qualify.

Cable Good ☐   Cable Bad ☐

	FROM	TO	Length
Cable Location (Second Leg)	_____	_____	_____

Power Reference 1	_____	Power Reference 2	_____
Power Test 1 (-)	_____	Power Test 2 (-)	_____
Power Loss 1 (=)	_____	Power Loss 2 (=)	_____

If either Power Loss 1 or Power loss 2 is greater than 13.0 dB, the cable does not qualify.

Cable Good ☐   Cable Bad ☐

4.8 | Troubleshooting Summary

To summarize, here's a checklist to assist with troubleshooting cable system failures. Network-specific cabling issues will be discussed in Chapters 5, 6, 7, and 8.

1. Know where your cable goes. If you don't know, consult your network documentation (see Chapter 2) or use cable tracing tools (see Chapter 3) and then record the cable location.

2. Define the most likely location of the cable failure, and isolate the problem to one segment of cable. Remember that repeaters can also fail (or blow a fuse), thus isolating one cable section from another.

3. Look for any recent cable or connector additions or rearrangements, such as a new Ethernet tap that is shorting the backbone cable.

4. Look for obvious disconnections:

   ARCNET: T-connectors, terminators, modular cords and connectors.

   Token ring: Media filters used with unshielded twisted pair cable, or hermaphroditic (data) connectors at the Multistation Access Units.

   Ethernet: BNC T-connectors, N connectors, terminators, transceiver, or AUI cables.

   StarLAN and IEEE 10BASE-T: Modular connectors, crossconnect fields and cables attached to 66-type punch-down blocks.

5. Consider the less-than-obvious problems, such as open or shorted BNC connectors, mis-wired modular plugs or open terminators.

6. Look for cable damage, such as cuts, frays, or breaks in the insulation.

7. When using TDRs, make measurements from both ends of the cable, and be aware of minimum and maximum cable distances that can be tested.

8. For suspected fiber optic cable failures, use a flashlight to verify fiber continuity. Never look directly into a live fiber, however, as eye damage may result. Also verify that the connectors are not dirty, and clean with isopropyl alcohol and a lint-free swab if necessary.

4.9 References

[4-1] Telecommunications Transmission Engineering, 2nd edition, volume 1, AT&T, 1977.

[4-2] Trompeter Electronics, Inc., (Westlake Village, CA) Catalog T-16, 1989.

[4-3] National Electrical Code—1987, National Fire Protection Association, Batterymarch Park, Quincy, MA, 1987.

[4-4] "What Does The New Code Mean to You," West Penn Wire, Washington, PA, 1988.

[4-5] "How to Specify, Bid and Install Plenum Cable," E.I. duPont de Nemours and Company, Inc., 1986.

[4-6] AT&T Premises Distribution System Wire Installation Manual, document 555-401-101, AT&T, 1987.

[4-7] Application Note 22W-6342: "Tektronix Metallic TDR's for Cable Testing," Tektronix, Inc., 1987.

[4-8] LANguage 89—Straight Talk from Tek on Cable Trouble-shooting, Tektronix, Inc., 1988.

[4-9] "A Guide to Fiber Optics System Design," Belden Electronic Wire and Cable, Belden/Cooper Industries, Inc., 1985.

[4-10] "A Basic Guide to Fiber Optics," Belden Electronic Wire and Cable, Belden/Cooper Industries, Inc., 1985.

[4-11] "A Guide to Fiber Optics System Installation," Belden Electronic Wire and Cable, Belden/Cooper Industries, Inc., 1986, 1987.

[4-12] AT&T Premises Distribution System Fiber Installation Manual, document 555-401-102, AT&T, 1988.

[4-13] IBM Token-Ring Network Optical Fiber Cable Options, document GA27-3747-0, 1986.

CHAPTER FIVE

Troubleshooting ARCNET

ARCNET (which stands for Attached Resource Computer Network) was developed by Datapoint Corporation in 1977, see reference [5-1]. It was designed as a token-passing bus architecture, transmitting at 2.5 Mbps, a rate equal to the transfer rate of the then-current Datapoint disks. ARCNET was maintained as a proprietary network until 1981 when Standard Microsystems Corporation (SMC) licensed the technology and began producing two integrated circuits: the COM9026—a local area network controller that implements the ARCNET protocol; and the COM9032—a local area network transceiver that generates the clock signals. For further technical details, see references [5-2], [5-3], [5-4], and [5-5]. NCR Microelectronics also manufactures a CMOS version of the LAN controller, the 90C26 (see reference [5-6]). In addition to the controller and transceiver, each ARCNET Network Interface Card (NIC) contains two more components: a driver for either coax, twisted pair or fiber optic cable, a RAM buffer (typically 2K) to store both incoming and outgoing frames, and miscellaneous logic to control the bus interface.

SMC introduced the first ARCNET NIC for the IBM PC in 1983, and along with other manufacturers, such as Datapoint, Contemporary Control Systems, Thomas-Conrad, LANMaster, Quam, Pure Data, Earth Computer, and others, supplies ARCNET cards for a variety of computer buses, including PC, AT, Microchannel, and industrial bus structures such as Intel Corporation's Multibus and the IEEE STD bus. ARCNET also boasts an organization of users and vendors, called the ARCNET Trade Association—telephone (312) 255-3003—which is responsible for conferences and architecture improvements. Current development includes protocol enhancements and increases in transmission rate beyond the current 2.5 Mbps.

5.1 ARCNET Topology

Of all the major networks, ARCNET is the most flexible in its architecture. Both star and bus topology networks, or a combination that might be described as a distributed star with branches, are possible. In addition, all three media choices: coax (RG-62/U), a single twisted pair (100 ohm impedance, 2 twists/foot, 22, 24, and 26 gauge solid or 24 and 26 gauge stranded) and duplex fiber optic cable (50, 62.5, 100, or 200 micron core) are available, and can be flexibly interconnected. A network requiring coax in the computer room, twisted pair throughout the office, and fiber optics outside to the guard station could be very easily designed. The appropriate media converters (called optical or twisted pair links by SMC) are used to connect dissimilar media types. The only major constraint on the transmission medium is that the signal propagation delay between any two workstations must not exceed 31 microseconds. In addition, the attenuation characteristics of the different types of cable affect the number of workstations that can be attached in a bus topology. The maximum signal attenuation between workstation and active hub, or between two workstations connected via a passive hub, must not exceed 11 dB. See reference [5-9], page 1-4.

Figure 5-1 shows the simplest topology, a star with a passive hub at the center and RG-62/U coax extending to three workstations. Maximum workstation to hub distance is 100 feet. Notice that the unused port must be connected to a termination resistor (93 ohms in this case) to provide an impedance match. More on this requirement in section 5-3.

Figure 5-1
ARCNET star topology with passive hub

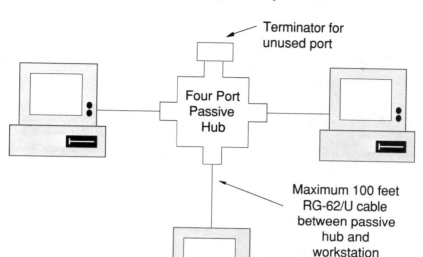

Terminator for
unused port

Four Port
Passive
Hub

Maximum 100 feet
RG-62/U cable
between passive
hub and
workstation

Figure 5-2 shows a similar star topology, but with an active hub. The active hub repeats the signal, allowing the hub to workstation distance to extend to 2,000 feet. Active hub ports are self-terminating, and do not require the termination resistors.

Bus topology ARCNET networks are shown in Figures 5-3a and 5-3b. The cable used can either be RG-62/U coax or unshielded twisted pair. Note that the number of workstations changes with the cable type selected: up to eight workstations on coax or up to ten workstations with twisted pair.

Figure 5-2
ARCNET star topology with active hub

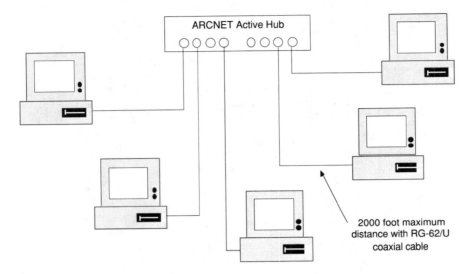

2000 foot maximum distance with RG-62/U coaxial cable

Figure 5-3a
ARCNET coaxial bus topology

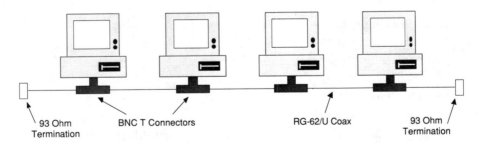

93 Ohm Termination

BNC T Connectors

RG-62/U Coax

93 Ohm Termination

Figure 5-3b
ARCNET twisted pair bus topology

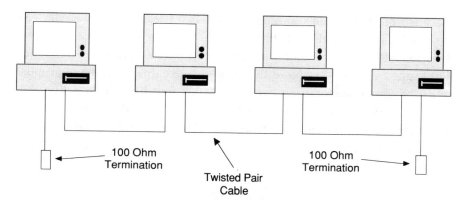

100 Ohm Termination

Twisted Pair Cable

100 Ohm Termination

Figure 5-4 shows a distributed star ARCNET topology which combines coaxial, twisted pair, and fiber optic media with both bus and star connections. The ability to interconnect these various media segments gives ARCNET its great flexibility.

Figure 5-4
ARCNET distributed star topology

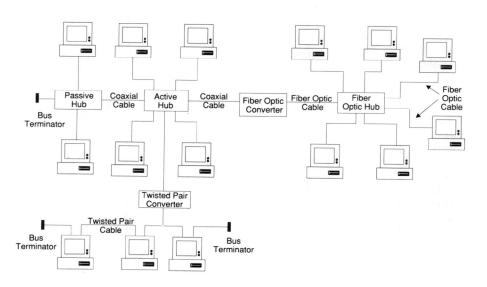

5.2 | ARCNET Cabling

Because of its flexible topology, a variety of transmission media can be used with ARCNET. Table 5-1 gives a summary of acceptable cables for ARCNET use, and was developed by Datapoint (see reference [5-8], pp. 1-6 and 1-7). Note that any given segment can have at most 11dB of signal attenuation; hence the 2,000 foot limit from active hub to workstation when using RG-62/U coax (5.5 dB/Kft * 2Kft = 11 dB total attenuation). Other manufacturers of ARCNET products may have different recommendations, or include other options such as fiber optics.

Table 5-1
Recommended ARCNET cabling

Cable Type	Nominal Impedance	Attenuation per 1,000 ft @ 5 MHz	Propagation Velocity	FCC RFI Compliance
RG-62 Belden #86262	93 ohms	5.5 dB	85%	OK
RG-59/U Belden #89108	75 ohms	7.0 dB	84%	OK
RG-11/U Belden #89292	75 ohms	5.5 dB	80%	OK
IBM Type 1 Belden #89688	150 ohms	7.0 dB	78%	OK with IBM balun
IBM Type 3 Telephone Twisted Pair; Belden #1155A	100 ohms	17.9 dB	66%	Requires filter/ balun

(source: Datapoint Corporation)

5.3 | ARCNET Hardware Components

A typical ARCNET network consists of a NIC in each workstation, active and/or passive hubs, repeaters or media converters, and the appropriate cables in between. We'll look at each component individually.

5.3.1 | ARCNET NICs

An example ARCNET NIC, the PC 550 from Standard Microsystems Corporation, is shown in Figure 5-5. Key components include the 8-position DIP switch used to set the node address; another bank of DIP switches used to set the base I/O port address and memory buffer address; the ARCNET LAN Controller IC, COM9026; the Local Area Network Transceiver IC, COM9032; jumpers used to set the IRQ line; the interface connector to the cable; and a socket for an autoboot PROM for diskless PCs.

Figure 5-6 details the wiring of the twisted pair interface used by the Standard Microsystems PC260/270 NIC for twisted pair cable. Note that the wire connections are polarity sensitive. The wires connecting pins 3 and 4 must go straight through, i.e. pin 3 must connect to pin 3 and pin 4 must connect to pin 4. A minimum of six feet of cable is required between two PC260s. Terminators for use with twisted pair NICs consist of a 100 ohm resistor connected between the center two pins (3 and 4 in this case) of the six pin modular connector.

Figure 5-5
ARCNET Network Interface Card

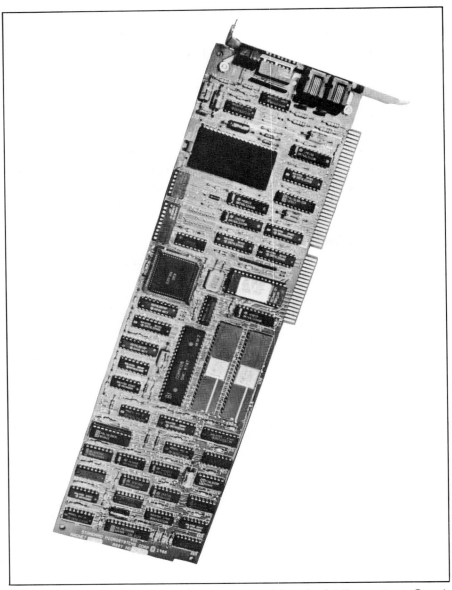

(photo courtesy of Standard Microsystems Corp.)

Figure 5-6
Pin assignments for Standard Microsystems PC260 twisted pair interface

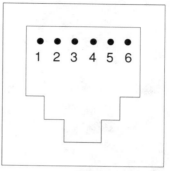

6 Pin Modular Jack
(Front View)

Pin	Signal
1	Not used
2	Not used
3	Data
4	Data
5	Not used
6	Not used

5.3.2 | ARCNET Passive Hubs

A four-port passive hub module from Contemporary Control Systems, Inc., is shown in Figure 5-7, with the internal wiring given in Figure 5-8. The passive hub is simply a resistive divider network designed to provide a match between the source impedance (93 ohms in the case of coaxial cable) and the load impedance. As an example, let's assume that we wish to calculate the impedance looking into port D of Figure 5-8.

Figure 5-7
ARCNET passive hub module

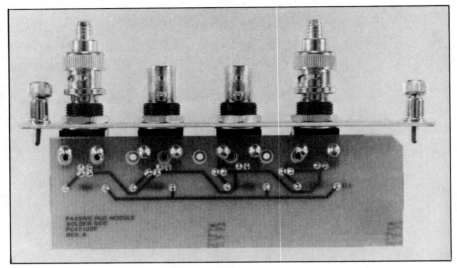

(photo courtesy of Contemporary Control Systems)

Figure 5-8
Four-port passive hub wiring (coax version)

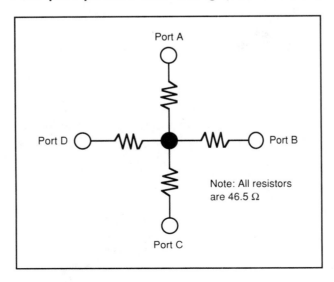

Figure 5-9
Four-port passive hub equivalent circuit (coax version), with B and D active ports and A and C terminated ports

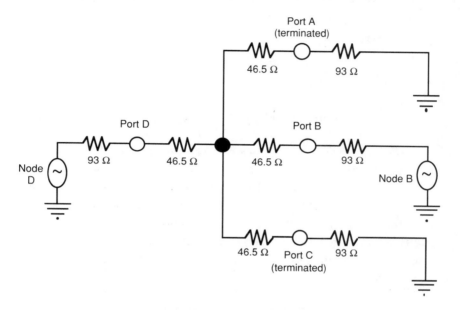

We'll further assume that ports A and C are terminated, and port B has another workstation attached, as shown in Figure 5-9. If the passive hub resistors have a value of 46.5 ohms, and each port has a 93 ohm impedance, the parallel combination of the three ports A, B, and C yields an effective load on port D of 93 ohms, thus achieving the impedance match. Equation 5-1 shows the result:

$$Z_{in} = 46.5 + \cfrac{1}{\cfrac{1}{139.5} + \cfrac{1}{139.5} + \cfrac{1}{139.5}} = 93 \text{ ohms} \qquad \text{Equation 5-1}$$

See reference [5-10], Section 8 for further details.

155

Other manufacturers, Datapoint and SMC in particular, use 33 ohm and 36 ohm resistors in their passive hub networks. In the case of the Datapoint design, terminators at unused ports are not required. Check the documentation with your network hardware for more specific details.

5.3.3 | ARCNET Active Hubs

A variety of manufacturers sell active hubs, which are bit level repeaters that regenerate the signal. Most active hubs have 8- or 16-port capacities. Figure 5-10 shows one example, the Mod Hub 16 from Contemporary Control Systems, Inc., which can accept combinations of coaxial, twisted pair, and fiber optic cable inputs. Built-in diagnostics, usually implemented visually with LEDs, distinguishes some products over others. As a minimum, the hub should indicate the presence of activity on each port, plus whether or not a network reconfiguration is underway. More on reconfiguration in section 5.5.

Figure 5-10
ARCNET Modular Active Hub

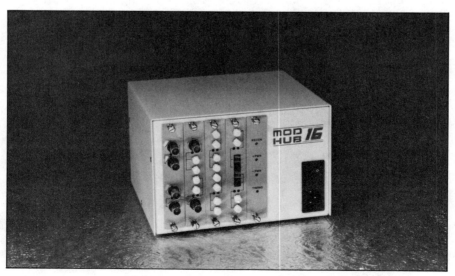

(photo courtesy of Contemporary Control Systems, Inc.)

5.4 | ARCNET Addressing

The heart of ARCNET is its token-passing bus architecture that passes the permission to transmit (token) in a logical ring, but is physically connected as a bus (or star). As such, each workstation's opportunity (or turn) to transmit is independent of its physical location in the network. Each NIC must be assigned a unique address between 1 and 255 with an eight-position DIP switch; address 0 is reserved for broadcast messages. Duplicating a node address is one of the easiest ways to disable an ARCNET. For the logical ring to operate, each NIC must know its own address (Source ID or SID set by the DIP switches) plus the address of the next NIC (Next ID or NID) in the logical ring progression.

A sample ARCNET LAN with four nodes, addressed 4, 32, 65, and 203, is shown in Figure 5-11. The physical topology is shown in Figure 5-11a, and the logical topology is shown in Figure 5-11b. Each NIC passes the token to its NID node; the highest-addressed node then wraps around to the lowest-addressed node, thus completing the logical ring progression.

Figure 5-11a
ARCNET node addressing example

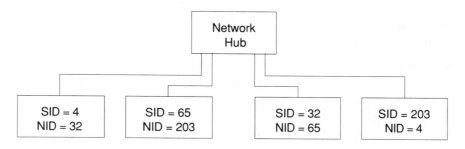

Figure 5-11b
ARCNET token passing example

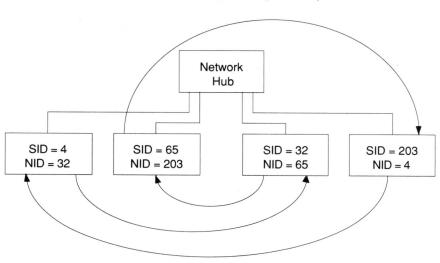

5.5   Network Reconfiguration

The logical ring must be modified any time a node either wishes to enter or exit the network. The process defined as system reconfiguration, or "recon," is as follows:

Any node that turns on, or one which has not received an Invitation to Transmit frame for 840 milliseconds, causes a system reconfiguration transmission: 8 MARKs + 1 SPACE repeated 765 times. This transmission is longer than any other type of transmission, disrupting the normal passing of the token, and causing all stations to set their Next ID (NID) register to their own (or Source) ID-SID so that NID = SID. In addition, a timer is initialized as follows:

$$\text{Timeout} = 146 * (255\text{-SID}) \text{ microseconds}$$

The highest node address times out first, and issues the first Invitation to Transmit frame, or token. If a response is not heard within 74 microseconds, the first node assumes that the NID address does not exist;

therefore it increments NID and tries again. Any response will cause the node to save the current value of NID in its buffer, and pass the token to the NID station. That station will then begin searching for its upstream neighbor in the logical ring topology.

In the network in Figure 5-11, with node addresses 4, 32, 65, and 203, node 203 would issue the first Invitation to Transmit, this time to node 204. Since node 204 does not exist, node 203 would then increment NID to 205, 206, ...255 then to 1, 2, ... 4 until node 4 seizes control of the process and begins its nearest neighbor search. The process would continue until node 4 finds node 32, node 32 finds node 65, and node 65 finds node 203. Node 203 already knows about node 4, thus completing the logical ring.

If a node is removed from the network, a similar (but less disruptive) search takes place. Again using our example network, if node 32 was turned off, node 4 would continue to increment its NID register until it passed control of the network to node 65. No other changes in the logical ring are required.

By now, the havoc caused when two nodes are given the same address should be evident—the network reconfiguration algorithm will never stabilize.

System reconfiguration time depends upon the total number of nodes and the cable propagation delay, and ranges from 24–61 milliseconds. As a result, a normal network reconfiguration will be almost transparent to the users, and any deviation from the prescribed reconfiguration protocols will result in network disruption.

5.6 | Typical ARCNET Hardware Failures

One of the most common passive hub hardware failures (which is not really a network failure at all) is the omission of a termination resistor at an unused passive hub port or at the end of a bus topology cable, thus affecting the impedance balance and causing signal reflections. To test the terminator, use a VOM and measure the DC resistance between the two contacts of the internal resistor. For a BNC terminator, measure between the center pin and the outside shell for a value close to 93 ohms; for a modular (RJ-11) terminator, measure between the two center pins (2 and 3 or 3 and 4, as appropriate) for a value close to 100 ohms. The correct impedance is 93 ohms for coax buses, and 100 ohms for twisted pair buses and twisted pair repeaters. Active hubs for coax cable are self-terminating and do not require the termination resistor.

Another hardware problem that is easy to avoid is the tendency to exceed the simple rules for ARCNET configuration. For example, maximum 10 NICs per twisted pair segment, twisted pair bus length less than 400 feet, etc. Many ARCNET difficulties can be avoided by simply obeying the configuration rules.

The other major hardware failure is a dysfunctional (or non-functional) NIC or active hub. Either of these problems is relatively straightforward to diagnose, as most manufacturers include an LED on the NIC or Active Hub for diagnostics. Unfortunately, there is no standard for these LED indicators, therefore consult the installation manual for your network hardware for proper interpretation. For many active hubs, another LED indicates that a network reconfiguration is in process.

5.7 | Isolating the Failing Component

Because of its modular architecture, ARCNET network failures can be very easy to isolate. Since most NICs and active hubs include diagnostic LEDs, the first step is to observe the LED at each port and determine if an improper state exists.

As an example, refer to Figure 5-12 and assume that the active hub indicates that a network reconfiguration is in process. The reconfiguration (sometimes labeled "RECON") LED normally lights for a few seconds, although as we have seen, the actual network reconfiguration would be completed in 61 milliseconds at most. The "RECON" LED only indicates that a reconfiguration has occurred—it does not indicate its source. Most likely, a defective receiver section of a NIC is causing the problem. The next challenge is to find the failure.

Figure 5-12
Isolating ARCNET network failures

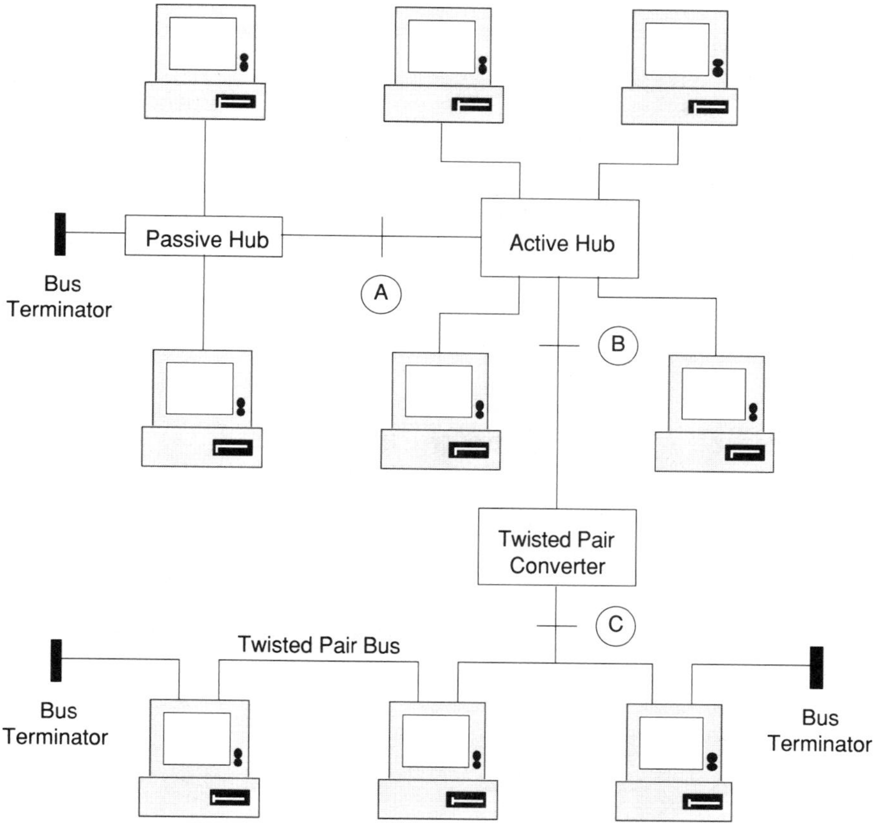

To isolate the problem, the network must first be segmented. Again using Figure 5-12, disconnect the cable between the active hub and passive hub (point A) and see if the problem clears. If it does, then the problem lies in the disconnected section—that is, some component connected to the passive hub. Reconnect the cable between the passive and active hubs at point A, and start disconnecting workstations from the passive hub ports one at a time. Remember to terminate the unused port when the cable is disconnected. If the network recovers (that is, "RECON" goes out), the problem has been isolated; if not, continue with the process.

Now return to the first scenario, and assume that segmenting at point A did not clear the problem. Next, disconnect at point B (the input of the twisted pair converter), and check the network. If the problem clears, reconnect at point B, and disconnect at point C, the output of the twisted pair converter. Remember to terminate any unused port on the converter. If the problem now clears, reconnect at point C and methodically segment the twisted pair bus, terminating each open endpoint, until the faulty NIC or cable section is isolated. If a cable section appears to be the problem, test it as we discussed in Chapter 4. If a NIC is suspect, replace with a known good spare, being careful to check all option settings, and especially avoid duplicating another NIC node address.

5.8 ARCNET Software Considerations

As we have seen, one strength of the ARCNET network is its simplicity in hardware configuration. We see this also in the software, and specifically in the ARCNET protocol as developed by Datapoint. We will also investigate some of the ARCNET timing constraints that affect its performance.

5.8.1 Frame Formats

The ARCNET protocol implemented on the COM9026 is a character-oriented protocol having five different types of frames, as shown in Figure 5-13. All ARCNET frames begin with an Alert Burst of six ONES. Each character within the frame consists of an 11-bit sequence: ONE + ONE + ZERO + 8-Bit Character. As a result, the network throughput is actually 1.8 Mbps (8/11 * 2.5 Mbps). The five frame formats are defined as follows:

- Invitation to Transmit (ITT)—passes the token from one node to another.

- Free Buffer Enquiry (FBE)—asks an intended destination node if it can accept a data packet from the node currently holding the token.

- Data packet (PAC)—the data itself, up to 508 octets, (delineated in the COUNT field) transmitted from the token holder to the intended destination. (An octet is defined as eight bits.) The COUNT is actually a Continuation Pointer (CP), used to locate the packet in the memory buffer. Packets of length 0–253 use a one octet COUNT; packets from 257–508 octets use a 2-octet COUNT. Note that packet lengths of 254–256 are not allowed. For packets of 253 octets or less, CP = 256 − length; for packets greater than 256 octets, the first octet CP = 0, and the second octet CP = 512 − length. The first octet of data is a system code that is a unique protocol identifier administered by the ARCNET Trade Association.

- Acknowledgement (ACK)—indicates correct receipt of a Packet or an affirmative response to a FBE.

- Negative Acknowledgement (NAK)—negative response to a FBE.

5.8.2 ARCNET Protocol Operation

When a node receives a token, it can either play (by initiating the transmit sequence) or pass (by sending the Invitation to Transmit to another node). If transmission is desired, the source issues a FBE, to the intended destination to confirm its ability to accept a message. Either an ACK or NAK is returned. If an ACK is received from a FBE, a packet is then transmitted. Upon reception, the destination node verifies the Cyclic Redundancy Check, and sends an ACK if the data passes the CRC. If the data fails the CRC, the destination node is silent, signaling the transmitting node that the transmission failed, and that the transmission must be re-attempted the next time that the node holds the token. See references [5-2] and [5-10] for additional details.

Figure 5-13
ARCNET frame formats

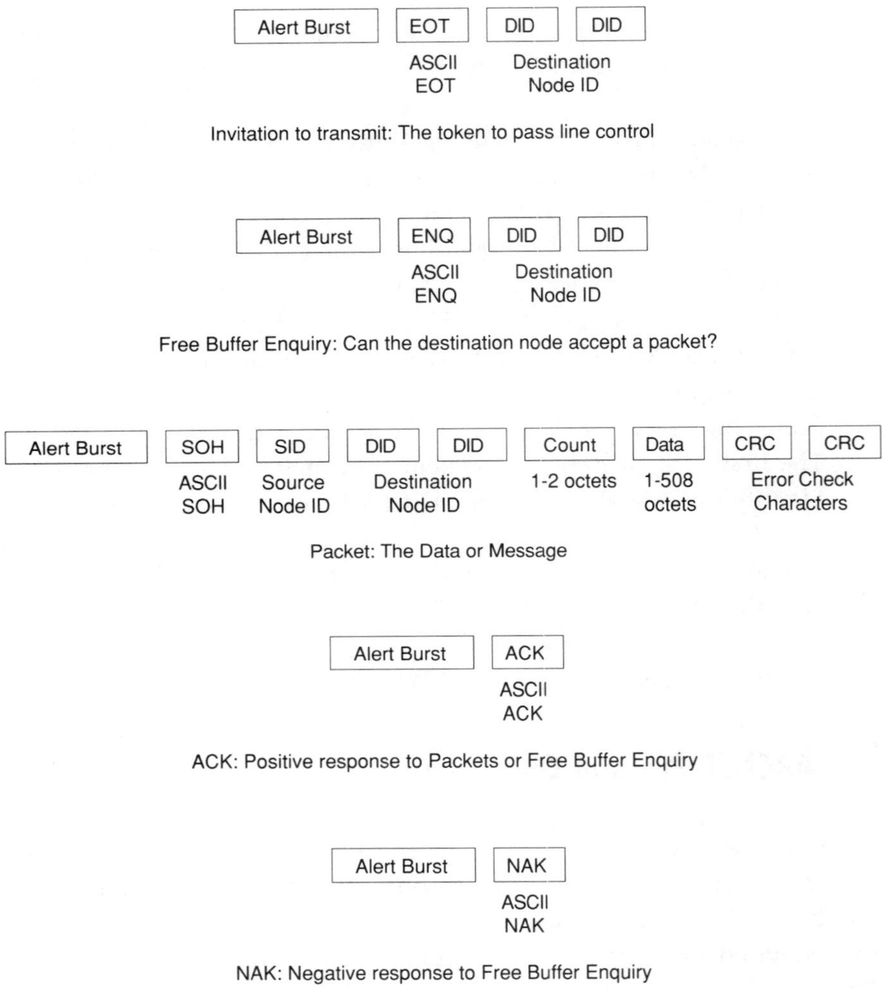

Alert Burst	EOT	DID	DID

ASCII   Destination
EOT   Node ID

Invitation to transmit: The token to pass line control

Alert Burst	ENQ	DID	DID

ASCII   Destination
ENQ   Node ID

Free Buffer Enquiry: Can the destination node accept a packet?

Alert Burst	SOH	SID	DID	DID	Count	Data	CRC	CRC

ASCII Source Destination 1-2 octets 1-508 Error Check
SOH Node ID Node ID   octets Characters

Packet: The Data or Message

Alert Burst	ACK

ASCII
ACK

ACK: Positive response to Packets or Free Buffer Enquiry

Alert Burst	NAK

ASCII
NAK

NAK: Negative response to Free Buffer Enquiry

5.8.3 | Network Response Times

ARCNET, being a token passing (deterministic) network, has the advantage of easy calculations of network parameters that yield overall response times. From Figure 5-13 we saw that there are five unique types of ARCNET transmissions. Each of these begin with an Alert Burst (six ONES) and then a transmission of eleven bits per character. Each bit requires 400 nanoseconds of time (1/2,500,000), making a total of 4.4 microseconds (11 x 400 nanoseconds) of time required to send each character. For the five different frame types shown in Figure 5-13, the individual response times are shown below:

- **Invitation to transmit (ITT)**

  Alert burst: 6 bits = 2.4 μs
  EOT, DID, DID   3 * 11 = 33 bits = 13.2 μs
  _____
  Total = 15.6 μs

- **Free buffer enquiry (FBE)**

  Alert burst: 6 bits = 2.4 μs
  ENQ, DID, DID   3 * 11 = 33 bits = 13.2 μs
  _____
  Total = 15.6 μs

- **Packets (PAC)**

  Alert burst: 6 bits = 2.4 μs
  SOH, SID, DID, DID, CNT[†]   5 * 11 = 55 bits = 22.0 μs
  n characters   n * 11 = 11n bits = 4.4n μs
  CRC, CRC   2 * 11 = 22 bits = 8.8 μs
  _____
  Total = 33.2 μs
  +
  4.4n μs

  [†] CNT is one octet in this example

165

- **Acknowledgement (ACK):**

  Alert burst: 6 bits = 2.4 μs
  ACK   1 * 11 = 11 bits = 4.4 μs
  _____
  Total = 6.8 μs

- **Negative Acknowledgement (NAK):**

  Alert burst: 6 bits = 2.4 μs
  NAK   1 * 11 = 11 bits = 4.4 μs
  _____
  Total = 6.8 μs

In addition to the transmission times associated with the individual frames, there are several other delays built into the protocol (see reference [5-9], Chapter 4 and reference [5-10], Chapter 5):

- Turnaround time (Tta) = 12.6 microseconds—measured from the end of a received transmission to the start of the response.

- Token propagation time (Tpt) = 0–31 microseconds—measured from the transmission of the token at one node to the reception of the same token at another node. This delay is a measure of the propagation delay of the cable and hubs, and must not exceed 31 microseconds.

- Message propagation time (Tpm) = 0–31 microseconds—measured from the transmission of a message at one node to the reception of the same message at the destination node, and may differ from Tpt since the destinations will generally not be the same. Note that the maximum propagation delay (31 microseconds) is the same, however.

- Broadcast delay time (Tbd) = 15.6 microseconds—measured after a node broadcasts a message until the start of the next token pass.

Note that there is no FBE sent before the broadcast message, and no ACK generated after; Tbd is thus fixed at 15.6 microseconds.

- Response timeout (Trp) = 74.6 microseconds—the maximum time allowed for a response to a transmission, equal to Tpm + Tta + Tpm (twice the message propagation time plus the turnaround time).

- Recovery time (Trc) = 3.4 microseconds—measured between a response timeout and the subsequent pass of the token.

- Idle line (Til) = 82.2 microseconds—the maximum time the network is allowed to be idle; if Til expires, then the reconfiguration sequence is initiated.

As two examples of ARCNET response time calculations, let's look at a Token Pass and a Token Pass plus Message. For additional examples, see reference [5-9], pp. 4-10 to 4-19, and reference [5-10], pp. 57-62.

- Token Pass—the originating node passes the token to the next station (NID) in the logical ring:

ITT	15.6 microseconds
Tta + Tpt	12.6 + Tpt
	———————————————————
Total	28.2 + Tpt microseconds

Given the worst case Tpt at 31 microseconds, maximum Token Pass time would be 59.2 microseconds.

- Token Pass plus Message—a workstation initiates a packet transmission to another workstation:

ITT	15.6	microseconds
Tta + Tpt	12.6 + Tpt	
FBE	15.6	
Tta + Tpm	12.6 + Tpm	
ACK	6.8	
Tta + Tpm	12.6 + Tpm	
PAC	33.2 + 4.4n	
Tta + Tpm	12.6 + Tpm	
ACK	6.8	
Tta + Tpm	12.6 + Tpm	

Total	$141.0 + 4.4n + Tpt + 4Tpm$ microseconds

Again, assuming the maximum case: $n = 508$ characters and 31 microseconds for Tpt and Tpm, the Token Pass and Message would occur in 2531.2 microseconds.

5.8.4 Memory Buffers

The maximum length Data Packet (508 octets) requires an external RAM buffer that is a minimum of 2K bytes in size. This buffer must be located somewhere in the PCs address space, usually in segment D, address D0000 hex. Care must be taken that this buffer does not interfere with any existing (or recently added) PC boards and their required address space. If a doubt exists concerning a possible conflict, remove all add-on cards in the PC and add them back in one at a time, starting with the ARCNET card.

5.8.5 Software Options

ARCNET boards are also sensitive to I/O-related options such as IRQ lines, DMA channels, and I/O Base Addresses of the PC. These options must also be consistent with the network operating system or higher layer software (for example, NetWare, ViaNet, or NetBIOS). Refer to a NIC installation manual (reference [5-11]) or manufacturer if any questions arise.

5.9 | Protocol Analysis with NetWare

According to many market and user surveys, Novell's NetWare is the most popular network operating system for LANs. Many different versions exist, including Entry Level System (ELS), Advanced NetWare, NetWare for VMS, System Fault Tolerant (SFT) NetWare, NetWare for Macintosh, and NetWare 386. We will consider the formats of Advanced NetWare in this section.

Figure 5-14 shows how NetWare compares with the OSI Reference Model. Note the broad support for 802.3, 802.5, and other types of networks. At this writing, NetWare drivers are available for over 100 different NICs—certainly an important reason for its wide acceptance. See references [5-12] and [5-13] for further details.

Figure 5-15 shows the structure of the Sequenced Packet Exchange (SPX) protocol packet. The first part of the packet is the Internetwork Packet Exchange (IPX) header, an implementation of the Xerox Networking Systems (XNS) Internet Datagram Protocol (IDP), which consists of fifteen 16-bit words or 30 octets. The Network, Host, and Socket fields are used to identify the specific network on the internet (32 bits), the host's node address (48 bits), and the application process queue (16 bits), respectively. IPX provides connectionless communication service.

The SPX header is an implementation of Xerox's Sequenced Packet Protocol (SPP), and is built on top of IPX. The twelve octets of the SPX header provide for connection-oriented data transfer.

Figure 5-14
Comparing the NetWare Protocol Suite with OSI

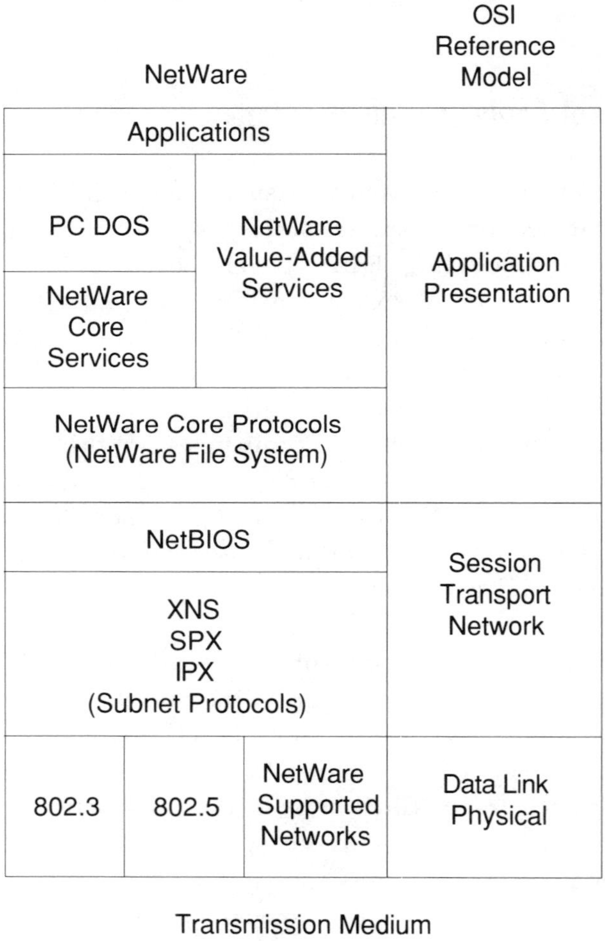

NetWare			OSI Reference Model
Applications			Application Presentation
PC DOS	NetWare Value-Added Services		
NetWare Core Services			
NetWare Core Protocols (NetWare File System)			
NetBIOS			Session Transport Network
XNS SPX IPX (Subnet Protocols)			
802.3	802.5	NetWare Supported Networks	Data Link Physical

Transmission Medium

(courtesy of Novell, Inc.)

170

Figure 5-15
The NetWare Sequenced Packet Exchange Packet

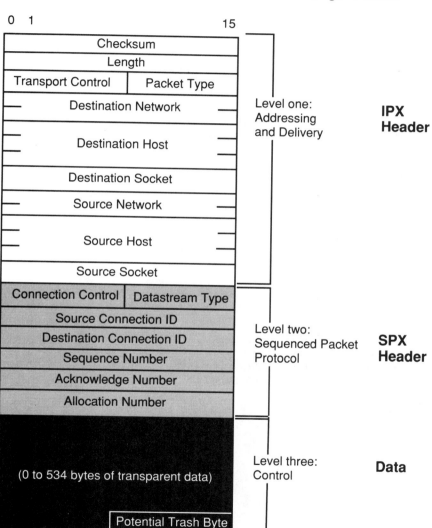

Immediately following the IPX and SPX headers are up to 534 octets of transparent data. For those keeping score, the longest NetWare packet length is therefore 576 octets (30 octets for the IPX header, 12 octets for the SPX header, plus 534 octets of data). Figure 5-16 shows a NetWare packet encapsulated within an ARCNET frame. Note the addition of the ARCNET fragmentation header. Since the ARCNET data field can contain at most 508 octets, a maximum (576 octet) length NetWare packet must be divided into two frames for transmission over an ARCNET network. The Fragmentation header controls this, by giving a 1 octet fragment number (non-fragmented, fragment 1 of 2, or fragment 2 of 2) plus a 2 octet sequence number.

Figure 5-16
Encapsulating the SPX Packet within an ARCNET frame

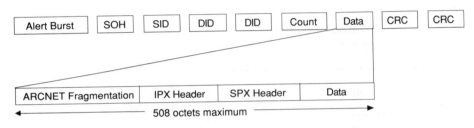

Figure 5-17
Capture range of the Network General Sniffer Protocol Analyzer for ARCNET networks

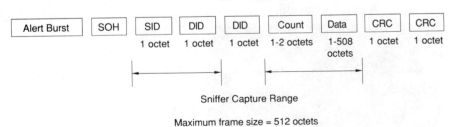

Figure 5-17 shows the capture range of the Network General Sniffer protocol analyzer for ARCNET. Figures 5-18a and 5-18b show a detail printout of two NetWare frames transmitted over an ARCNET network and captured by the Network General Sniffer protocol analyzer.

The first frame is a Get Station Number Request. The second frame is a Get Station Number Reply. The notations along the left-hand side of the figure indicate the protocol layer being decoded from Figure 5-14. DLC indicates Data Link Control (ARCNET), NOV indicates the Novell ARCNET fragmentation header, XNS indicates the Xerox Network Systems header (IPX), and NCP indicates the NetWare Core Protocols in use. See reference [5-14] for further information.

Figure 5-18a
Novell NetWare "Get Station Number Request" packet transmitted over ARCNET and captured by the Network General Sniffer protocol analyzer

```
DLC:   ----- DLC Header -----
DLC:
DLC:   Frame 11 arrived at 13:39:34.3424; frame size is 45 (002D hex) bytes.
DLC:   Destination: Station 44, NetWare-XT
DLC:   Source     : Station 20, IBM PC
DLC:   ARCNET system code = FA
DLC:
NOV:   ----- Novell ARCNET fragmentation header -----
NOV:
NOV:   Unfragmented frame
NOV:   Sequence number = 8
NOV:
XNS:   ----- XNS Header -----
XNS:
XNS:   Checksum = FFFF
XNS:   Length = 37
XNS:   Transport = 0
XNS:   Packet type = 17 (Novell Netware)
XNS:
XNS:   Dest   network = 00001111, host = 10005A0033BF, socket = 1105 (?)
XNS:   Source network = 00002222, host = 000000000020, socket = 16385
XNS:
XNS:   ----- Novell Advanced NetWare -----
XNS:
XNS:   Request type = 2222 (Request)
XNS:   Seq no=5    Connection no=1     Task no=1
XNS:
NCP:   ----- Get Station Number Request -----
NCP:
NCP:   Request code = 19
NCP:
NCP:   [Normal end of Netware "Get Station Number Request" packet.]
NCP:
```

Figure 5-18b
Novell NetWare "Get Station Number Reply" packet transmitted over ARCNET and captured by the Network General Sniffer protocol analyzer

```
DLC:  ----- DLC Header -----
DLC:
DLC:  Frame 12 arrived at 13:39:34.3457; frame size is 49 (0031 hex) bytes.
DLC:  Destination: Station 20, IBM PC
DLC:  Source     : Station 44, NetWare-XT
DLC:  ARCNET system code = FA
DLC:
NOV:  ----- Novell ARCNET fragmentation header -----
NOV:
NOV:  Unfragmented frame
NOV:  Sequence number = 28633
NOV:
XNS:  ----- XNS Header -----
XNS:
XNS:  Checksum = FFFF
XNS:  Length = 41
XNS:  Transport = 0
XNS:  Packet type = 17 (Novell Netware)
XNS:
XNS:  Dest   network = 00002222, host = 000000000020, socket = 16385
XNS:  Source network = 00001111, host = 10005A0033BF, socket = 1105 (?)
XNS:
XNS:  ----- Novell Advanced NetWare -----
XNS:
XNS:  Request type = 3333 (Reply)
XNS:  Seq no=5    Connection no=1    Task no=0
XNS:
NCP:  ----- Get Station Number Reply -----
NCP:
NCP:  Request code = 19 (reply to frame 11)
NCP:
NCP:  Completion code = 00 (OK)
NCP:  Connection status flags = 00 (OK)
NCP:  ASCII Station Number = 01
NCP:  Station number = 1
NCP:
NCP:  [Normal end of Netware "Get Station Number Reply" packet.]
NCP:
```

5.10 | Troubleshooting Summary

In summary, here's a quick checklist to assist in troubleshooting your ARCNET network:

1. Check for duplicate node addresses. Make sure that the DIP switches are making positive contact make sure that they are actuated as far as possible (either in/out or up/down).

2. Check for unterminated passive hubs, T-connectors, cable ends or unused jacks on twisted pair hubs or NICS.

3. Verify correct IRQ and DMA channel options, plus I/O base address, and memory (on-board RAM) buffer locations.

4. Observe the status of the diagnostic LEDs on the NIC or active hub, and verify correct network operation.

5. Check the network topology for any recent violations, such as number of PCs per segment, length of the segment, etc.

6. Verify power connections to any active hubs; also check for any blown fuses or incorrect power (120/240 VAC) settings.

7. If the entire network has failed, start at the server and disconnect segments until proper operation is restored. Then begin adding back in disconnected sections until the failing element is isolated and replaced.

5.11 | References

[5-1] Some of the material in this chapter first appeared in "Troubleshooting ARCNET," by Mark A. Miller, *LAN Technology Magazine*, Volume 5, Number 5, May 1989.

[5-2] COM9026 Local Area Network Controller circuit description, Standard Microsystems Corporation, 1984.

[5-3] COM9032 Local Area Network Transceiver circuit description, Standard Microsystems Corporation, 1984.

[5-4] COM90C65 Local Area Network Controller/Transceiver/Support Logic Data Sheet, Standard Microsystems Corporation, 1989.

[5-5] Technical Note TN5-2, "Using the COM9026 and COM9032," Standard Microsystems Corporation, 1985.

[5-6] NCR90C98 ARCNET Controller/Transceiver Data Sheet, NCR Corporation, 1988.

[5-7] ARCNET Designer's Guide, Publication 900.006A, Standard Microsystems Corporation, 1987.

[5-8] ARCNET Cabling Guide, Document number 51087, 2nd Edition, Datapoint Corporation, 1988.

[5-9] ARCNET Designer's Handbook, Document 61610, Datapoint Corporation, 2nd edition, 1988.

[5-10] ARCNET Factory LAN Primer, Contemporary Control Systems, 1987.

[5-11] ARCNET—PC110/PC210 Network Controller Board Installation Guide, Publication 900.022, July 1987.

[5-12] Advanced NetWare Theory of Operations, version 2.1, Novell, Inc., 1987.

[5-13] NetWare System Calls for DOS, document 101-000571-001, Novell, Inc., 1989.

[5-14]   ARCNET Network Portable Protocol Analyzer Operation and Reference Manual, Network General Corporation, 1986-1988.

CHAPTER SIX

Troubleshooting the Token Ring

The token ring network adheres to the IEEE 802.5 Standard, and is supported by a number of LAN manufacturers, including IBM, Proteon, Racore, Gateway Communications, 3Com, Ungermann Bass, and others (see reference [6-1]). We will look at how specific details of the 802.5 Standard fit the OSI model later in this chapter.

The IEEE 802.5 Committee was formed in 1980, with IBM and Texas Instruments announcing an agreement in 1982 to jointly develop a chipset in support of the token ring. That agreement culminated with the TMS380 five-chip set in 1985. IBM uses the TMS380 in the RT/PC adapter, but its own internal versions (not available commercially) for the other token ring products. The major difference between the two versions is the memory interface: the TMS380 uses Direct Memory Access (DMA), while the IBM implementation uses shared memory. Recent developments in late 1988 included an increase in the transmission rate from 4 Mbps to 16 Mbps and the announcement by Texas Instruments of the TMS380C16—a single chip version operating at the higher rate. IBM also has a 16 Mbps chip used with its 16/4 Mbps adapters, although there was no formal development agreement with Texas Instruments. Before we investigate hardware and software troubleshooting, we will take a brief look at the token ring network architecture.

6.1 | Token Ring Architecture

Its name implies a ring, however the token ring is physically a star, and electrically a ring. Figure 6-1 shows an example network, with two Multistation Access Units (abbreviated MSAU so as not to confuse it with the Medium Attachment Unit (MAU) used with 802.3 networks) and various workstations. Media repeaters (for copper or fiber) can be added between two MSAUs to increase the transmission distance. Each node acts as a bit repeater—receiving the serial bit stream from its Nearest Active Upstream Neighbor (NAUN) node, processing as necessary, and sending the bit stream on down the cable to the next node in line. Only a few bit times of delay are required in each workstation for these functions. The serial transmission follows a complete ring or loop (hence the name token ring), with the sending station eventually receiving its transmitted information back after this information completes one round trip around the ring.

Figure 6-1
Token ring architecture

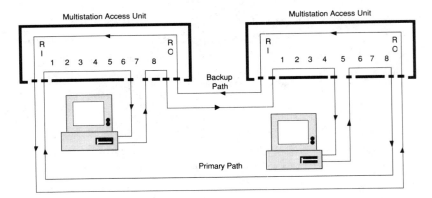

The Token is merely a specific bit sequence that circulates among the nodes, giving permission to transmit. Token ring networks are often described as being distributed polling environments for this reason. Each workstation is thus polled to determine if it needs access to the network. When the node is in possession of the token, it can transmit a message that is in its output buffer. Otherwise, the node is in bit repeat (and/or receive and process) mode.

The star-wired ring architecture has several troubleshooting advantages over other topologies:

- The wiring center (MSAU in this case) allows ready access to both ends (workstation and wire center) of the cable for testing.

- A faulty node or wire center can be easily bypassed by rearranging jumpers on the patch panel; or otherwise eliminating the failing section automatically at the direction of network management software.

6.2 | The Token Ring Standard

As mentioned previously, the token ring network adheres to the IEEE 802.5 Standard (see reference [6-2]), which has some interesting characteristics from a network troubleshooting perspective that are worth considering.

6.2.1 | The Physical Layer

The 802.5 Physical Layer standard includes the following characteristics:

- **Symbol Encoding**—Differential Manchester encoding with no DC component (therefore allowing inductive or capacitive coupling between cable and network interface) is used. The Differential Manchester code is defined as follows: a ZERO is represented by a transition at the beginning of the bit cell; a ONE has no beginning transition. In addition, a forced transition in the middle of the bit provides timing information. Violations to the Differential Manchester code will be used to provide special framing characters, and the timing will be important when we discuss the roles of the Active and Standby Monitors. Refer to Figure 6-2 for an example of the symbol encoding.

Figure 6-2
Differential Manchester encoded signal

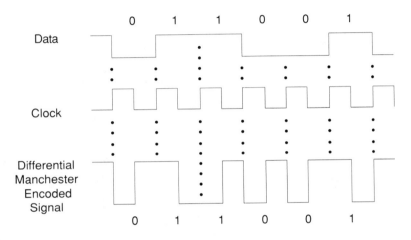

- **Signal Rate**—4 Mbps; plus a 16 Mbps data rate has also been approved.

- **Cable**—Balanced shielded twisted pairs, 150 ± 15 ohms impedance (although unshielded twisted pairs are also implemented in practice).

- **Connector**—a four conductor, hermaphroditic (genderless) connector shown in Figure 6-3, wired as follows:

Signal Lead	Pin Designation
Receive +	Red (R)
Receive -	Green (G)
Transmit +	Orange (O)
Transmit -	Black (B)

Figure 6-3
The Hermaphroditic Connector

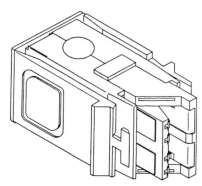

Most importantly, when the connector is disconnected from its mate, shorting bars connect pins R and O and pins G and B. We will use this feature when we test for defective cables.

- **Latency Buffer**—in order for the Token (a 24-bit sequence) to properly circulate when all stations are repeating, the ring must have a minimum of a 24-bit time propagation delay. This delay guarantees that the Token will not return (that is, overlap) to the sending station before it is completely transmitted. Since most rings are not physically long enough (at 4 Mbps, the cable would have to be about 4,500 feet long to "hold" the entire Token), the Active Monitor station inserts a minimum of 24-bit times of delay.

- **Phantom Power**—the NIC supplies a DC current via the four-wire transmit/receiver circuit to a relay in the MSAU. When the station is not plugged in or is turned off, the relay bypasses that MSAU port maintaining the continuity of the ring. When the station is plugged in and turned on, the relay changes state, enabling the NIC to transmit and receive. Figure 6-4 shows the relay states for both active and inactive nodes. For unpowered MSAUs, like IBM's, an initialization tool should be used to set the correct state of the electronic relay when the MSAU is first installed. For powered MSAUs, like Proteon's, the relays are initialized when the MSAU is powered up.

6.2.2 | The Medium Access Control Layer

The MAC layer, as the name implies, controls access to the transmission medium, or cable, and performs the following functions:

- **Frame Formats**—three separate transmission frames are defined in 802.5: the Token, a 24-bit sequence authorizing network access; the Frame used for either network management (MAC frames) or data transmission (LLC frames); and the Abort Sequence, used when a frame transmission must be prematurely terminated. We will discuss the use of these frames in section 6.5.

- **Error Control**—generation of the Frame Check Sequence, a 32-bit Cyclic Redundancy Check.

- **Ring Maintenance Functions**—including active and standby monitor functions, error isolation, and recovery and ring management. The functions of the ring monitors are especially interesting, and are discussed in section 6.2.4.

6.2.3 | The Logical Link Control Layer

The Logical Link Control (LLC) layer defines virtual data paths between communicating end points in collaboration with the physical data paths defined in the MAC and Physical layers. Multiple links to multiple logical entities (called Service Access Points or SAPs) are possible. As an example, one NIC, having its unique 48-bit address (defined at the MAC layer) can provide a communication path into several different higher layer protocols—that is, NetBIOS or IBM's Advanced Program-to-Program Communication (APPC). The SAP delineates that higher layer. To review from Chapter 1, there are three different types of LLC services:

- **Type 1 (Unacknowledged Connectionless)**
  LLC frames are sent and received with no delivery acknowledgement.

- **Type 2 (Connection-Oriented)**
  Sequential transmission of frames with acknowledgements.

- **Type 3 (Acknowledged Connectionless)**
  Datagram service with transmission acknowledgements, but no virtual circuit connection.

As we saw in Chapter 1, a LAN station Class I supports Type 1 LLC services, while a LAN station Class II supports either Type 1 or Type 2. Both the TI and IBM chipsets support Class II service.

6.2.4   The Ring Monitors

The Active Monitor is the active node with the highest address that wins a claim token process between all active nodes. It performs the following functions: provides the network Master clock from which all other workstations receive their timing; monitors the network, and must see a Frame or Token every 10 milliseconds; removes any continuously—circulating priority Tokens or Frames (that is, those with a priority greater than zero); inserts a latency buffer (24 bits long when operating at 4 Mbps, 32 bits long at 16 Mbps) to guarantee a ring length and insure token circulation; and periodically notifies the other nodes of its existence by sending the Active Monitor Present MAC frame, one of the 25 MAC frame types.

All other nodes become Stand-by Monitors that determine if the Active Monitor is functioning properly.

Ring error isolation, recovery, and management involve a number of MAC-defined frames that are "built-in" to the token ring chipsets. These services are detailed in section 6.8.

6.3 | Token Ring Hardware Components

The hardware elements for token ring networks are somewhat more sophisticated than those for other networks because of the network management functions built into the token ring chipsets. Therefore, we will briefly discuss the chipset prior to looking at other hardware components.

6.3.1 | Token Ring Network Controller Chips

The Texas Instruments TMS380 chipset implements the IEEE 802.5 Standard for Token Ring LANs. Two versions of the chipset exist. The TMS380 is a five-chip set that operates at 4 Mbps and consists of:

TMS38051: Ring interface transceiver
TMS38052: Ring interface controller
TMS38010: Communication protocol processor
TMS38021: Protocol handler for 802.5 functions
TMS38030: DMA controller between the NIC and host system bus

For the IBM products, a front end performs the TMS38051 and TMS38052 functions; a 16-bit processor does the communication processing like the TMS38010; dual protocol handlers perform the TMS38020 802.5 functions; and an attachment interface provides a shared memory interface to the host. The TMS380C16 Second Generation Token Ring COMMprocessor is a 16 Mbps device that incorporates the functions of the TMS38010, TMS38021, and TMS38030 into a single 132-pin device fabricated in one micron CMOS technology. In addition, the TMS38051 and TMS38052 Ring Interface transceiver and controller chips have been combined into the TMS38053 Ring Interface. The Ring Interface device processes the signal from the transmission media, and hands off a data stream to the COMMprocessor. Using these second generation devices dramatically shrinks the area required for the NIC to less than ten square inches.

Cost reductions would likely follow as well. See references [6-3], [6-4], and [6-5] for further information.

6.3.2 | Network Interface Cards

Figure 6-4 shows an example of a token ring NIC, the p1345 PC/AT Interface from Proteon. Note the locations of the various components; the TMS380 is in the center section of the board.

Figure 6-4
Token ring network interface card

(photo courtesy of Proteon, Inc.)

6.3.3   Multistation Access Units (MSAUs)

The wiring hub of the token ring is called a multistation access unit, or MSAU. An example of an MSAU, the Proteon p2710 Intelligent Wire Center, is shown in Figure 6-5. The eight ports for workstations, plus the Ring In (RI) and Ring Out (RO) connectors used for connections to other MSAUs are visible on the front panel. Connections to power and the network manager workstation used with the TokenVIEW-4 program are on the rear.

Figure 6-5
Token ring multistation access unit

(photo courtesy of Proteon, Inc.)

TokenVIEW-4 is one example of a token ring network management product that uses the troubleshooting capabilities incorporated into the 802.5 standard. The Proteon Intelligent Wire Centers also include relays in the RI and RO ports to facilitate remote fault isolation. The IBM and compatible units use the hermaphroditic connectors (with the internal shorting bars) for RI and RO instead. Recall from Figure 6-

1 that the first RI should be connected to the last RO to provide a backup wiring path for co-located MSAUs.

Figure 6-6
Internal wiring of the MSAU

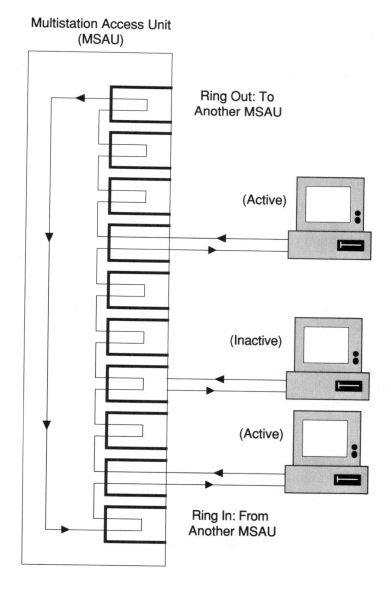

Multistation Access Unit
(MSAU)

Ring Out: To
Another MSAU

(Active)

(Inactive)

(Active)

Ring In: From
Another MSAU

The internal wiring of an MSAU is shown in Figure 6-6. Note that workstations attached (and activated) have opened the relay connections at the ports; disconnected or inactive ports have the relay contacts closed to maintain the electrical continuity of the ring. When the station inserts into the ring, an audible "click" can be heard when the relay operates. It is a good idea to listen for this sound from the MSAU enclosure to verify proper port operation.

6.3.4   Cabling Systems

As we saw in section 6.2.1, the 802.5 standard only specifies shielded twisted pairs, having a characteristic impedance of 150 ± 15 ohms, although other types are implemented in practice. IBM defines its allowed cable types by number, summarized below:

Type 1:   2 shielded, solid wire, twisted pairs, 22 AWG. Available for plenum or non-plenum interior use and underground or aerial exterior use. Use of Type 1 permits transmission at 16 Mbps, and a maximum of 260 stations on the network.

Type 2:   2 shielded, solid wire, twisted pairs, 22 AWG, plus 4 twisted pairs of solid 26 AWG wires added between the shield and the insulating cable sheath. Type 2 also supports 16 Mbps transmission.

Type 3:   Unshielded, telephone grade (22 or 24 AWG) twisted pairs, typically found inside a building. Requires a media filter at (or within) the NIC, and limits the transmission rate to 4 Mbps, and the number of workstations to 72.

Type 5:   100/140 micron fiber optic cable, used to connect distant MSAUs with fiber optic repeaters.

Type 6:   Patch cables consisting of data grade, stranded, shielded twisted pairs, 26 AWG. When used, the distance limits are 66% that of Type 1.

Type 8: Undercarpet cable, data grade twisted pair cable, 26 AWG. When used, the distance limits are 50% that of Type 1.

Type 9: Shield twisted pair, 26 AWG approved for plenum installations. When used, the distance limits are 66% that of Type 1.

6.3.5 Repeaters

Both copper and fiber optic repeaters are available to connect distant wiring closets of MSAUs. Specific details on distance limitations, etc. are beyond the scope of this book; see references [6-6], [6-7], and [6-8] for further information.

6.4 Token Ring Hardware Troubleshooting

As we have seen, the IEEE 802.5 Standard incorporates many built-in features that facilitate troubleshooting. Anytime that a ring is dysfunctional, you should first look at any element that could have suffered from human intervention—for example, unplugged cables, unpowered MSAUs (IBM's are not powered, Proteon's are), etc. Because of the myriad of patch cord connections typically associated with a token ring network, the first step in hardware troubleshooting is to obtain copies of the network documentation. IBM provides many excellent documentation suggestions (see references [6-6], [6-7], and [6-8]), to make this task easier. Thereafter, a straightforward process to isolate the defective ring portion (called the failure domain) remove (or patch around) the failing section, repair the defective component, and restore the ring to full operation can be initiated.

6.4.1 Identifying Failure Domains

The term "failure domain" is described in the IEEE 802.5 Standard, and consists of the station that is reporting the failure, it's Nearest Active Upstream Neighbor (NAUN) station, plus the cable (and possibly repeaters) in between.

Translated, this means that a node or cable failure upstream will be noted by a downstream station. When this failure is recognized, the downstream station transmits a MAC frame called a Beacon to tell other stations on the network that a hard failure has been identified. Another part of the Beacon process includes an autoreconfiguration, where the nodes with the failure domain automatically perform cable and node diagnostics. Failure recovery is thus automatic in many cases.

Software diagnostics, such as the diagnostic disk that accompanies most token ring cards, or a protocol analyzer, are able to decode the Beacon frame, which includes the NAUN station address and Beaconing station address. Once these two end points are defined, the hardware failure must lie somewhere in between.

When a single wiring closet is used for the entire network, the failure can be isolated to an individual MSAU, which can then be bypassed by rearranging jumper cables. When multiple wiring closets are used, first isolate the problem to a single closet, and then proceed to identify the failing MSAU. Further troubleshooting involves testing (or re-placing) both NICs, MSAUs, or repeaters, and thorough testing of the cable system in between making certain that any filters used with un-shielded twisted pair cable are checked as part of the cable plant testing. Reference [6-9] provides further details.

6.4.2   Cable System Testing

Since many token ring failures involve cable and wiring difficulties, IBM developed a special device, called the IBM Cabling System Tester (Part Number 4760500) shown in Figure 6-7, to expedite the process. The device comes in two parts: the Tester itself, and a Data Wrap Plug that is used at one end of the cable to insert a known impedance be-tween wires. The Data Wrap Plug permits viable measurements with the Tester, since a disconnected hermaphroditic connector will auto-matically short the Red to Orange and Green to Black wires.

Figure 6-8 describes two such tests that can be made with the Cabling System Tester.

Figure 6-7
IBM Cabling System Tester

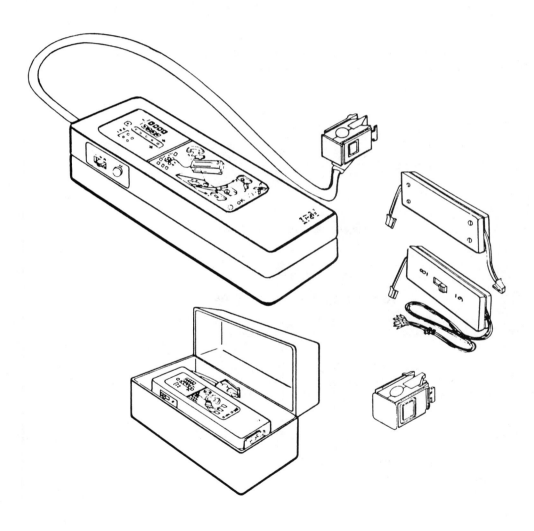

Figure 6-8
Token ring cable testing

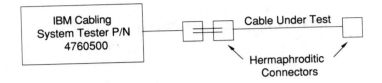

Test 1: Checks for shorts between the data conductors and shield, open conductors or mis-assembled connectors.

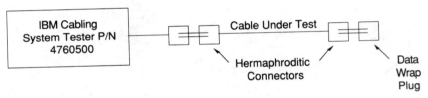

Test 2: Checks for an open shield, transposed pairs or shorted pairs.

Figure 6-9
Token ring connector pinouts at the NIC

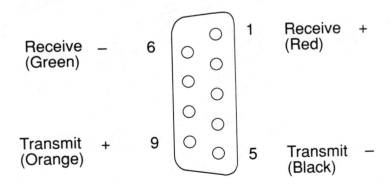

Figure 6-9 shows the pinouts of the DB-9 connector used at the NIC to connect to the MSAU port. A quick test of the shorting bars within the hermaphroditic connector can be made using a VOM to measure the resistance between pins 1 and 9 and pins 5 and 6 on the DB-9 connector at the other end of the pigtail cable. If the shorting bars are operating properly, both of these measurements will be very close to a short (0 ohms) since Transmit + should be shorted to Receive +, and Transmit—should be shorted to Receive -.

6.5 Token Ring Frames

The token ring employs three frame formats: the Token, the Frame, and the Abort Sequence, shown in Figures 6-10a, b, and c, respectively. In addition, two types of Frames are possible: the Logical Link Control (LLC) Frames, which transmit user data, and the Medium Access Control (MAC) frames, which provide ring management. We will discuss each type of frame separately.

Figure 6-10a
Token ring Token format

Starting Delimiter	Access Control	Ending Delimiter	
1	1	1	octets
VV0VV000	PPPTMRRR	VV1VV1IE	

V = Differential Manchester Violations	P = Priority Mode T = Token Bit M = Monitor Count R = Priority Reservation	V = Differential Manchester Violations
0 = Binary ZERO		1 = Binary ONE I = Intermediate E = Error Detect

Figure 6-10b
Token ring Frame format

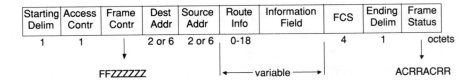

Starting Delim	Access Contr	Frame Contr	Dest Addr	Source Addr	Route Info	Information Field	FCS	Ending Delim	Frame Status
1	1		2 or 6	2 or 6	0-18		4	1	octets

FFZZZZZZ

← variable →

ACRRACRR

F = Frame Format
  00 = MAC (Ring data)
  01 = LLC (User data)
  1X = future use
Z = Control bits
A = Address recognized; initially 0, changed to 1 when station recognizes its address
C = Frame copied; initially 0, changed to 1 when station copies frame to its RX buffer
R = Reserved bits
RI = Route Information; used for additional routing when a frame traverses multiple rings via bridges. When RI is present, the Least Significant Bit (LSB) of the Source address = 1, and the RI is placed in all messages:

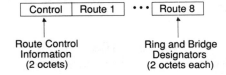

| Control | Route 1 | ••• | Route 8 |

Route Control Information (2 octets)

Ring and Bridge Designators (2 octets each)

Figure 6-10c
Token ring Abort Sequence

Starting Delimiter	Ending Delimiter
1	1 octets
VV0VV000	VV1VV1IE

6.5.1 | The Token Format

The Token circulates around the ring, controlling access to the network. The 24 bits of the Token are divided into three octets: the Starting Delimiter, which contains violations to the Differential Manchester Code plus binary ZEROs; the Access Control field, which grants network access; and the Ending Delimiter, which contains Differential Manchester Code violations, binary ONES, plus two additional bits, Intermediate and Error detect, described below.

The Access control field begins with three Priority (P) bits that set the priority of that token. Each workstation is assigned a priority (see the Change Parameters MAC frame) for their transmissions, 000 being the lowest and 111 being the highest. The Priority Reservation (R) bits can be used by a workstation to request the reservation of the next token as a transmission passes by. In order for a workstation to transmit, its priority must be greater than or equal to the priority of that token. The Token (T) bit delineates either a Token (T=0) or a Frame (T=1).

The Monitor (M) bit is used to prevent high priority tokens or any frames from continuously circulating around the ring, and is set to M=0 by the transmitting station, and set to M=1 by the Active Monitor. If the monitor sees an incoming priority Token or Frame with M=1, it assumes that the transmitting station did not remove the token or frame after one round trip, and removes that Token or Frame, purges the ring, and issues a new Token.

The Ending Delimiter includes Differential Manchester Code violations and binary ONES; an Intermediate frame (I) bit, which when set indicates that this frame is part of a multi-frame transmission; and an Error detect (E) bit that is set when a frame contains a Frame Check Sequence (FCS) error, non-integral number of bytes or a Differential Manchester Code violation between Starting and Ending delimiters.

6.5.2 | The Frame Formats

The first two octets of the Frame, the Starting Delimiter and Access Control fields, are from the Token format described above. The two types of Frames, MAC and LLC, are identified by the first two bits of the third octet, or Frame Control field:

$$00ZZZZZZ = \text{MAC frame}$$
$$01ZZZZZZ = \text{LLC frame}$$
$$1XZZZZZZ = \text{Reserved for future use}$$
$$Z = \text{Represent control bits}$$

Next comes the Destination and Source Address fields which can be 2 or 6 octets in length, although the longer addresses are commonly used. The Address field format is the same as that used for the IEEE 802.3 networks and is described in Figure 7-11b. The Routing Information field is optional, and is used for multi-ring networks as described in Figure 6-10b. The Information field is variable in length, although it is generally limited in practice by the manufacturer and the transmission rate (4 Mbps or 16 Mbps). Within the Information field is an LLC or MAC Protocol Data Unit (PDU), described below.

The Frame Check Sequence (FCS) field is a 32-bit Cyclic Redundancy Check. The Ending Delimiter field is also from the Token frame format. Last, the Frame Status field provides feedback to the transmitter regarding the condition of that frame. The Address recognized (A) bits are set equal to ONE by the receiving station to indicate that the intended receiver recognized its address. The Frame copied (C) bits are set equal to ONE by the receiving station to indicate that the receiver copied the frame into its buffer. Both the A and C bits are repeated for redundancy. By reading the A and C bits, the transmitter can thus verify the proper reception of a frame.

6.5.2.1 The LLC Frame Format

The Logical Link Control Frame is shown in Figure 6-11. Imbedded within the Information field of the 802.5 frame are:

- the LLC Protocol Data Unit (PDU), which contains the Destination and Source Service Access Point Addresses (DSAP and SSAP)

- a Control field that defines three types of PDUs: Information (I), which carry sequenced user information; Supervisory (S), which control the exchange of Information PDUs; and Unnumbered (U) for unsequenced information transfer and other data link control functions; and finally another Information field. This Information field within the LLC PDU contains user data from the higher layers—that is, 3 through 7. Reference [6-10] is devoted to detailed explanations of the above items.

Figure 6-11
The 802.2 LLC PDU within an 802.5 frame

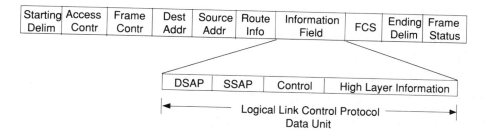

6.5.2.2 The MAC Frame Format

The MAC Frame is shown in Figure 6-12. The Information field within the MAC PDU consists of a Length field, indicating the length in octets of the PDU; a Class field, indicating the Source and Destination Class (for example, Ring Station, Network Manager, Ring Parameter Server, Ring Error Monitor, etc.); Commands that the intended receiver is to perform; and Parameters, called Subvectors, that further elaborate on the Commands. More details on these functions in section 6.9.

Figure 6-12
The MAC PDU within an 802.5 frame

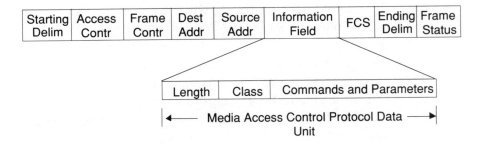

6.5.3 | The Abort Sequence Format

Certain error conditions, such as hard errors internal to the workstation, cause the transmission of the abort sequence shown in Figure 6-10c. Note that the Starting Delimiter and Ending Delimiter fields are the same as in the Token frame, discussed in section 6.5.1.

6.6 | Ring Management

Each token ring NIC, regardless of manufacturer, includes the Network Management functions incorporated into the 802.5 Standard. These functions include monitoring soft and hard errors; maintaining details of the configuration, such as the Nearest Active Upstream Neighbor (NAUN); and control of various parameters such as the token priority, ring number, etc. The basis for these functions is a Network Management "Agent" located in each NIC, that communicates with the Network Management "Product" located somewhere on the network. As of this writing, only two vendors have developed these "products": Proteon with the TokenVIEW-4 Program, and IBM with the IBM LAN Manager Program.

Figure 6-13
Network Management Agent and Product Relationships

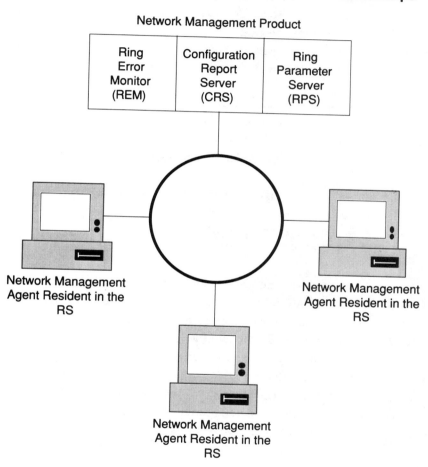

Figure 6-13 illustrates the relationship between the Agent on the NIC or Ring Station (RS), and the Product (attached somewhere on the network). Four different functions are implemented in the Product:

- the Active and Standby Monitors, which supervise the network operation
- the Ring Error Monitor (REM), responsible for collecting error reports from the NICs and Active and Standby Monitors

- the Configuration Report Server (CRS), which keeps track of the current network configuration, and controls individual NIC parameters such as its access priority, or signals a particular station to remove itself from the ring
- the Ring Parameter Server (RPS), which assigns operational parameters to the station at the time of insertion onto the ring.

Since the Product may exist anywhere on the ring, the Agent communicates with the Product through a series of twenty-five MAC frames that are transmitted to one of several functional (or well-known) addresses, shown here as 12 hexadecimal characters (or 6 octets):

C00000000001:   Active Monitor
C00000000002:   Ring Parameter Server
C00000000008:   Ring Error Monitor
C00000000010:   Configuration Report Server

The Agent, when desiring (or requested) to communicate with the Product, builds a MAC frame as shown in Figure 6-12, and transmits it to the appropriate functional address above. The host system (for example, a PC on the network) would be oblivious to these transmissions—after all, they are used for network management, not for the transmission of user data. Should a fault such as a noisy section of cable occur on the network, the human network administrator can access the software network management product for diagnostic assistance. In addition, protocol analysis tools have the ability to capture, record, and decode the various MAC frames to assist the user with fault isolation and network optimization. Since the Active Monitor, Ring Parameter Server, Ring Error Monitor, and Configuration Report Server are unique addresses, any information sent to one of the above entities can be captured for further analysis- more on this in section 6.10.

6.7 Token Ring Processes

In order to better understand the various MAC frames, it would be a good idea to first review the various processes that occur between the individual workstations on the token ring network. The eight processes are summarized below; for further information, see Section 3 of reference [6-3].

6.7.1 Ring Insertion

When any Host system wishes to attach to the ring, it issues an OPEN command to the network, which initiates the Ring Insertion Process. There are five unique phases to the process:

Phase 0: **Lobe Media check**—verification of the cable by looping the station transmit signal to the station receiver at the wiring concentrator. The Lobe Media Test MAC frame is used.

Phase 1: **Physical insertion**—the phantom drive DC current is applied at the NIC to the transmit pair to activate the relay at the wire concentrator port, thus physically connecting the station to the network.

Phase 2: **Address verification**—the station verifies that its address is unique within the ring. The Duplicate Address Test MAC frame is used.

Phase 3: **Participation in Neighbor Notification**—the station learns of its Upstream Neighbor's Address, and sends its address to the nearest downstream neighbor.

Phase 4: **Request Initialization**—A Request Initialization MAC frame is sent to the RPS, which responds with an Initialize Ring Station MAC frame containing that station's parameters, such as the local ring number. If no RPS is present, the station would insert onto the ring with its default parameters.

When Phase 4 is completed, the station is then both physically and logically attached to the network.

6.7.2 | Claim Token

One of the active RS must be designated as the Active Monitor (AM); all others are Standby Monitors. When a RS detects the absence of the AM, it originates the Claim Token (also called Monitor Contention) process by transmitting a Claim Token MAC frame. The active RS with the highest address wins this process and becomes the new Active Monitor.

6.7.3 | Ring Purge

The AM uses the Ring Purge process in two cases: to put the ring in a token-passing mode after it wins the Monitor Contention process, or when it detects a token error condition. The Ring Purge MAC frame is initiated by the AM, and is repeated by all downstream stations. When the Ring Purge frame returns to the AM without errors, the AM then transmits a new token, thus initiating token passing.

6.7.4 | Neighbor Notification

This process allows each RS to obtain the 6 octet (or 12 hex character) address of its Upstream Neighbor, and also provides the CRS with an ordered list of all active stations.

6.7.5 | Beacon

The Beacon process is used to alert downstream stations that a hard error has occurred, causing severe network failure. Examples would be a broken or shorted cable, or a defective NIC. The Beacon MAC frame also informs the downstream stations about the nature of the failure. Should the Beacon frame be sent from a station's downstream neighbor (that is, point to a fault at the upstream station or the cable in between), the upstream neighbor will begin a process to automatically test and possibly remove itself from the ring.

6.7.6 | Transmit Forward

Transmit forward is used to transmit (or relay) information around the ring to test the communication path between stations.

6.7.7 | Hardware Error

Hardware error is used to detect a wire fault (absence or improper DC phantom drive from the NIC); frequency error (a frequency difference between the incoming signal and that station's crystal oscillator); or loss of signal (either insufficient signal level or major phase difference).

6.7.8 | Soft Error Counting

Soft error counting is a log of network errors that degrades performance such as corrupted tokens, but doesn't cause a network failure. The log is used by higher layer protocols to initiate a recovery process, and by the CRS to isolate potential problem areas.

6.8 | MAC Frames

The MAC frames provide the communication capabilities for the token ring processes that were described above, and can be divided into four categories: Medium Control, concerned with reliable operation of the network; Station Initialization, used when a station wishes to join the ring; Error Monitoring, indicating soft errors that have occurred;

and finally Network Management, for control of the network configuration and station parameters. Recall that the MAC frames are transmitted from the Network Management Agent (on the NIC or RS) to one of several functional addresses: AM, RPS, REM, or the CRS. Delving into these frames with a protocol analyzer, for example, will provide further insight into how well the network is functioning internally. The twenty-five MAC frame formats are shown below. For further information on the MAC frames, see section 3 of reference [6-3].

6.8.1   Medium Control Frames

- **Beacon (RS to all RS)**—transmitted when an RS detects a hard failure, such as a wire fault, signal loss, or streaming station.
- **Claim Token (RS to all RS)**—transmitted by any station that detects the absence of the AM, and wishes to start the Claim Token process; or during the Contention process to determine the new AM.
- **Ring Purge (AM to all RS)**—used by the AM to recover from a temporary error condition, release a new token, and reinitialize the token passing process; or at the conclusion of the Claim Token process.
- **Active Monitor Present (AM to all RS)**—transmitted every 7 seconds or at the end of the Ring Purge process to indicate the presence of the Active Token Monitor.
- **Standby Monitor Present (RS to all RS or AM)**—transmitted in response to an Active Monitor Present or another Standby Monitor Present frame during the Neighbor Notification process.

6.8.2   Station Initialization Frames

- **Lobe Media Test (RS to itself)**—used during the initial phase of the ring insertion process to test the transmission media from the station to the wire center and back.

- **Duplicate Address Test (RS to all RSs)**—used to verify the uniqueness of that station's address.
- **Request Initialization (RS to RPS)**—asks the RPS for operational parameters (local ring number, physical drop number and error report timer value) during the Ring Initialization process.
- **Initialize Ring Station (RPS to RS)**—transmits the parameters from the RPS to the station.

6.8.3 Error Monitoring Frames

- **Report Error (RS to REM)**—indicates a count of soft errors that may be recoverable by higher layer protocols.
- **Report Monitor Error (RS to REM)**—informs the REM of a problem in the Claim Token process, or a problem with the AM.
- **Report Neighbor Notification Incomplete (RS to REM)**—indicates that the station has not received a transmission from its upstream neighbor during the Neighbor Notification process.

6.8.4 Network Management Frames

- **Report New Monitor (AM to CRS)**—transmitted at the conclusion of the Claim Token process by the winning station.
- **Report SUA Change (RS to CRS)**—reports a change in the stations stored upstream address as a result of information gathered during the Neighbor Notification process.
- **Remove Ring Station (CRS to RS)**—sent from the Configuration Report Server to force a station to de-insert from the ring.
- **Change Parameters (CRS to RS)**—allow the Configuration Report Server to change the local ring number, physical drop number, soft error report timer value, function class and access priority number; may also be used during the Station Initialization process.
- The following frames are used by the Configuration Report Server to gather specific information about a particular station:

- **Request Station Address (CRS to RS)**
- **Report Station Address (RS to CRS)**
- **Request Station State (CRS to RS)**
- **Report Station State (RS to CRS)**
- **Request Station Attachment (CRS to RS)**
- **Report Station Attachment (RS to CRS)**

- **Transmit Forward (CRS to RS)**—used to test the path between various stations by retransmitting a given message.
- **Report Transmit Forward (RS to CRS)**—a confirmation from the station to the CRS that a frame has been forwarded in the Transmit Forward process.
- **Response (RS to CRS or RPS)**—acknowledges a response to a Change Parameters (from CRS) or Initialize Ring Station (from RPS) frame.

6.9   Token Ring Software Considerations

We looked at the three token ring frame formats (shown in Figure 6-10) as part of our discussion on the IEEE 802.5 Standard. While many software failures would involve decoding at OSI layers 3-7 with a protocol analyzer, and will be discussed in section 6.10, there are several software-configurable parameters that may cause difficulties.

6.9.1   NIC Address

The token ring frame format specifies a 6 octet (48 bit) address for both Source and Destination nodes. These addresses can be either universally administered (and burned into ROM on the NIC) or locally administered (set in RAM on the NIC). While it is safest to always use the ROM address (in theory, these are absolutely unique and never duplicated), an occasion may arise requiring the locally administered case. If this occurs, care should be taken to see that the address selected is not a duplicate, and that it falls in the correct range for that particular network; for example, IBM requires that the address fall in the range from 400000000000 to 40007FFFFFFF Hex (see reference [6-11]). Proteon recommends an address between 4000C9000400 and 4000C900FFFF (see reference [6-12]).

6.9.2 | Shared Memory (RAM) Address

The IBM token ring chipset shares its memory with the PCs address space; NICs based upon the TMS380 chipset use DMA. When the IBM NICs are used, be careful to select the RAM address so that a conflict with other system boards will not occur. See reference [6-11] for details; for Proteon NICs, see reference [6-12].

6.9.3 | NIC Priority

The Token Format includes two fields (the Network Priority and Priority Reservation) that make eight different priorities (000 = lowest and 111 = highest) for Tokens. These fields allow a high priority transmission to grab the next Token, regardless of its physical position in the ring. In most cases, all nodes will have the same priority (such as a default of 000); however in fine-tuning the network, it may be advisable to set a Host or Bridge at a higher priority. Should a particular node experience response time delays, when the network is heavily utilized, verify that the software driver has not incorrectly set that NIC's priority lower than the other nodes on the network.

6.9.4 | Routing Information

The Routing Information field is inserted in the Frame anytime the Source to Destination route includes one or more bridges. Parameters that identify the bridge-ring paths are obtained by special frames used to discover routes. Should a particular workstation experience difficulty accessing another node via a bridge, double-check the routing information.

6.10 | Protocol Analysis with NetBIOS Frames

NetBIOS, the Network Basic Input Output System, was developed by Sytek, Inc., and IBM as a programming interface to IBM's PC Network LAN. In its original release, NetBIOS was provided on the PC Network NIC itself; for the token ring network, NetBIOS is emulated within the PC. Many other vendor's also offer NetBIOS emulators (see reference [6-14], Chapter 5).

Table 6-1
NetBIOS frames available with the IBM Token Ring Network

Command Name	Code	Function
ADD_GROUP_NAME_QUERY	X'00'	Check for duplicate group name on network
ADD_NAME_QUERY	X'01'	Check for duplicate name on network
ADD_NAME_RESPONSE	X'0D'	Negative response: add name is duplicate
NAME_IN_CONFLICT	X'02'	Duplicate names detected
NAME_QUERY	X'0A'	Request to locate a name on the network
NAME_RECOGNIZED	X'0E'	Name Recognized: NAME_QUERY response
SESSION_ALIVE	X'1F'	Verify session is still active
SESSION_CONFIRM	X'17'	SESSION_INITIALIZE acknowledgement
SESSION_END	X'18'	Session termination
SESSION_INITIALIZE	X'19'	A session has been set-up
DATA-ACK	X'14'	DATA_ONLY_LAST acknowledgement
DATA_FIRST_MIDDLE	X'15'	Session data message-first or middle frame
DATAGRAM	X'08'	Application-generated datagram
DATAGRAM_BROADCAST	X'09'	Application-generated broadcast datagram
DATA_ONLY_LAST	X'16'	Session data message—only or last frame
NO_RECEIVE	X'1A'	No receive command to hold received data
RECEIVE_CONTINUE	X'1C'	Indicates receive outstanding
RECEIVE_OUTSTANDING	X'1B'	Re-transmit last data—receive command up
STATUS_QUERY	X'03'	Request remote node status
STATUS_RESPONSE	X'0F'	Remote node status information
TERMINATE_TRACE	X'07'	Terminate traces at remote nodes
TERMINATE_TRACE	X'13'	Terminate traces at local and remote nodes

Many application programs are deemed "NetBIOS compatible," which is another way of saying that they rely upon the NetBIOS functions for network communication. When compared with the OSI model, the NetBIOS program would be defined as a Session layer protocol—one that is responsible for establishing and terminating the communication session between two users on the network, or between one user and the network server. Functions at the Transport and Network layers, specifically end-to-end reliability and internetworking, respectively, are not rigorously addressed by NetBIOS; and frequently other protocols, such as TCP/IP, are used in addition. References [6-15] and [6-16] discuss using NetBIOS with TCP/IP; more on TCP/IP is in Chapter 8.

When using NetBIOS, the Host machine builds a Network Control Block and Transmits the Appropriate NetBIOS frame. Table 6-1, taken from reference [6-14], lists the NetBIOS frames available with the IBM token ring network; see Chapter 3 in that reference for further details.

Figure 6-14
NetBIOS commands encapsulated in the token ring frame

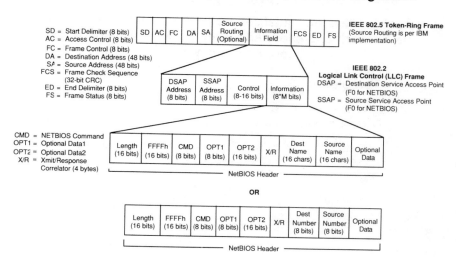

Figure 6-14, also taken from reference [6-14], shows how a NetBIOS frame would be encapsulated within the token ring Information field. Note the NetBIOS command field—the 1 octet code specifying the NetBIOS frame in use. Figure 6-15 shows the capture range of the Network General Sniffer protocol analyzer. Figures 6-16 and 6-17 illustrate the NetBIOS Session Initialize and Session Confirm frames, as captured by the Network General Sniffer on a token ring network. The notations along the left-hand side of the figures indicate the protocol layer being decoded. DLC indicates Data Link Control (token ring), LLC indicates Logical Link Control, and NET indicates NetBIOS. See reference [6-17] for further information.

Figure 6-15
Capture range of the Network General Sniffer Protocol Analyzer for Token Ring Networks

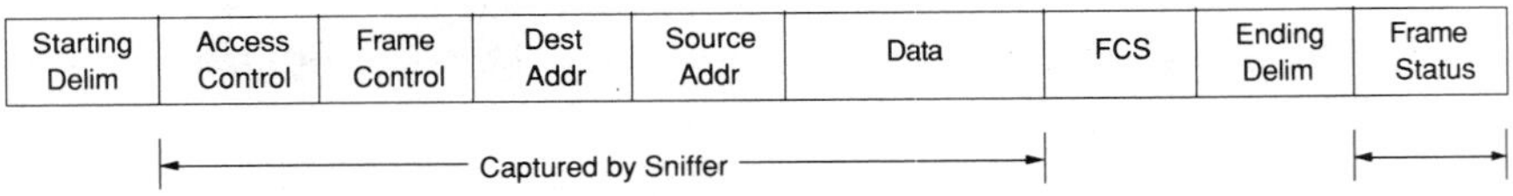

Starting Delim	Access Control	Frame Control	Dest Addr	Source Addr	Data	FCS	Ending Delim	Frame Status

```
|------------------ Captured by Sniffer ------------------|        |------
```

Figure 6-16
A NetBIOS "Session Initialize" frame transmitted over a Token Ring network and captured by the Network General Sniffer protocol analyzer

```
DLC:  ----- DLC Header -----
DLC:
DLC:  Frame 33 arrived at 10:35:24.136  ; frame size is 32 (0020 hex) bytes.
DLC:  AC: Frame priority 0, Reservation priority 0, Monitor count 1
DLC:  FC: LLC frame, PCF attention code: None
DLC:  FS: Addr recognized indicators: 00, Frame copied indicators: 00
DLC:  Destination: Station IBM   118E9A
DLC:  Source     : Station IBM   12F7EC
DLC:
LLC:  -----LLC Header-----
LLC:
LLC:  DSAP = F0, SSAP = F0, Command, I frame, M(R) = 0, N(S) = 0
LLC:
NET:  -----NETBIOS Session Initialize -----
NET:
NET:  Header length = 14, Data length = 0
NET:  Delimiter = EFFF (NETBIOS)
NET:  Command = 19
NET:  Flags = 00
NET:  0... .... = NO.ACK ability
NET:  .... 000. = Largest frame value = 0
NET:  .... ..0 = Pre version 2.0
NET:  Max data receive size = 1750
```

```
NET:   Transmit correlator = 5B0B
NET:   Response correlator = 000C
NET:   Remote session number = 4
NET:   Local session number = 1
NET:
```

Figure 6-17

A NetBIOS "Session Confirm" frame transmitted over a Token Ring network and captured by the Network General Sniffer protocol analyzer

```
DLC:   ----- DLC Header -----
DLC:
DLC:   Frame 34 arrived at  19:35:24.138  ; frame size is 32 (0020 hex) bytes.
DLC:   AC: Frame priority 0, Reservation priority 0, Monitor count 1
DLC:   FC: LLC frame, PCF attention code: None
DLC:   FS: Addr recognized indicators: 11, Frame copied indicators: 11
DLC:   Destination: Station IBM    12F7EC
DLC:   Source     :  Station IBM    118E9A
DLC:
LLC:   ----- LLC Header -----
LLC:
LLC:   DSAP = F0, SSAP = F0, Command, I frame, N(R) = 1, N(S) = 0
LLC:
NET:   ----- NETBIOS Session Confirm -----
NET:
NET:   Header length = 14, Data length = 0
NET:   Delimiter = EFFF (NETBIOS)
NET:   Command = 17
NET:   Flags = 00
NET:   0... .... = NO.ACK ability
NET:   .... ...0 = Pre version 2.0
NET:   Max data receive size = 1750
NET:   Transmit correlator = 000C
NET:   Session correlator = 0000
NET:   Remote session number = 1
NET:   Local session number = 4
NET:
```

6.11 | Troubleshooting Summary

To summarize, here's a checklist to assist with diagnosing token ring network failures:

1. Perform the NIC board diagnostics, if a diagnostic disk is available.

2. Check IRQ, DMA Shared Memory, and I/O Base Address for conflicts with other boards. If in doubt, remove all boards but the NIC, and reinsert one board at a time. Visually inspect the NIC for any jumpers that may have fallen off, or any DIP switches not firmly set.

3. Verify status of power (and fuse) to the MSAUs if they require commercial (110/220 VAC) power.

4. Look for a break in any daisy-chained MSAU power connections.

5. Proteon Wire Centers (their name for MSAUs) include an LED at each port to indicate an in-ring condition of that workstation, plus a switch to force that node off the ring. If using Proteon products, check the LEDs on each port for the correct status.

6. If using unpowered MSAUs, unplug all cable connections to the MSAU, reset each port with the initialization tool, and reinsert the cable connectors.

7. If the NIC and cable have been tested and pass, but the failure still exists, move the NIC to another port on the MSAU and re-test.

8. Verify that an audible "click" is heard (verifying relay operation) from the MSAU port when a station inserts into the ring.

9. Replace any type-3 (twisted pair) media filters if a cable problem proves elusive.

10. For a quick check of the wiring on the NIC to MSAU cable, and to verify that the shorting bars of the hermaphroditic connector are working, check for a short between pins 1 and 9 and 5 and 6 on the DB-9 connector end of that cable.

11. Check for duplicate node address with the NIC diagnostic disk, network management software, or protocol analyzer if software-configurable node addressing has been used.

6.12 | References

[6-1]   Some of the material in this chapter first appeared in "Troubleshooting the Token Ring," by Mark A. Miller, *LAN Technology Magazine*, volume 5, number 6, June 1989; and "Token Ring Management with the TMS380 Chipset," by Mark A. Miller, *LAN Technology Magazine*, Volume 5, Number 6, July 1989.

[6-2] Institute of Electrical and Electronics Engineers, Inc., Token Ring Access Method and Physical Layer Specifications, IEEE Std 802.5—1989.

[6-3] TMS380 Adapter Chipset User's Guide, Document SPWU001D, Texas Instruments, 1986.

[6-4] TMS380 Adapter Chipset User's Guide Supplement, Document SPWU003, Texas Instruments, 1987.

[6-5] TMS380 Second Generation Token Ring, Texas Instruments, 1989.

[6-6] IBM Cabling System Planning & Installation Guide, Document GA27-3361, 1986.

[6-7] IBM Token Ring Network Introduction & Planning Guide, Document GA27-3677, 1986.

[6-8] Using the IBM Cabling System with Communication Products, Document GA27-3620-1, second edition, 1986.

[6-9] IBM Token Ring Network Problem Determination Guide, Document SY27–0280-1.

[6-10] Institute of Electrical and Electronics Engineers, Logical Link Control, IEEE Standard 802.2—1985.

[6-11] IBM Token-Ring Network PC Adapter Guide to Operations, document 639099, 1986.

[6-12] Proteon ProNET-4 Model p1345 IBM PC/AT Interface System Installation Guide, document 42-040149-00, December 1988.

[6-13] J. Scott Haugdahl, Inside the Token Ring, 2nd Edition, Architecture Technology Corporation, Minneapolis, 1988.

[6-14] J. Scott Haugdahl, Inside NETBIOS, Architecture Technology Corporation, Minneapolis, 1988.

[6-15] RFC-1002: Protocol Standard for a NetBIOS Service on a TCP/UDP Transport: Detailed Specifications, DDN Network Information Center, March 1987.

[6-16] RFC-1001: Protocol Standard for a NetBIOS Service on a TCP/UDP Transport: Concepts and Methods, DDN Network Information Center, March 1987.

[6-17] Token Ring Network Portable Protocol Analyzer Operation and Reference Manual, Network General Corporation, 1986-1988.

CHAPTER SEVEN

Troubleshooting Coaxial Ethernet

Ethernet was developed by XEROX beginning in 1975, (see reference [7-1]) and is currently supported by DEC, INTEL, and XEROX, plus a multitude of other vendors. Ethernet adheres to its own published specification, as defined in reference [7-2]. Ethernet also falls in the class of IEEE 802.3 networks 10BASE5, 10BASE2, and 10BROAD36, all of which use coaxial cable backbones (see references [7-3] and [7-4]). Recall from Chapter 1 that the 802.3 terminology specifies the transmission rate in Mbps (for example, 10 Mbps), baseband or broadband signaling (for example, BASE), and finally, the length of a segment in hundreds of meters (for example, 500 m).

StarLAN (IEEE 802.3 1BASE5) and Ethernet over twisted pair (the proposed IEEE 802.3 10BASE-T) are very similar to coaxial Ethernet. However, because the transmission media significantly impacts our troubleshooting approach, we will look at coaxial Ethernet and 802.3 networks in this chapter, and twisted pair Ethernet and StarLAN networks in Chapter 8.

In addition, we will differentiate between the Ethernet standard (from DEC, Intel, and Xerox) and the IEEE 802.3 family of standards, because there are notable technical differences.

7.1 Ethernet Topology

To concisely summarize the Ethernet specifications, we could describe a branching, non-rooted topology, (generally described as a bus) that covers a maximum diameter of 2.5 kilometers; a data rate of 10 Mbps over baseband cable; and a maximum number of 1024 workstations. Like all baseband LANs, transmission is of a half-duplex nature, with only one workstation being allowed to transmit at any one point in time.

7.1.1 | The CSMA/CD Protocol

Access to the media (or cable) is governed by a process known as Carrier Sense Multiple Access with Collision Detection (CSMA/CD). With that protocol, each workstation listens for the presence of another station's transmitted signal before doing anything else. If the network is active, the station defers. If the network appears inactive, the station transmits, but continues to "listen" during transmission for the presence of any other signals. Should another station be heard during transmission, a collision results.

Because of the analog process required to sense the presence of any other transmitting (and thus colliding) signal, time constraints for the network are based upon the assumption that two workstations at the opposite ends of the bus cable must be able to hear each other's signal in order to defer within a reasonable time.

7.2 | CSMA/CD Physical Channels

As mentioned above, there are several differences between the coaxial CSMA/CD networks, Ethernet, 802.3 10BASE2, and 802.3 10BASE5. The first difference is in nomenclature. The Ethernet attachment to the coaxial cable is called a transceiver; 10BASE5 and 10BASE2 refer to it as the Medium Attachment Unit (MAU), although for 10BASE2, the MAU may be built into the NIC. Likewise, Ethernet calls the cable between the transceiver and NIC the transceiver cable; 10BASE5 refers to it as the Attachment Unit Interface (AUI) cable. Since 10BASE2 usually attaches directly to the NIC, no AUI cable is then required. Other nomenclature differences are discussed in section 7.3.3.

Figure 7-1
Thick Ethernet and IEEE 802.3 10BASE5 topology

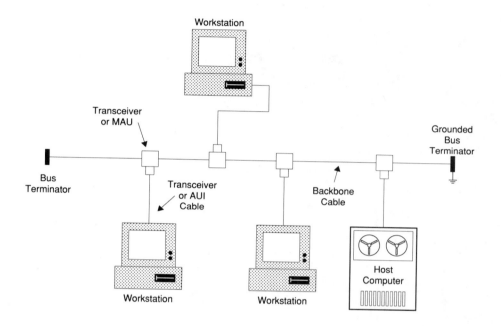

Some NICs (Western Digital's as one example) offer an extended transmission distance option. This enhancement does not adhere to either the Ethernet of 10BASE2 standard. If this option is desired, consult the NIC installation manual for further details. Figures 7-1 and 7-2 illustrate configurations for both thick and thin coaxial cable networks.

Figure 7-2
Thin Ethernet and 802.3 10BASE2 topology

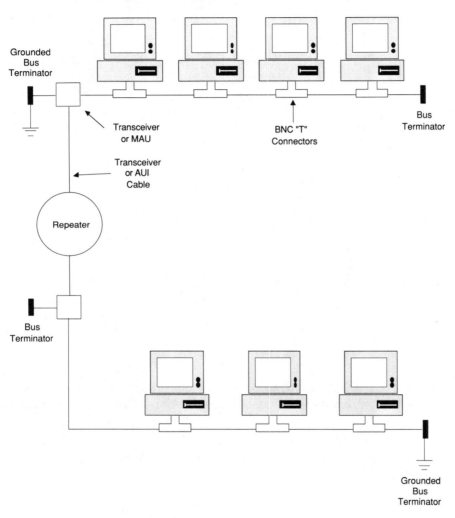

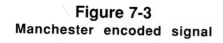

Figure 7-3
Manchester encoded signal

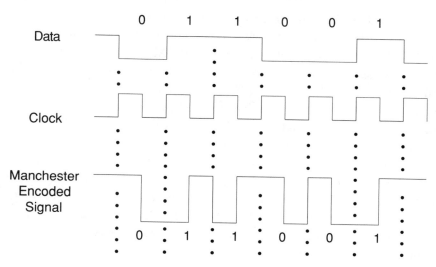

7.2.2 | The Ethernet Physical Channel

These physical limits are summarized below. See reference [7-2] section 7 for further information.

- Maximum length of the coaxial cable segment is 500 meters, where the cable has a propagation velocity of 0.77c (where c is the speed of light in a vacuum, 300,000 meters per second).

- The cable must be terminated in its characteristic impedance, 50 ± 2 ohms, and grounded only at only one point.

- Maximum of two repeaters along a path between two workstations.

- Maximum of 50 meters between a transceiver attached to the coaxial cable segment and its associated workstation.

- Maximum 100 transceivers per segment.

7.2.3 | The 802.3 Physical Channel

The 802.3 Specification for CSMA/CD networks defines two types of baseband Ethernet-like networks: 10BASE5 (10 Mbps transmission, 500 meter maximum segment length) and 10BASE2 (10 Mbps transmission, 185 meter segment length). These are described as ANSI/IEEE Std 802.3—1988 and IEEE 802.3a—1988, respectively (see references [7-3] and [7-4]). All use the Manchester encoding shown in Figure 7-3 for transmission of the data signals. The physical characteristics are slightly different from the Ethernet specification. Before looking at 802.3, a few definitions are required. A coax segment contains connections to the workstations via MAUs. Link segments (sometimes called inter-repeater links, or IRLs) are point-to-point connections between repeaters, and do not have user or host MAUs attached. Repeaters connect either coax segments or link segments, and may be attached at any MAU location on a coax segment, but only at the ends of a link segment. Repeater connections count toward the total number of MAU connections allowed on a coax segment.

7.2.3.1 | 802.3 10BASE5

- Maximum coaxial segment length is 500 meters, with a minimum velocity of propagation of 0.77c.

- Maximum of five segments (with four repeaters) along a path between any two workstations; three of which may be coax segments having a maximum delay of 2,165 nanoseconds, plus two link segments having a maximum delay of 2,570 nanoseconds. Note that the maximum length of a link segment is specified by its propagation delay, not its distance, although many manufacturers use 500 meters (for coax) in specifying the maximum network span, commonly quoted as 2,500 meters (5 segments x 500 meters per segment).

- When no link segments are used, three coax segments may exist on that path.

- Double-shielded, 0.4 inch diameter coaxial cable is typically used.

- Cable terminated at each end with 50 ± 2 ohms, grounded at only one point within the segment.

- Total of 100 MAUs on a cable segment.

- MAUs placed on the cable at increments of 2.5 meters throughout the entire cable length.

7.2.3.2   802.3 10BASE2

- Maximum coaxial segment length of 185 meters, with a minimum velocity of propagation of 0.65c.

- RG-58A/U coax, 0.2 inch diameter typically used, having a stranded center conductor.

- Maximum of five segments (with four repeaters) between two workstations: three tapped coax segments and two link segments—the same as 10BASE5.

- Cable terminated at each end in 50 ± 2 ohms, and grounded at only one point within the segment.

- Connected with BNC "T" adapters.

- Total of thirty workstations or nodes per cable segment.

- MAUs placed a minimum of 0.6 meters apart.

See Table 7-1 for a comparison between the three standards just discussed.

Table 7-1
Ethernet and IEEE 802 Parameters

Parameter	Ethernet Version 2.0	IEEE 802.3 10BASE5	IEEE 802.3 10BASE2
Cable Impedance	50 ohms	50 ohms	50 ohms
Maximum Coax Segment Length	500m (1640 ft.)	500m (1640 ft)	185m (600 ft)
Maximum Number of Coax Segments Without Link Segments (IRLs)	3	3	3
Maximum Number of Segments Including 2 Link Segments	3	5	5
Maximum Network Span (not including drop cables)	1500m (4920 ft)	2500m (8200 ft)	925m (3000 ft)
Maximum Number of MAUs Per Segment	100	100	30
Minimum Distance Between Nodes	2.5m (8 ft)	2.5m (8 ft)	0.6m (1.5 ft)
Transceiver	external	external	internal or external
Connector Type	N	N	BNC
Maximum Transceiver to Node Distance	50m (164 ft)	50m (164 ft)	50m (164 ft) if external transceiver is used

7.3 Ethernet Hardware Components

Ethernet and 802.3 hardware consists of the NIC, Repeaters, and Transceivers. We'll look at each individually.

7.3.1 The Ethernet Network Interface

Figure 7-4 is an example photo of an Ethernet or 802.3 NIC, the Western Digital Ethercard PLUS 16. Note that two connectors are provided for connection to the cable: the BNC for thin coax and the DB-15 connector for thick coax networks. A jumper on the board must be set for the appropriate cable type.

Figure 7-4
Western Digital Ethercard PLUS 16

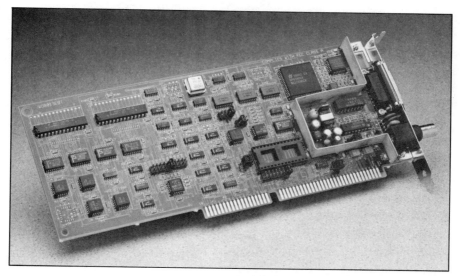

(photo courtesy of Western Digital)

7.3.2 | Repeaters

An Ethernet/802.3 repeater is shown in Figure 7-5, the Cabletron Systems MR-9000C.

Figure 7-5
Cabletron Systems MR-9000C Multiport Ethernet/802.3 Repeater

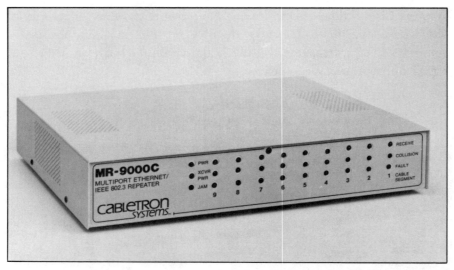

(photo courtesy of Cabletron Systems)

Notice the diagnostic LEDs on the front panel, they can be very useful is troubleshooting the network. In this case, PWR indicates power to the repeater itself; the XCVR PWR indicates proper power from the repeater to the transceiver; JAM indicates that the unit is propagating a collision from one segment to another; RECEIVE indicates that a frame of data has been received on that segment; COLLISION indicates a collision on that segment; and FAULT indicates that the repeater has automatically disconnected that segment because of a cable fault or 32 consecutive collisions. Become familiar with the normal states of these LEDs so that an abnormal condition will be readily apparent.

7.3.3 | Transceiver Characteristics

A Cabletron Systems transceiver and its attachment around the coaxial cable is shown in Figure 7-6. DB-15 connectors terminate a transceiver cable that extends from the transceiver to the Ethernet or 802.3 NIC, as shown in Figure 7-7.

Figure 7-6
Thick Ethernet Transceiver

(photo courtesy of Cabletron Systems)

Four pairs of wire are used on the interface: Transmit (called Data Out in 802.3), from NIC to transceiver; Receive (called Data In in 802.3), from transceiver to NIC; Collision Presence (called Control In in 802.3), which indicates a transmission collision with another node; and Power (called Voltage in 802.3), which provides power from the NIC to the transceiver.

Figure 7-7
Thick Ethernet Transceiver Attachment

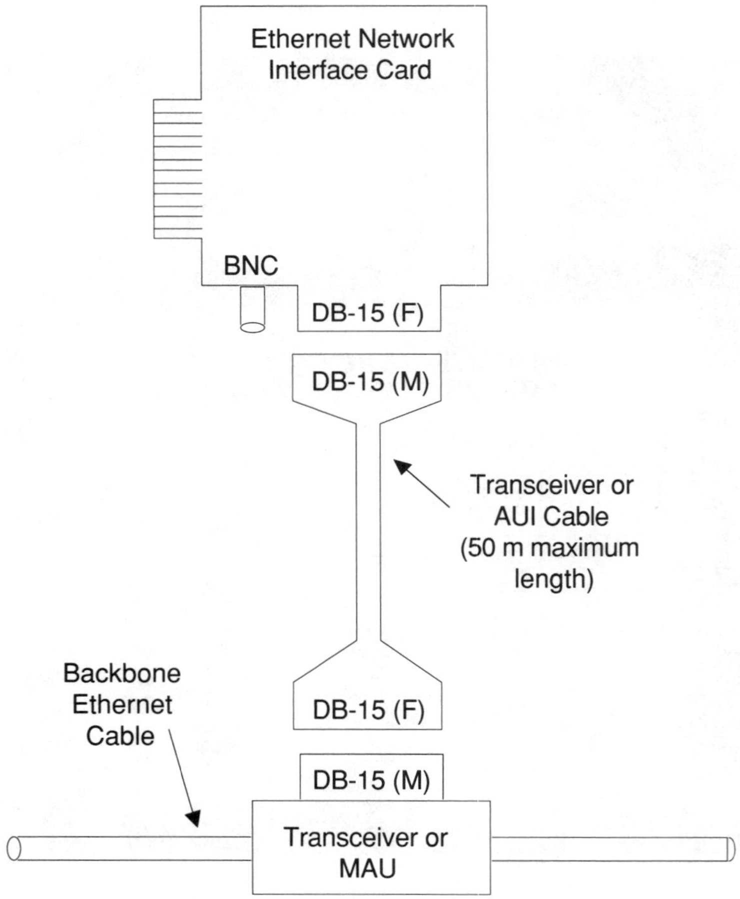

Pinouts for the transceiver are given in Figure 7-8. Note the differences between Ethernet version 2.0 and IEEE 802.3. It is very important that the cable from the transceiver to the NIC is wired for either Ethernet version 2.0 or IEEE 802.3 operation. Using one with the other may not work because of the differences in ground (shield) leads. As a general rule, cables that include pin 1 are for Ethernet V.2.0, while cables that include pin 4 are for 802.3.

Figure 7-8
Transceiver pinouts for Ethernet Version 2.0 and IEEE 802.3

Pin No.	Ethernet V2.0	IEEE 802.3
1	Shield	Control In Shield
2	Collision Presence +	Control In A
3	Transmit +	Data Out A
4	Reserved	Data In Shield
5	Receive +	Data In A
6	Power Return	Voltage Common
7	Reserved	Control Out A
8	Reserved	Control Out Shield
9	Collision Presence −	Control In B
10	Transmit −	Data Out B
11	Reserved	Data Out Shield
12	Receive −	Data In B
13	Power	Voltage
14	Reserved	Voltage Shield
15	Reserved	Control Out B
Connector Shell	——	Protective Ground

In addition, Ethernet v.2.0 transceivers generate a self-test signal known as Collision Presence Test, sometimes referred to as the "heartbeat." This signal confirms that the collision detect circuitry in the transceiver is operational (see reference [7-2] section 7.4.7). IEEE 802.3 transceivers generate a signal similar to Collision Presence Test, known as the Signal Quality Error (SQE) Test (see reference [7-3], section 7.2.2.2.4). The SQE Test signal is not allowed for transceivers that connect to 802.3 repeaters (see reference [7-4] section 9.1).

Many transceiver manufacturers (Cabletron and Interlan are two examples) have designed their transceivers to either provide this Collision Presence Test or SQE Test signal (when connecting to Ethernet version 2.0 NICs), or turn the signal off (when connecting to 802.3 repeaters). Make sure that this option is set correctly. Reference [7-7] provides information on this issue, plus useful comparisons between the Ethernet and 802.3 standards.

7.4 | Ethernet Hardware Troubleshooting

With the background above on the Ethernet and IEEE 802.3 differences, let's now look at what hardware failures can occur. Hardware faults generally occur in three different categories: cable failures, transceiver failures, or NIC failures. It is also helpful to isolate the location of the failure. For example, a network failure, where the entire network is non-functional; a segment failure, where only a portion of the network is at fault; or a workstation failure, where a single node cannot communicate with other nodes. We'll look at each category individually.

7.4.1 | Cable Failures

Since Ethernet is a bus topology, any damage to the bus will cause a major network failure. Both continuity (DC resistance) and time domain reflectometry (TDR) tests can be made as we studied in Chapter 4. Of these two tests, however, the TDR tests are considered more reliable.

For a continuity test, go to one end of the cable, disconnect that end's terminator and use a Volt-Ohm-Milliameter (VOM) to measure the DC resistance between the center conductor and shield of the cable. A properly terminated cable will measure around 50 ohms. If the cable is shorted, expect somewhere between 0–10 ohms, and if the cable is open (or the terminator at the far end is missing) a measurement significantly above 50 ohms will result. Should the status of the terminator be suspect, measure the DC resistance between the center conductor and outside shield of the terminator itself—it should be very close to 50 ohms. If not, replace the terminator.

7.4.2 | Testing Cable Segments

For a more accurate measurement than DC continuity, a Time Domain Reflectometer (TDR) should be used. In addition to shorts and opens, a TDR detects the location of any impedance mismatch along the cable. The resulting signal reflections can be caused by cable crimps, kinks, sharp bends, or an improper cable termination. It's also a good idea to use a TDR to inspect any newly installed cable, prior to bringing up the network, to verify proper installation. The TDR operates by sending a pulse of known amplitude and duration (and associated rise and fall times) from one end of the cable. When an open or a short is detected, a pulse reflects back to the TDR. An open connection reflects the same polarity, and a short reflects the opposite polarity.

Since the polarity and time delay (between initial pulse transmission and reflected pulse reception) is known, the distance to any open or short can be calculated using the cable's velocity of propagation. Most cable opens and shorts will occur at connector junctions or transceiver connections—any place where another mechanical device has entered the transmission path. See Chapter 4 for more details on TDR usage.

7.4.3 | Cable Connections

Thick Ethernet segments are joined by coaxial barrel connectors, thin segments are joined by BNC "T" connectors. Should the cable test open, look for any portion of the bus that might be disconnected from the rest. The most typical culprit is the "T" connector that is detached at the wrong end of the T, thus opening the bus instead of removing a single workstation. Obviously an open cable will bring down the network since two unterminated ends will result.

Many vendors recommend that all cable segments be cut from the same spool to insure manufacturing consistency. In addition, reference [7-3], section 8.6.2.1, recommends using connectorized lengths that are odd multiples of a half wavelength in the cable at 5 MHz—that is, lengths of 23.4 m, 70.2 m, and 117 m (± 0.5 m) for all thick coax sections. Add the various sections as necessary to achieve the 500 meter maximum segment length.

7.4.4 | Transceiver Failures

For most thin Ethernet networks (10BASE2), the transceiver may be built into the NIC itself, and a transceiver failure can only be corrected by replacing the entire NIC. For thick Ethernet and 10BASE5 networks, the mechanical connection necessitated by the transceiver attachment around the cable can cause problems, or the transceiver can fail internally. Should the entire cable show a short, a recently added transceiver may have shorted the cable's center conductor to the outer shield. Use a TDR to determine the location of the short, and if a transceiver is at that location, replace that transceiver.

If only one workstation cannot communicate with the network, the transceiver may be open. A TDR would not indicate the problem, since the open appears to the network to be a non-existent node. Some transceivers include LEDs that indicate network activity, node activity, confirm proper power feed from the NIC, etc. Make a visual inspection of these LEDs as part of your diagnostics. When in doubt, replace the transceiver with a known good spare.

Transceivers can occasionally fail internally without causing a cable short or open connection. For a quick test, remove the NIC (thus powering down the transceiver) and see if the network recovers. If the problem does not go away, remember that the transceiver could still be shorting the cable, and the only cure is to remove it from the cable.

7.4.5   NIC Failures

A faulty NIC is probably the easiest to fix, since a simple replacement is relatively fast, assuming that you have a spare on hand. Most NIC manufacturers include diagnostic disks with the boards that allow internal diagnostics without removing the interface board from the PC. One common difficulty, however, occurs because Ethernet/802.3 NICs must operate with either thick or thin coaxial cable. Most 802.3 NICs have two connectors on them: a DB-15 for connecting to the transceiver and thick cable, and a BNC when connecting to the thin cable. A jumper on the NIC must be optioned to select the correct cable connection. Should the jumper be set incorrectly, the NIC will not communicate with the network at all. Double check this option setting prior to closing the cover on the PC. See references [7-5] and [7-6] for further information.

7.4.6   Jabbering Nodes

Ethernets occasionally suffer from a problem known as a "jabbering node," where garbage data appears on the network, with no known origin. When this occurs, segmenting the network in a similar fashion to our fault isolation with ARCNET is required. Let's assume that we are testing the thick Ethernet network shown in Figure 7-9, and that the network is jammed with garbage data. One approach is to disconnect the repeater at point A and see if the problem clears. If it does, the jabbering node is located somewhere after the repeater connection. Let's assume that we now suspect the segment past the repeater. Reconnect the repeater at point A and then disconnect the individual sections that comprise that segment one at a time, making sure to terminate each new endpoint. When the problem is isolated to an individual cable section, reconnect that section and proceed to isolate the problem down to a particular node by powering down each node on that section individually. When the network recovers, the jabbering node has been identified. Further testing will determine if the transceiver, transceiver cable, or NIC is at fault.

Figure 7-9
Isolating jabbering nodes

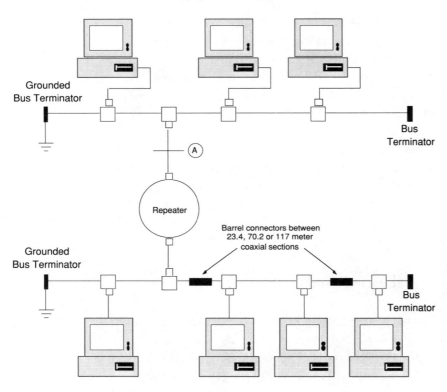

Grounded
Bus Terminator

Bus
Terminator

(A)

Repeater

Barrel connectors between
23.4, 70.2 or 117 meter
coaxial sections

Grounded
Bus Terminator

Bus
Terminator

Step 1: Isolate faulty segment.
Step 2: Isolate faulty cable section.
Step 3: Isolate faulty node.
Step 4: Isolate faulty transceiver, transceiver cable, or NIC.

7.5 | Ethernet Software Considerations

As we found with the hardware specifications, Ethernet and 802.3 do not have precisely the same Data Link Layer frame structure, either. Figure 7-10 shows the Ethernet frame, and Figure 7-11 shows the 802.3 frame for comparison.

Figure 7-10a
The Ethernet Data Link Layer frame

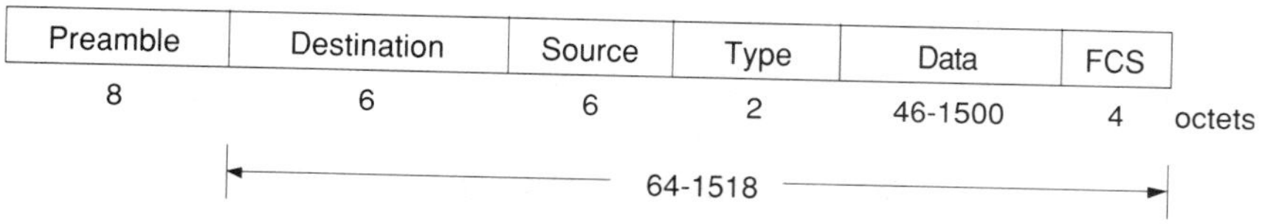

Preamble	Destination	Source	Type	Data	FCS	
8	6	6	2	46-1500	4	octets

64-1518

Figure 7-10b
The Ethernet Address fields

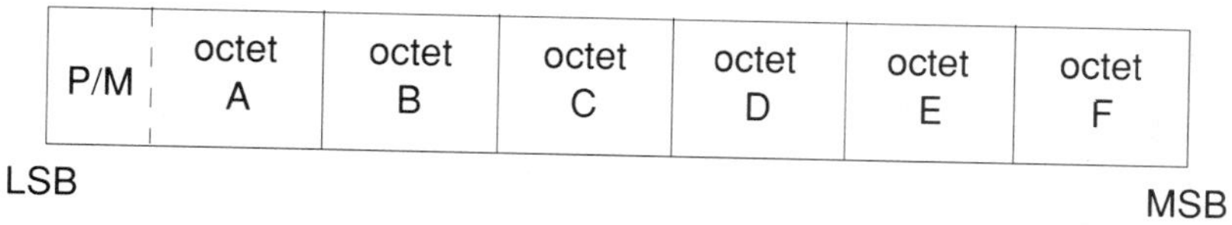

P/M	octet A	octet B	octet C	octet D	octet E	octet F

LSB   MSB

Figure 7-11a
The 802.3 Data Link Layer frame

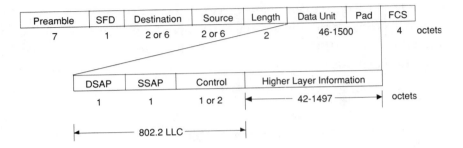

Figure 7-11b
The 802.3 Address fields

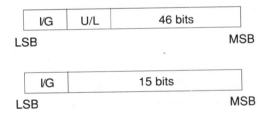

7.5.1 | The Ethernet Frame

The Ethernet frame begins with a Preamble (8 octets) that is an alternating 1010... pattern that ends in 10101011. The Preamble provides synchronization. The Destination address is a 6 octet field that can either define a Physical Address or a Multicast Address, determined by the least significant bit of the first byte of that field. A Physical Address (usually burned into a ROM) sets that LSB=0, and is unique across all Ethernet networks. A Multicast Address can be to a group or broadcast to all stations, and has the LSB=1. In the case of a broadcast address, the destination field is set to all ONEs—that is, FFFFFFFFFFFF hex. The

Physical Addresses are further subdivided: the first three octets (A, B, and C in Figure 7-10b) are currently assigned by the IEEE (formerly by Xerox Corporation), and the last three octets (D, E, and F) are assigned by the manufacturer. Should the NIC become defective and the node address need to remain consistent (such as a well-known address for a gateway), the ROM containing the original address can be removed from the old board and inserted on the new board; or the address can be set in a register using the diagnostic disk. Regardless of technique, care should be taken when any human intervention replaces the address administration safeguards that were developed. The Source address is specified next, and is the address of the station originating the frame.

The Type field, sometimes referred to as the Ethertype, is a 2 octet field that specifies the higher layer protocol used in the Data field. This field is administered by Xerox Corporation. Some familiar Ethertypes would be 0800 hex (for the IP of TCP/IP), 0600 hex (XNS), and 6003 hex (DECnet).

The Data field is the only variable length field, and can range from a minimum of 46 octets to a maximum of 1500 octets. The contents of this field is completely arbitrary, as specified by the higher layer protocol used within that frame.

The last field is a Frame Check Sequence that is a 32-bit CRC based upon the contents of the Address, Type, and Data field.

The allowable frame length not including the Preamble ranges from 64 to 1518 octets. Frames outside that range are considered invalid. Short frames (sometimes called fragments or runts) generally arise from collisions. Long frames (sometimes called jabbers) usually indicate a defective transmitter at one of the NICs.

7.5.2 The 802.3 Frame

Again referring to figures 7-10 and 7-11, note the differences between the Ethernet and 802.3 frames. The 802.3 frame begins with a Preamble (7 octets) that is an alternating pattern 1010..., this time ending in 1010. The Start Frame Delimiter (SFD) is next, defined as 10101011. Note that if the 802.3 Preamble and SFD fields are combined, a pattern identical to the the Ethernet Preamble will result.

Next is the Destination Address fields shown in Figure 7-11b, which can be either 2 or 6 octets in length, although 6 octets is the most common. The Individual/Group (I/G) field corresponds to the Physical/Multicast designation of Ethernet; the Universal/Local (U/L) field indicates whether the address is administered universally (through the IEEE) or locally (by the network administrator).

The Source Address comes next, and must match the Destination Address field in length (either 2 for Destination and 2 for Source; or 6 for Destination and 6 for Source, but not 2 and 6). The Length field is 2 octets long and indicates the number of Logical Link Control (LLC) octets in the Data field. A minimum of 46 octets of data is required; when the LLC data is less than 46, the Pad field is used. Maximum length of the Data and Pad fields combined is 1500 octets. Finally, Frame Check Sequence (FCS), based upon a 32-bit Cyclic Redundancy Check, is computed based upon the contents of the Destination Address, Source Address, Length, Data, and Pad fields. See Reference [7-3] section 3.2 for further details.

7.5.3 Data Link Layer Analysis

One difference in the Data Link Layer frames of Ethernet and 802.3 occurs is the Ethernet Type and 802.3 Length fields. In the case of Ethernet, the Type defines the higher layer protocol that is used within the data field. In contrast, the same position within an 802.3 field is occupied by the Length (or number of bytes) of the Data fields. For 802.3

the designation of higher layer protocol type is done by the 802.2 Logical Link Control protocol data unit and its Destination Service Access Point (DSAP) and Source Service Access Point (SSAP) fields.

In general, older DEC Ethernet backbones used the Ethernet frame format, newer ones can use either Ethernet or 802.3 frames. Most NIC card vendors support 802.3. From the Data Link Layer frame point of view, however, the bit stream of both formats will be the same in length. Because of the differences in the Ethernet and 802.3 frame formats, any NIC that wishes to communicate with an Ethernet host must transmit the appropriate Ethertype, whereas NICs communicating with 802.3 hosts will transmit the Length of the Data field in the same position. An Ethernet host that was expecting an appropriate Ethertype and actually received a Length would thus be confused. As an example of maximum flexibility, Novell provides a special utility known as ECONFIG, which allows the network administrator to configure the NIC to either the Ethernet or IEEE 802.3 frame format specifications. As of this writing, NetWare for VMS supports drivers for 3COM, Western Digital, Interlan, and Novell NICs. Contact Novell for further information.

7.6 | Protocol Analysis with DECnet

The DECnet protocol suite is used very frequently on Ethernet networks because of the historical ties to Digital Equipment Corporation. Figure 7-12 illustrates how the DECnet Phase V Protocol Suite aligns with the OSI model; see references [7-8] and [7-9] for further details.

Figure 7-12
The DECnet Protocol Suite compared with the OSI Model

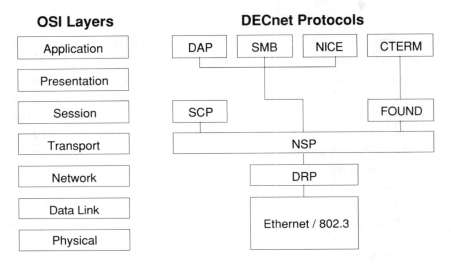

DECnet Phase I was introduced in 1976 and has continued to be enhanced through the announcement of DECnet Phase V in September 1987. Of greatest significance in this announcement is DEC's commitment to become fully compliant with the OSI model. The individual layers are defined as follows:

Physical layer: DECnet recognizes standards from EIA, CCITT, and ISO, such as EIA-232-D, V.24, X.21, and ISO 8802-3.

Data Link layer: DDCMP (the Digital Data Communications Message Protocol from DEC), HDLC (High Level Data Link control from ISO) and IEEE 802 (ISO 8802-3) are supported in Phase V, plus Ethernet for DECnet Phase IV compatibility.

Network layer: The ISO 8473 (Internetwork Protocol) supports Phase V, and DECnet Routing Protocol (DRP) supports Phase IV.

Transport layer: ISO 8073 (Transport Protocol Classes 0, 2, and 4) support Phase V, and the Network Services Protocol (NSP), originally defined in Phase I, maintains compatibility with Phase IV.

Higher layers (Session, Presentation, and Application) maintain compatibility with Phase IV protocols, and support standard OSI protocols defined for those layers. Among those most frequently seen for Phase IV include:

- Session Control Protocol (SCP)
- Data Access Protocol (DAP), for remote file access
- Network Information and Control Exchange Protocol (NICE), for network management
- Maintenance Operation Protocol (MOP)
- Command Terminal Protocol (CTERM)—a virtual terminal protocol used in conjunction with the session layer Foundation Services Protocol (FOUND)
- Server Message Block (SMB)

Reference [7-8] provides further details on DECnet Phase V.

Figure 7-13
DECnet Protocols within an Ethernet frame

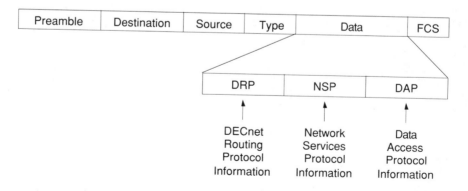

Figure 7-13 shows the DECnet fields encapsulated within an Ethernet frame. Figure 7-14 shows the capture range of the Network General

Sniffer protocol analyzer, and Figure 7-15 illustrates a summary trace file captured by the Sniffer protocol analyzer. The notations along the left-hand side of the figure indicate the protocols being decoded. DLC indicates Data Link Control (Ethernet), DRP indicates DECnet Routing Protocol, NSP indicates Network Services Protocol, and DAP indicates Data Access Protocol. See reference [7-10] for further information.

Figure 7-14
Capture range of the Network General Sniffer Protocol Analyzer for Ethernet networks

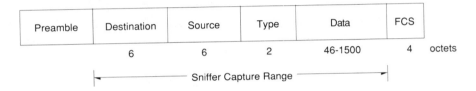

Figure 7-15
The DECnet protocols over Ethernet as captured by the Network General Sniffer protocol analyzer

```
DLC:  ----- DLC Header -----
DLC:
DLC:  Frame 15 arrived at  01:51:31.3222 : frame size is 60 (003C hex) bytes.
DLC:  Destination: Station DECnet00FF04
DLC:  Source     : Station DECnet000104
DLC:  Ethertype = 6003 (DECNET)
DLC:
DRP:  ----- DECNET Routing Protocol -----
DRP:
DRP:  Data length = 36
DRP:  Data Packet Format = 26
DRP:          0... .... = no padding
DRP:          .0.. .... = version
DRP:          ..1. .... = Intra-Ethernet packet
DRP:          ...0 .... = not return packet
DRP:          .... 0... = do not return to sender
DRP:          .... .110 = Long Data Packet Format
DRP:  Data Packet Type = 6
DRP:  Destination Area    = 00
```

```
DRP:  Destination Subarea   = 00
DRP:  Destination ID        = 1.255
DRP:  Source Area           = 00
DRP:  Source Subarea        = 00
DRP:  Source ID             = 1.1
DRP:  Next Level 2 Router   = 00
DRP:  Visit Count           = 0
DRP:  Service Class         = 00
DRP:  Protocol Type         = 00
DRP:
NSP:  ----- Network Services Protocol -----
NSP:
NSP:  Message Identifier = 60
NSP:            0... .... = Non-extensible field
NSP:            .110 .... = Begin-End Data Message
NSP:            .... 00.. = Data Message
NSP:            .... ..00 = always zero
NSP:  Type       = 0 (Data Message)
NSP:  Sub-type = 6 (Begin-End Data Message)
NSP:  Logical Link Destination = 4221
NSP:  Logical Link Source      = C320
NSP:  Data Acknowledgment Number
NSP:     Acknowledge Qualifier       = ACK
NSP:     Message Number Acknowledged = 2
NSP:  Link Acknowledgment
NSP:     Acknowledge Qualifier       = ACK
NSP:     Message Number Acknowledged = 2
NSP:  Data Segment Number = 3  (normal ACK expected)
NSP:  [4 data bytes]
NSP:
DAP:  ----- Data Access Protocol -----
DAP:
DAP:  Code = 4  (Control)
DAP:  Control Function = $CONNECT;  Initiate Data stream
DAP:
```

7.7 Troubleshooting Summary

To summarize, here's a checklist to assist with diagnosing coaxial cable Ethernet and 802.3 failures:

1. Clean the gold fingers and reseat the NIC in the PC bus.

2. Check the board jumper that selects the thin coaxial (BNC) or thick coaxial (DB-15) cable connection.

3. Run the NIC board diagnostics, if available. If loop-around testing is used, use the appropriate cable terminator.

4. Check IRQ, DMA, Shared Memory, and I/O Base Addresses for conflicts with other boards. If in doubt, remove all boards but the NIC, and reinsert one board at a time.

   Visually inspect the NIC for any jumpers that may have fallen off, or any DIP switches not firmly set. Activate the DIP switches (forward and then back to the original position) to confirm good contact. If more than one NIC is resident in a workstation or server, verify that the shared memory buffers have unique addresses.

5. Confirm the order of CONFIG.SYS and AUTOEXEC.BAT files, plus any device drivers that are being used.

6. Verify that the transceiver, transceiver cable, and any applicable option (for example, "Heartbeat" or SQE-Test) are set consistently for Ethernet version 2.0 or IEEE 802.3 operation.

7. Verify that power and transceiver or AUI cables to any repeaters are properly connected and that SQE-Test signals to repeaters are properly administered.

8. Use a TDR to test for any shorted transceivers or other cable faults such as crimps, kinks, or opens.

9. Verify that the minimum distance for transceiver placement (such as 2.5 meters for thick cable) has not been violated, and that the transceivers are placed at multiples of 2.5 meters (for example, at the 2.5, 5.0, 7.5, 10.0, etc., meter markings on the cable).

10. Verify that the network configuration rules have been followed (for example, no more than three coax segments plus two IRLs, etc.).

11. Check for any unterminated cable ends.

12. Test terminators with an ohmmeter for a resistance between 48-52 ohms.

13. Check for any disconnected or poorly assembled T connectors used with a thin segment.

14. Verify that RG-58A/U (50 ohm thin cable) and not RG-59A/U (75 ohm thin cable) has been used.

15. Check for duplicate node addresses with the NIC diagnostic disk or protocol analyzer if software-configurable node addressing has been used.

7.8 References

[7-1] Some of the material in this chapter first appeared in "Troubleshooting Coaxial Ethernet," by Mark A. Miller, *LAN Technology Magazine*, Volume 5, Number 7, July 1989.

[7-2] The Ethernet, A Local Area Network—Data Link Layer and Physical Layer Specification, version 2.0, November 1982. Published by DEC, INTEL and XEROX, DEC document number AA-K759B-TK.

[7-3] Institute of Electrical and Electronics Engineers, Carrier Sense Multiple Access with Collision Detection (CSMA/CD), ANSI/IEEE Std 802.3 - 1988, ISO 8802-3: 1989.

[7-4] Institute of Electrical and Electronics Engineers, Supplements to Carrier Sense Multiple Access with Collision Detection, ANSI/IEEE Std 802.3a, b, c, and e—1988.

[7-5] Western Digital Corporation, EtherCard PLUS 16 Installation Guide, 1988.

[7-6] 3COM Corporation, EtherLink II Installation Guide, 1987.

[7-7] Cabletron Systems, Inc., MT-800 Multiport Ethernet/IEEE 802.3 Transceiver User Manual, 1988.

[7-8] DECnet DIGITAL Network Architecture (Phase V), Digital Equipment Corporation, Naynard, NA, 1987, order number EK-DNAPV-GD, September 1987.

[7-9] DECnet Protocol Suite, PA-1307, publication 21407-001, Network General Corporation, Mountain View, CA 1989.

[7-10] Ethernet Network Portable Protocol Analyzer Model PA-302 Operation and Reference Manual, Network General Corporation, Mountain View, CA, 1986-1988.

CHAPTER EIGHT

Troubleshooting StarLAN and Twisted Pair Ethernet

Chapter 7 studied troubleshooting the coaxial cable-based Ethernet standards 10BASE5 and 10BASE2. In this chapter we will study problems and solutions inherent to 1BASE5 (StarLAN) and the 10BASE-T (Twisted Pair Ethernet) Standards. Even though the 10BASE-T standard is an IEEE Project 802.3 development, most vendors are referring to it as "twisted pair Ethernet." We will follow their lead in the nomenclature used in this chapter. We'll look at the StarLAN network first (see reference [8-1]).

8.1   StarLAN Topology

StarLAN was first released in 1985 as a cost-effective, twisted pair alternative to the coaxial, cable-based LANs that had dominated the industry. Adhering to the IEEE 802.3 1BASE5 specification, StarLAN is supported by a wide variety of companies including AT&T, Interlan, Western Digital, Hewlett-Packard and others. The Intel 82588 and National Semiconductor DP8390 are two examples of StarLAN Controller ICs.

Figure 8-1a
StarLAN daisy-chain topology

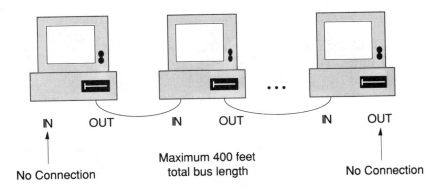

IN   OUT   IN   OUT   IN   OUT

No Connection   Maximum 400 feet   No Connection
total bus length

Figure 8-1b
StarLAN star topology

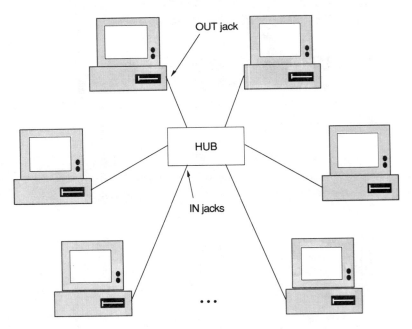

OUT jack

HUB

IN jacks

Maximum 800 feet (250 meters)
between Workstation and Hub

StarLAN is a logical bus network that can have two topologies: a daisy-chained bus (although not part of the 1BASE5 standard) connecting up to 10 workstations (shown in Figure 8-1a); or a star-wired arrangement that connects either 10, 11, or 12 workstations (depending on the manufacturer) into a central hub (shown in Figure 8-1b). Daisy-chains are also allowed from the workstations attached to the central hub. Even though the topology looks like a star, it is logically a bus just like Ethernet. See reference [8-2] for further details.

8.2 | The StarLAN Physical Channel

StarLAN adheres to the IEEE 802.3 1BASE5 Standard: 1 Mbps transmission, 250 meters between workstation and hub, maximum workstation-to-workstation distance of 500 meters via a single hub. Longer distances are possible when hubs are connected in a hierarchical topology. The StarLAN characteristics are summarized below (for further information, see reference [8-3]).

• Signaling rate of 1 Mbps, using Manchester encoding. See figure 7-3 for an illustration of the Manchester-encoded signal.

• Transmission via standard, unshielded, inside-building telephone wiring, typically 22, 24, or 26 gauge.

• Two transmission channels: one twisted pair for the upward link, and the other for the downward link. Most manufacturers designate the pairs Transmit and Receive, respectively.

• The data pairs are allowed to coexist in the same cable as audio and telephone.

• Hubs function as repeaters, and propagate the signals received from the workstations to higher-level hubs. At the header hub, signals are looped around and sent down link to lower-level hubs and workstations. The hubs also perform collision detection (remember, this is a CSMA/CD network). Stations are informed of collisions via a specially coded "collision presence" signal.

- Up to five levels of hubs can be cascaded, according to 1BASE5, although some vendor implementations allow more (Western Digital allows ten levels of hubs).

8.3 StarLAN Hardware Components

The hardware elements for StarLAN include the network interface card, wiring hub, and the cabling itself. We'll look at each item separately.

8.3.1 Network Interface Cards

Figure 8-2 shows examples of a StarLAN NICs, the StarLink Plus, and StarCard Plus from Western Digital Corporation. In addition to the usual jumpers and CSMA/CD controller chip (National Semiconductor DP8390), the StarLink Plus NIC has IN, OUT, and PHONE jacks. The StarCard Plus has OUT and PHONE jacks. The StarLink NIC could be connected at any point in a daisy chain, where the StarCard is intended to be an endpoint in a star environment. The IN and OUT ports are for network cabling, and the PHONE port is for telephone connections. Not all vendors support the PHONE port and integrated voice/data wiring.

8.3.2 Wiring Hub

Figure 8-2 also shows an example of a StarLAN hub. The hub includes multiple IN ports (11 in this case) for connections to either single or daisy-chained workstations, one OUT port for connection to a higher-level (uplink) hub, a power connector, plus diagnostic LEDs. Note the power requirements of the hub if the entire network (or one star of a multi-star configuration) has failed, check for the absence of power at the hub.

Figure 8-2
StarLAN network hardware

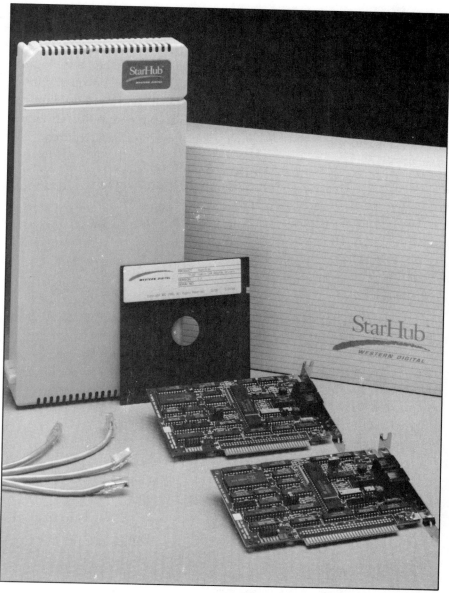

(photo courtesy of Western Digital)

8.3.3 | StarLAN Cabling

Figures 8-3a, 8-3b, and reference [8-4] detail the 8-pin modular connector (specified as ISO/DIS 8877, and usually called an RJ-45) and cable pair assignments used with StarLAN. Note that "Transmit" and "Receive" definitions depend upon the orientation of the user. Figure 8-3b describes the NIC, therefore for this case, the OUT port uses pins 1 and 2 for transmit, whereas on the IN port, pins 1 and 2 are used for receive. The RJ-45 cable itself must have pin-to-pin continuity. In other words, pin 1-to-pin 1, pin 2-to-pin 2, etc., connections are required.

Figure 8-3a
The RJ-45 modular jack (front view)

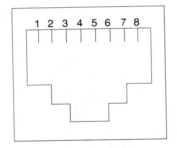

Figure 8-3b
StarLAN NIC port assignments

Pin	In Port	Out Port	Phone Port
1	Receive +	Transmit +	NC
2	Receive -	Transmit -	NC
3	Transmit +	Receive +	NC
4	NC	Ring	Ring
5	NC	Tip	Tip
6	Transmit -	Receive -	NC
7	NC	Power	Power
8	NC	Power	Power

NC = No Connection
Tip/Ring = Analog Telephone Connections
Power = Power feed for telephone (as required)

8.3.4   Telephone Connections

In the IEEE 802.3 1BASE5 standard (reference [8-3], page 153) pins 4 and 5 are defined as "not used" by 1BASE5, and pins 7 and 8 are "reserved". Notice from Figure 8-3b that some NICs (AT&T and Western Digital, in particular) allow for analog telephone wiring on pins 4 and 5 plus power (if required) for the telephone accessories, such as a speakerphone, on pins 7 and 8.

While StarLAN was designed to coexist with analog telephone cabling, some caution must be exercised when doing so. Modular phone connectors are designed so that smaller plugs (for example, 4 pin or RJ-11) plugs can fit into larger (for example, 8 pin or RJ-45) jacks. In addition, the two center pins (pins 2 and 3 on the 4-pin connector, 3 and 4 on the 6-pin connector, or 4 and 5 on the 8-pin connector) are used to carry the Tip and Ring of the analog telephone circuit. In addition, depending upon the type of telephone system (PBX, Key System, etc.), other signals for either power or station signaling may exist on the pins other than the center two, 3 and 6, for example. Should this be the case, interference between the StarLAN transmit and receive signals (pins 1 and 2, and 3 and 6) and the telephone or power signals may result. Possible damage to both systems could occur. To summarize, use caution when integrating StarLAN and telephone systems into the same building wiring plan.

8.4   Twisted Pair Ethernet Topology

An AT&T study presented to the 1BASE5 Committee concluded that the vast majority of all workstations are within 100 meters of a wiring closet. This report is often cited as the impetus behind the "Ethernet over twisted pair" or the IEEE 802.3 10BASE-T project. As of this writing the standard is still in the draft stage (see reference [8-5]); however many vendors, including SynOptics, Western Digital, AT&T, Hewlett-Packard and Racal-Interlan are vigorously marketing products as an alternative to conventional coaxial cable-based Ethernet and 802.3 networks. Several objectives are common among the various products: transmission distance between workstation and wire closet of approximately 100 meters; the ability to easily interconnect and cascade wire closet hardware; and the continuing use of existing 802.3 10BASE5 or 10BASE2 NICs, thus minimizing additional investment. Figure 8-4 shows a typical twisted pair Ethernet network topology.

Figure 8-4
Twisted pair Ethernet topology

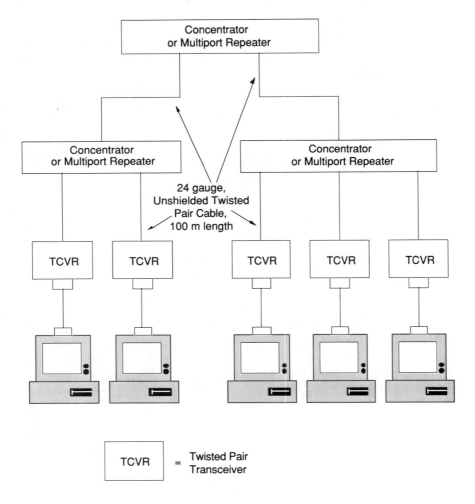

8.4.1 | The Twisted Pair Ethernet Physical Channel

The proposed 10BASE-T standard specifically addresses a twisted pair Medium Attachment Unit (MAU). Any existing 802.3 NICs which meet the current specification at the AUI interface can be used with the new standard. In other words, 10BASE-T provides a means for attaching AUI-compatible devices to twisted pair media, instead of the usual coaxial media.

The maximum distance between the AUI interface (called a Twisted Pair Medium Attachment Unit, or TPMAU) and a central wiring closet is the 100 meters mentioned above. At the wire closet, a Multiport Repeater (MPR) exists to connect all workstations on that floor. Wire closets on other floors can be cabled in a similar fashion, and interconnected with each other. The resultant network topology is a distributed star, with offshoots of bus segments possible. Compatibility at the 802.3 AUI interface is assured, therefore 10BASE-T networks can also connect with existing thin or thick coaxial networks.

The transmission media distance limitations are primarily governed by the minimum propagation velocity of the cable, expressed as a percentage of the speed of light, c = 300,000 km/sec. For twisted pair cable, the factor is 0.59c, 0.66c for fiber optics; 0.65c for the 10BASE2 (thin) coaxial; and 0.77c for 10BASE5 (thick) coaxial. Also a factor in the distance calculation is the maximum round trip signal propagation time for 10 MBPS 802.3 networks. This is one of the principle characteristics that makes CSMA/CD networks operate properly—the transmitting station must receive any collision information from the most remote station before it ceases transmitting even the shortest permissible frame (64 octets, or 512 bits). Because the 802.3 networks allow a great deal of flexibility in their choice of transmission media, care must be taken to insure that the propagation delay specifications (and the resulting cable length limits) are not exceeded.

8.4.2 | Twisted Pair Ethernet Architectures

Because of the great interest among users and vendors in the twisted pair Ethernet concept, many vendors developed and began marketing products prior to the finalization of the 10BASE-T standard. As a result, some interoperability problems may occur if hardware from different vendors (all claiming some degree of compliance to 10BASE-T) is used.

As of this writing, two different architectures are emerging. The LattisNet architecture from SynOptics Communication, Inc., is a hierarchical topology. Host computers that are 802.3 compliant at the AUI interface connect to a local concentrator. Larger networks may be constructed with up to four levels of concentrators. Retiming must be provided in every other concentrator in the hierarchy. Equalization (correction for signal distortion) is done at the Receive end of each twisted pair link.

Another architecture is the StarLAN 10 network developed by AT&T. In StarLAN 10, the AUI-compatible devices connect to a twisted pair transceiver, which then connects to a Multiport Repeater (MPR). The MPR is similar to other 802.3 repeaters, therefore yielding a flat (instead of hierarchical) topology. Equalization occurs at the transmitter end of the link via a process called predistortion.

8.4.3 | Twisted Pair Ethernet Interface ICs

Four manufacturers are currently producing integrated circuits in support of twisted pair Ethernet networks: AT&T Microelectronics has developed three devices: the T7200 Multiport Repeater Unit; the T7210 Manchester Decoder and Interface, which interfaces directly with an Intel 82586 LAN Controller IC; and the T7220 Twisted Pair Medium Attachment Unit, which is an interface between the twisted pair cable and AUI functions.

Intel's 82504TA device is identical to the AT&T T7210. The NCR Microelectronics 92C02 requires external analog drivers to the outside world. SynOptics Communication's IC supports the LattisNet product line, and is used by a variety of manufacturers, including Racal-Interlan, Western Digital, Tiara, and others. Since all four manufacturers support the proposed 10BASE-T standard to varying degrees, it would be wise to consider chip-level compatibility in the purchase of NICs that use these ICs. Hopefully, this will avoid any interoperability problems.

8.5   SynOptics LattisNet Hardware Components

One implementation of twisted pair 802.3 networks, the LattisNet product from SynOptics Communications, Inc., maintains compatibility with 802.3 at the transceiver output to the NIC (DB-15 connector), see references [8-6] and [8-7] for further information.

LattisNet uses a hierarchical star topology with a central concentrator, and subsequent concentrators, much like StarLAN. Up to four levels of concentrators, or seven concentrators in the longest path between two workstations are allowed. Links between concentrators may be 24 gauge, unshielded, twisted pairs or fiber optic cable, and connections to thin or thick baseband, broadband, or fiber optic segments are also supported.

8.5.1   LattisNet Network Interface Cards

One example of an Ethernet NIC that supports twisted pair cable is the Racal-Interlan NI5210-UTP, shown in Figure 8-5. Note that the BNC connector that would usually attach to the thin coaxial cable has been replaced with an RJ-45 modular jack. In addition, the DB-15 (AUI) connector is present, allowing the NIC to be used with conventional coax 802.3 networks as well. The LattisNet interface IC discussed in section 8.5.1 is connected to the modular jack, thus bringing the twisted pair transceiver function directly onto the board. See reference [8-8] for further details.

Figure 8-5
LattisNet-compatible NIC

(photo courtesy of Racal-Interlan)

8.5.2 LattisNet Transceivers

When conventional 802.3 NICs are used in LattisNet, a means of converting between the unshielded twisted pair, shielded twisted pair, or fiber optic media, and the conventional DB-15 (AUI) interface must be provided. This is the function of the transceivers shown in Figure 8-6.

Figure 8-6
LattisNet transceivers

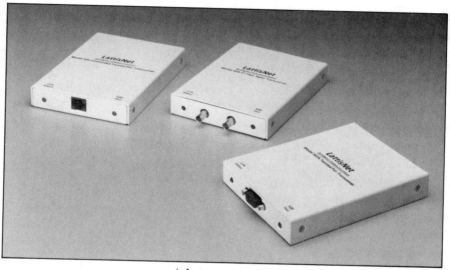

(photo courtesy of SynOptics Communications)

8.5.3 | LattisNet Concentrators

The LattisNet concentrator, for connection to the multiple NICs and transceivers, is shown in Figure 8-7. Because of its modular construction, the concentrator allows for connections into transceivers for coaxial 802.3 networks, plus shielded and unshielded twisted pair and fiber optic links to other concentrators or transceivers. Note the existence of the LEDs on the modules—they are an integral part of any LattisNet maintenance procedures.

Figure 8-7
LattisNet concentrators

(photo courtesy of SynOptics Communications)

8.5.4 | LattisNet Cabling

Figures 8-8a and 8-8b show the cable configurations and pinouts for the LattisNet hardware. Since many network difficulties will invariably involve the cable plant, a few comments are in order.

First, note the pinouts of the RJ-45 connectors used between the concentrator and twisted pair transceiver. There is only one port (unlike StarLAN's IN and OUT). The Transmit signal is defined as going from the transceiver to concentrator, or from concentrator to next highest concentrator; the Receive signal goes in the opposite direction. One significant requirement of the 24-gauge cables is that they must have pin-to-pin continuity, i.e., pin 1 must connect to pin 1 for proper network operation. Secondly, the transmit and receive pairs must be twisted, no flat wire or silver satin cabling is allowed.

Figure 8-8a
SynOptics LattisNet cabling

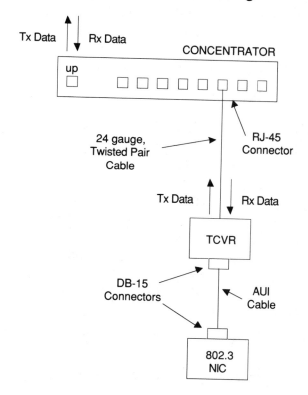

Figure 8-8b
SynOptics LattisNet port pinout

PIN	Color	Signal
1	White/Orange	TxData +
2	Orange/White	TxData -
3	White/Green	RxData +
4	Blue/White	NA
5	White/Blue	NA
6	Green/White	RxData -
7	White/Brown	NA
8	Brown/White	NA

NA = Not Assigned

In addition, the output of the twisted pair transceiver is the DB-15 connector used with other 802.3 devices connecting to the AUI cable. LattisNet is compliant with 802.3 at this interface, meaning that any vendor's 802.3 NIC can attach to the output of the LattisNet transceiver.

8.5.5 Using Twisted Pairs

A detailed discussion on the reuse of twisted pairs within a building is beyond the scope of this handbook, however, there are some factors that impact the LattisNet Operation that should be considered. SynOptics defines three electrical specifications for any twisted pair cable used with LattisNet: a characteristic impedance at 10 MHz between 85 and 115 ohms; an attenuation at 10 MHz less than 11 dB per 360 feet; and near-end crosstalk (NEXT) attenuation between pairs of at least 30.5 dB at all frequencies up to 10 MHz. SynOptics provides lists of approved cables, and will also test any proposed cable for customers. See appendixes A and B in reference [8-6] for further details.

8.6 AT&T StarLAN 10 Hardware Components

As mentioned previously, AT&T developed the original 1 Mbps StarLAN to take advantage of the large, installed base of twisted pair building wiring. At the same time that the StarLAN standard (IEEE 802.3 1BASE5) was developed, a multiport repeater standard (IEEE 802.3c) was also approved. This development allowed future CSMA/CD network developments to concentrate on transmission medium improvements, leaving the core multiport repeater standard intact. With that direction, AT&T undertook development of the 10 Mbps StarLAN product. The resultant network is a flat topology, unlike the LattisNet hierarchical topology, see reference [8-9] for further information.

8.6.1 | StarLAN 10 Network Interface Cards

The components of StarLAN 10 are functionally similar to LattisNet, with workstations connected to wire or fiber optic hubs and twisted pair MAUs for connecting between conventional AUI devices, and fiber optic repeaters to extend the 100 meter twisted pair cable limit.

Figure 8-9
AT&T StarLAN 10 product line

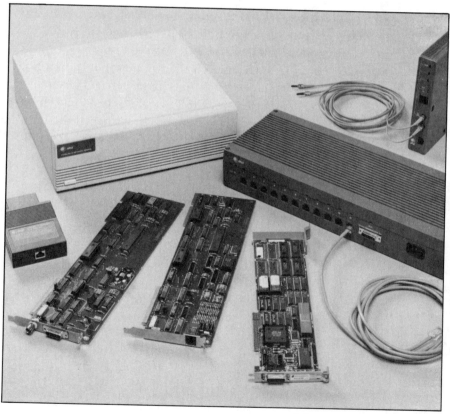

(photo courtesy of AT&T)

StarLAN 10 and LattisNet have some significant electrical differences, however. StarLAN 10 and 10BASE-T uses transmit equalization, adjusting the signal for the degradation of the twisted pair cable at the transmitter end with predistortion. (Recall that LattisNet uses equalization at the receive end.) While this factor may not cause significant advantages of one network over the other, it nevertheless may raise questions regarding interoperability.

Several different NICs (which AT&T labels Network Access Units or NAUs) are available for StarLAN 10, shown in Figure 8-9. At the bottom, left to right, is a PC Ethernet NAU with both BNC and DB-15 connectors, the PC NAU having an RJ-45 interface (OUT port) for attachment directly to the StarLAN 10 hub, and finally the MC100 for Micro Channel. Not shown is the 3B2 NI which allows AT&T 3B2 minicomputers to connect to StarLAN 10. Also not shown is the PC Fiber NAU, which takes 62.5/125 micron fiber optic cable from a fiber optic hub direct to the workstation. The fiber optic cable is terminated with standard ST fiber connectors and follows the Fiber Optic Inter-Repeater Link (FOIRL) Standard. In the upper-left corner of the figure the 10:1 bridge for interconnecting the 1 and 10 MBPS StarLAN products.

8.6.2 StarLAN 10 Attachment Unit Interface Adapter

The StarLAN 10 AUI adapter connects between a standard 802.3 device and the twisted pair cable, similar to the LattisNet transceivers. The adapter is shown on the left side of Figure 8-9. Internal jumpers enable/disable the Signal Quality Error (SQE) test signal, configure the RJ-45 port for either IN or OUT, and control the jabber reset function.

This last option is very useful for network troubleshooting. A jabber is a continuous transmission from a faulty NIC, which will result in jamming the network. When the AUI Adapter detects a jabber from its attached device, it disables the transmit function, thus preventing a failure of the entire network. Resetting this jabber function manually (the option which AT&T calls power cycle, as opposed to automatic) allows the network administrator to quickly isolate the defective NIC by powering the workstation down and then up again. However, this procedure may not be convenient for a major host such as a minicomputer. More on jabber conditions in section 8.7.3.

8.6.3 StarLAN 10 Hubs

The StarLAN 10 hubs are available for both twisted pair and 62.5/125 micron fiber optic cable. Twisted pair hubs have ten IN ports (for connection to workstations or other hubs) and one switchable port (for connection to either an IN or OUT port of another device). In addition, one AUI port allows connection to any other type of 802.3 media, including thin and thick coax, fiber optic or broadband cable. The fiber optic hub contains six fiber ports, one IN/OUT port, and one AUI port.

All StarLAN 10 hubs are actually multiport repeaters, which can be connected to conventional 802.3 backbones or other hubs. The heart of these hubs is the AT&T T7200 Multiport Repeater Unit. This 68 pin IC provides the intelligence necessary for proper hub control and diagnostics. Under normal conditions, the hub accepts data from one IN port, and repeats the signal to all other ports except that input port. If a collision occurs, the repeater sends a jam signal to all workstations on the network.

Hub diagnostics are driven by an LED controller on the T7200. Four different conditions are monitored: traffic and collision activity, jabbed ports, FIFO errors (regarding clock recovery and data reception), and medium attachment unit lockup. We will discuss the use of the hub's diagnostic LEDs for troubleshooting StarLAN 10 networks in section 8.7.3.

8.6.4 StarLAN 10 Fiber Adapter

AT&T's great interest in fiber optics is demonstrated with the Fiber Adapter shown in the upper right-hand corner of Figure 8-9. This device accepts an input from a twisted pair device (such as a NIC) and converts the signal for transmission via 62.5/125 micron fiber to a

Fiber Hub or another Fiber Adapter. Maximum distance between two fiber devices is 2,027 meters (6,649 feet).

8.6.5 StarLAN 10 Cabling

StarLAN 10 follows the cable nomenclature of the 1 Mbps product and defines the modular 8-pin jacks (RJ-45) as either IN or OUT ports. Cable pinouts for these connectors is shown in Figure 8-10; color codes for the cables depend upon the type of the cabling system used (either PBX or Key system), and are described in detail in reference [8-10]. OUT jacks are located on StarLAN 10 NICs, and IN jacks are located on wire hubs.

Twisted pair MAUs and hub ports have switchable jacks that can be selected for either IN or OUT functions. The network is configured by connecting the OUT jack of one device to the IN jack of another with modular 8 wire patch cords. Patch cables must have pin-to-pin continuity, as with LattisNet. Unused IN or OUT jacks are self-terminating, and do not require terminating resistors.

Connection of other media types is straightforward. The 62.5/125 micron multimode fiber optic cables connect from the transmit (TX) port of one device to the receive (RX) port of another. Coaxial cables attach via the DB-15 AUI connectors.

Figure 8-10
AT&T StarLAN 10 hub port pinouts

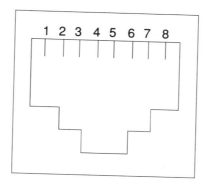

Pin	OUT Jack Assignments	IN Jack Assignments
1	OUTGOING DATA 1 (+)	INCOMING DATA 1 (+)
2	OUTGOING DATA 2 (-)	INCOMING DATA 2 (-)
3	INCOMING DATA 1 (+)	OUTGOING DATA 1 (+)
4	(No Connection)	(No Connection)
5	(No Connection)	(No Connection)
6	INCOMING DATA 2 (-)	OUTGOING DATA 2 (-)
7	(No Connection)	(No Connection)
8	(No Connection)	(No Connection)

8.7 StarLAN and Twisted Pair Ethernet Hardware Troubleshooting

Even though the 1BASE5 and twisted pair Ethernet networks are similar, there are some differences in troubleshooting procedures. We'll address StarLAN first.

8.7.1 StarLAN Hardware Troubleshooting

Most StarLAN installations use 24 gauge unshielded telephone cable that is terminated with RJ-45 modular connectors. While the cabling seems very straightforward, it can cause difficulties. The second typical failure is that of the Network Interface Card (NIC) itself. We'll look at each area individually.

8.7.1.1 NIC Problems

In addition to incorrect cable connections to the NIC, the usual pitfalls of the Interrupt Request (IRQ), I/O Base Address, and DMA Channel must be optioned properly for the host PC. In addition, some NICs have a RAM buffer or BIOS ROM that must share the PC's address space. Use caution to avoid memory conflicts with other devices in the PC. The System Sleuth software program described in Section 3.6 is a valuable tool to use for this task.

Most StarLAN NICs come with a diagnostic disk to facilitate troubleshooting. Probably the most useful test to run is the internal loopback, which will exercise both transmitter and receiver sections. Since the transmitter and receiver sections are somewhat independent, it is possible for one to fail while the other operates properly. If any workstation can transmit but not receive, run a loop-around test for further confirmation.

8.7.1.2 Daisy-Chain Difficulties

As we saw in Figure 8-1a, the daisy-chain cabling is the easiest connection for StarLAN workstations. One caution: various manufacturers place different limits on the length of the daisy chain, ranging from 400 to 800 feet. Check your NIC installation guide for details. While it seems simple on the surface, several characteristics of the StarLAN NICs should be noted. First, the daisy-chain must begin with a connection from one OUT connector to the next IN connector. If a dangling cable is attached to either the first IN or last OUT, network difficulties will result.

Remember from our discussion of bus topology networks that all buses must be terminated at the ends with the characteristic impedance of the cable to prevent signal reflections. The AT&T and Western Digital StarLAN NICs do this automatically—when a modular cord is not plugged into the IN port, a bus terminator is automatically inserted at both transmit and receive pairs. Plugging a dangling cord into the first workstation's IN port would thus eliminate the bus termination. The OUT interface shorts the transmit and receive pairs together (thus completing the bus) when a modular cord is not plugged into the port. This also allows for proper termination at that workstation's IN port. Plugging an extra modular cord into an unused OUT connector will defeat this feature as well. Racal-Interlan and other manufacturers take a different approach, requiring a terminator resistor in any unused IN connector and a loopback plug in any unused OUT connector. Check the NIC documentation for details on your particular network.

For identical reasons, workstations connecting to a hub must cable between the OUT port on the NIC to the IN port of the hub. For networks with multiple layers of hubs, the OUT port on one hub connects to an IN port of the higher-layer hub. Again using the AT&T products as an example, a StarLAN network can have several IN ports with no modular cords attached, but only one unused OUT port. Violations of this rule will invariably cause a network failure. See Figure 8-11 and reference [8-4], section 4, for further details.

Figure 8-11
StarLAN daisy-chain wiring

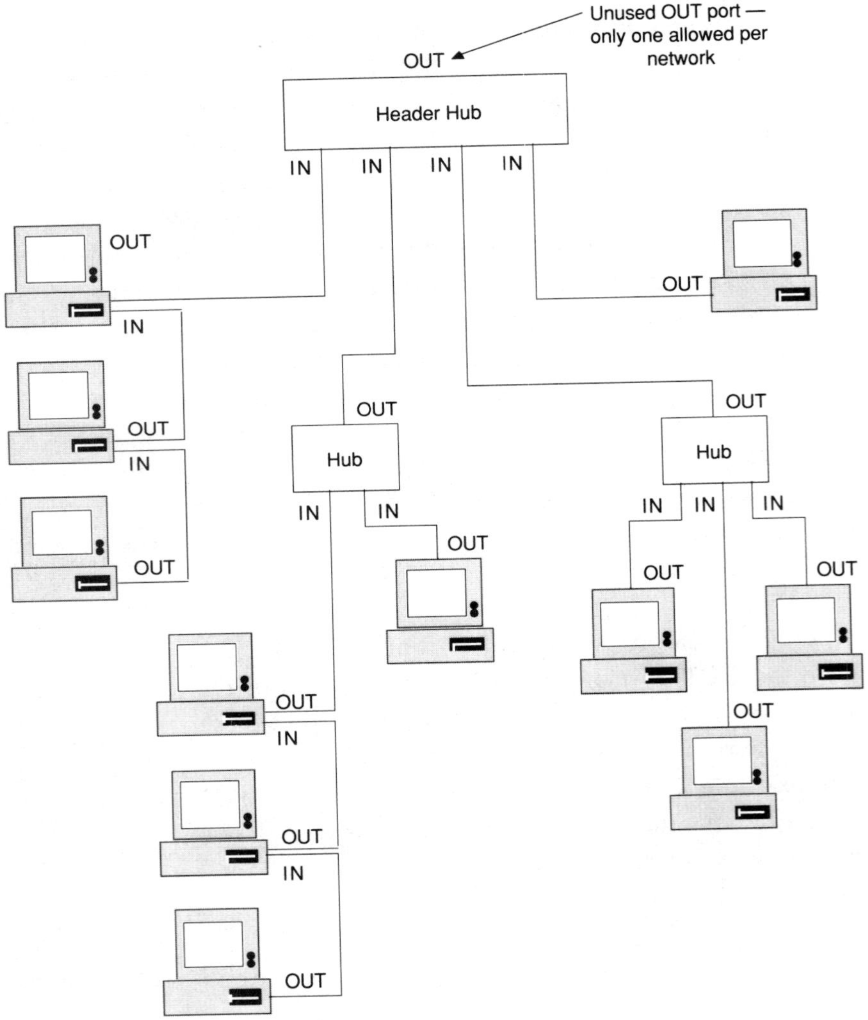

8.7.1.3 **Other Hardware Problems**

The first step in identifying any network failure is to isolate the problem to one particular section of the network. With StarLAN's modular architecture, this is relatively easy. LEDs indicate power and traffic conditions at that hub, thus any abnormal condition should be readily apparent.

To segment a StarLAN network, start at the central hub, and proceed to isolate the problem to a particular hub, hub port, and finally a NIC and workstation. Thorough network documentation is essential for this step. As you disconnect individual segments of the network, make sure that no configuration rules (e.g., no more than one unused OUT port, etc.) are violated. If a failure can be isolated to one particular hub, check the power connection and also observe any diagnostic LEDs that indicate abnormal network traffic conditions. Beyond that, go to the individual ports and workstations to troubleshoot as discussed previously.

8.7.2 LattisNet Hardware Troubleshooting

Because of its distributed star topology, LattisNet failures are very straightforward to diagnose. The first step is to segment the network, much like we did with ARCNET, and isolate the failure to a particular concentrator, cable section, or transceiver. In order to do that in an orderly fashion, obtain the network documentation to determine which concentrator is the central (or highest) point in the multi-tiered star architecture. SynOptics makes the fault isolation task even easier by providing diagnostic LEDs on the concentrators and transceivers for a visual indication of network status. One caution however, the phantom power circuit used to power the Link Status LEDs does not guarantee that the circuit is properly wired. Several conditions, such as a broken conductor, will still illuminate that LED. Reference [8-6] describes these conditions in greater detail.

Secondly, if LattisNet is connected to a coaxial backbone, disconnect the two segments, shown as point A in Figure 8-12. This will isolate the failure to either the coaxial or twisted pair segment. If the LattisNet recovers, the failure exists on the coaxial cable section; proceed to troubleshoot the coax segment as discussed in Chapter 7.

Figure 8-12
Troubleshooting with LattisNet

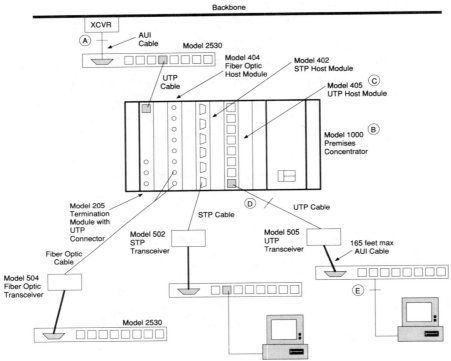

(courtesy of SynOptics Communication)

If the network is still inoperable, go to the central concentrator (point B) and begin disconnecting the various host modules one at a time. When the network recovers, the faulty downstream concentrator or device has been identified.

Let's assume that the unshielded twisted pair module (point C) looks like the culprit. Reinsert the module into the concentrator chassis to recreate the failure, then proceed to disconnect the downward links (point D) one at a time. If other concentrators are downward of point D, disconnect their attached workstations (point E) individually as well. When the network recovers, the problem is identified. Only three possible causes remain: the concentrator port, the cable (and possibly the transceiver), or the PC and its NIC. Replace each of these individually until the failure is completely eliminated.

Should a failing section be encountered, simply unplug it and see if the network failure goes away. If the problem clears, you have just isolated the defective section. Continue to segment the network in this fashion until the failing part is identified. Should the failure be at the NIC, use the diagnostic disk that came with the board for further troubleshooting.

8.7.3 StarLAN 10 Hardware Troubleshooting

The first procedure in troubleshooting StarLAN 10 is to check the configuration for any recent changes, additions, or deletions. Three areas are critical. First, verify that all switches controlling the IN/OUT ports on hubs or twisted pair MAUs are set in the correct position. Remember that IN ports must connect to OUT ports. Also check fiber hubs to verify that all TX (transmit) fibers terminate on the appropriate RX (receive) fiber port. Secondly, verify that the SQE (Signal Quality Error) Test signal from any 802.3 transceiver that connects into the StarLAN 10 hub is turned off, since the hub is actually a multiport repeater. Third, check for any violations to the delay rules. In order to operate properly, the maximum allowable delay along any path between two workstations is 460 bit times. See reference [8-9] for details on these calculations. If any of these three problems are identified, correct them and see if the network returns to normal operation.

If a problem still exists, then the diagnostics built into the hub can be of great help. Three LEDs are common to both the wire and fiber hubs, traffic, collision, and jabber. A fourth LED, Link Status, determines the health of each individual fiber link, and exists only on the fiber hubs.

Using Figure 8-13 as an example, begin troubleshooting at the fiber hub, since it is a common point to all other network components. First, check the the traffic LED. It should either be on, or blinking, thus indicating that the network is operational. If it is off, no power is getting to the hub itself—check the power cord, and replace as necessary.

Figure 8-13
Troubleshooting with StarLAN 10

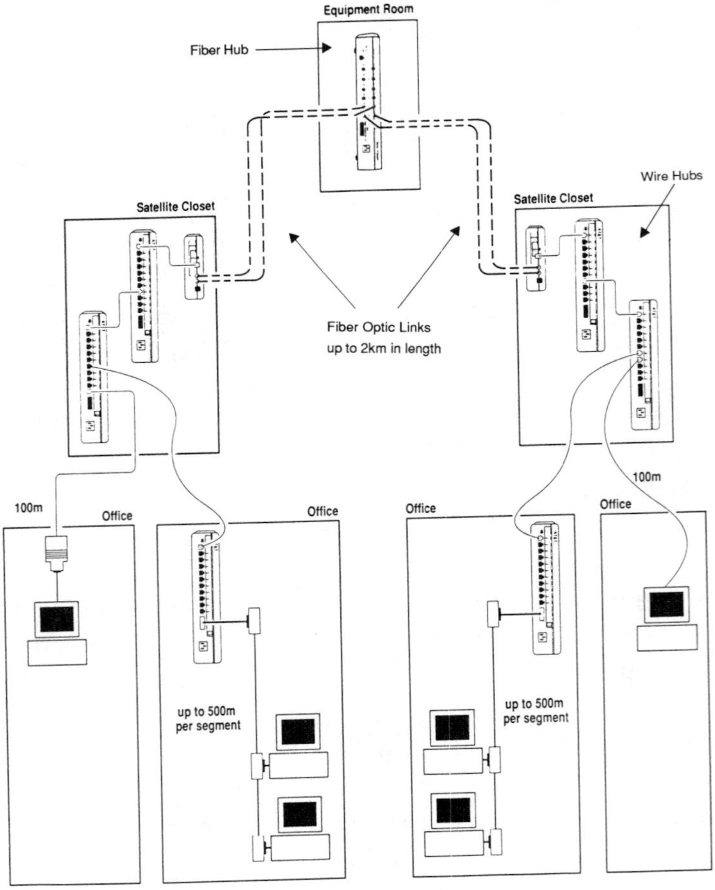

(Courtesy of AT&T)

Second, observe the collision LED. It should normally be off, but may occasionally blink when collisions occur. If there is only one active port, and collisions are still indicated, several causes are possible. The wiring associated with that port may be defective, SQE may be incorrectly turned on, or the NIC may be defective.

Third, inspect the jabber LED. A jabber occurs when the maximum allowable frame length has been exceeded, or 32 successive collisions generate otherwise unacceptable frames. In most cases, faulty wiring or a defective NIC is the cause. The jabber LED signals this failure, and most importantly, indicates that the portion of the network associated with that port (plus all of its downstream stations) has been disconnected from the network.

This is a provision of the 802.3 repeater standard known as the Auto Partitioning/Reconnection Algorithm, (see reference [8-3], section 9.6.6), and implemented by the T7200 IC in the hubs. If a jabber LED is lit on the fiber hub in Figure 8-13, the defective section is somewhere downstream from that port. Further isolate the problem by inspecting the jabber LED on the wire hub, and then finally verifying the twisted pair MAU or NIC. Remember that the twisted pair MAUs also have a jabber option switch that must be set appropriately, as discussed in Section 8.6.2. Another approach is to wait until a user calls to complain of unsuccessful network access. Since the network has disconnected that jabbed node, the caller has then isolated the network failure for you.

Finally, check the Link Status LEDs. Should this LED not be on for any particular fiber optic link, double check the fiber connectors, try another fiber port, or test the fiber optic cable itself.

8.8 | StarLAN and Twisted Pair Ethernet Software Considerations

Both StarLAN and the 10BASE-T proposal are actually Physical layer specifications, the Data Link layer frame format could be either the IEEE 802.3/802.2 or Ethernet. As a result, the techniques for Data Link layer and also Higher layer protocol analysis using a protocol analyzer like the Network General Sniffer, Hewlett-Packard 4972A or Excelan LANalyzer are also applicable to StarLAN and LattisNet architectures. One caution at the Data Link layer, diagnostic disks supplied with some StarLAN NICs allow the user to change the burned-in ROM 48-bit source address. Use extreme caution if this is done because other workstations and hosts in the network will be depending on the consistency of that address, and not react favorably to a sudden change. Should an unusual failure like that occur, ask the question, "what might have changed in my software parameters?" and proceed as we have discussed previously.

8.9 | Protocol Analysis with TCP/IP

The first network demonstrating the viability of packet switching in the United States was ARPANET, sponsored by the Advanced Research Projects Agency of the Department of Defense (DoD). ARPANET became operational in 1969 with four nodes, and it still exists today. The DoD developed the Transmission Control Protocol/Internet Protocol (TCP/IP) suite to solve the problem of interconnection of the major research universities and defense contractors, many of whom had dissimilar computer hardware and operating systems. ARPANET and TCP/IP became the link tying all of those systems together (see reference [8-11]). At about the same time, Ethernet was developed and the Ethernet-TCP/IP alliance was formed. With more of the Ethernet networks converting to the 802.3 family, it makes sense to consider software analysis of TCP/IP over 802.3 network transmission.

Figure 8-14 shows how the TCP/IP suite fits into the OSI model. Starting at the Data Link layer, ARCNET, IEEE 802, or Ethernet LANs have been frequently implemented for network access, see references [8-12], [8-13], and [8-14].

Figure 8-14
TCP/IP and the OSI Model

OSI Layer	Protocol Implementation
Application	Application-specific protocols, e.g., Virtual Terminal, Electronic Mail, File Transfer
Presentation	
Session	
Transport	Transmission Control Protocol (TCP)
Network	Internet Protocol (IP)
Data Link	Network Interface Cards: Ethernet, StarLAN, Token Ring, ARCNET
Physical	Transmission Media: Twisted Pair, Coax, or Fiber Optics

At the network layer, the Internet Protocol (IP) provides datagram service between hosts (or LANs) and network nodes. IP is responsible to route packets from one network to another, and as such, contains 32-bit addresses for the source and destination network and host.

The Transmission Control Protocol (TCP) provides transport layer service, supporting process-to-process communication between the two hosts. TCP provides virtual circuit service between the two host applications (called ports), thus assuring a reliable, byte-streamed connection. Higher-layer protocols such as the File Transfer Protocol (FTP), Simple Mail Transfer Protocol (SMTP), and Virtual Terminal Protocol (TELNET) are often associated with TCP/IP, although for LAN use,

NetBIOS and Server Message Block (SMB) protocols are beginning to emerge as well, see reference [8-15].

As mentioned above, TCP/IP as a protocol suite is most closely associated with Ethernet and 802.3 LANs. Figure 8-15 shows how the IP and TCP headers, plus the TCP data (from a higher layer protocols such as FTP, SMTP, or TELNET) would be encapsulated into the 802.3 frame.

Figure 8-15
Encapsulating a TCP/IP Datagram within an IEEE 802.3 frame

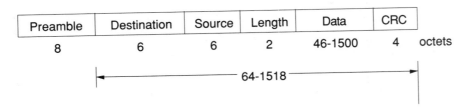

The IP Header contains a minimum of 20 octets, and consists of fields describing the IP version, Internet header length; type of service requested; total length of the IP datagram; identification, flags, and fragment offset controlling the fragmentation and reassembly of the datagrams; a time to live; the protocol used within the IP data field; a header checksum; source and destination addresses specifying the network and host IDs; and various options, padding, and data from the higher layers (TCP, for example). See reference [8-16] for further details.

The TCP Header also contains a minimum of 20 octets, and consists of fields defining the source and destination ports (application programs); the sequence and acknowledgement numbers; a data offset; six flags controlling the setup and termination of the session; the receiver window size; a checksum; a pointer to urgent data; and finally, options, padding, and data from the higher layers. See reference [8-17] for additional information.

Figure 8-16 shows the capture range of the Network General Sniffer protocol analyzer when operating on an 802.3 network. Figure 8-17 shows an 802.3 frame with TCP/IP headers plus 256 bytes of data that was captured by the Sniffer protocol analyzer. Each layer of protocol, Data Link Control (DLC), Logical Link Control (LLC), Internet Protocol (IP), and Transmission Control Protocol (TCP), is identified along the left-hand margin. With the numerous fields and options associated with the TCP/IP protocols, the advantages of using a protocol analyzer for software analysis becomes obvious. See reference [8-18] for further details.

Figure 8-16
Capture range of the Network General Sniffer Protocol Analyzer for 802.3 networks

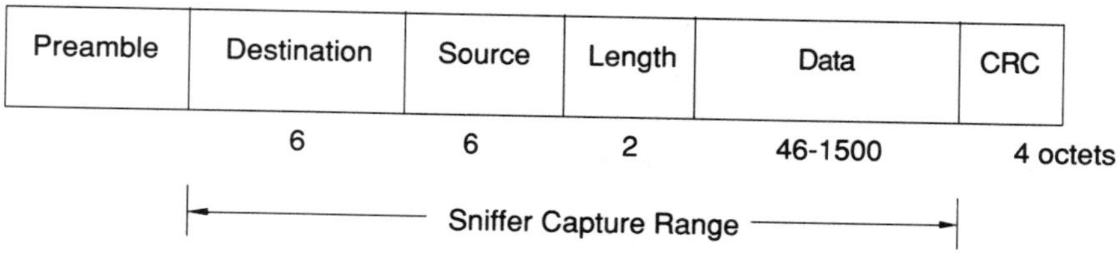

Preamble	Destination	Source	Length	Data	CRC
	6	6	2	46-1500	4 octets

Sniffer Capture Range

Figure 8-17
A TCP/IP Datagram transmitted over an IEEE 802.3 network and captured by the Network General Sniffer protocol analyzer

```
DLC:  ----- DLC Header -----
DLC:
DLC:  Frame 2 arrived at  14:30:33.0340 ; frame size is 313 (0139 hex) bytes.
DLC:  Destination: Station 3Com  138372
DLC:  Source    : Station 3Com  138162
DLC:  802.2 LLC length = 299
DLC:
LLC:  ----- LLC Header -----
LLC:
LLC:  DSAP = 06, SSAP = 06, Command, Unnumbered frame: UI
LLC:
IP:   ----- IP Header -----
IP:
IP:   Version = 4, header length = 20 bytes
IP:   Type of service = 00
IP:        000. .... = routine
IP:        ...0 .... = normal delay
IP:        .... 0... = normal throughput
IP:        .... .0.. = normal reliability
IP:   Total length = 296 bytes
IP:   Identification = 0
IP:   Flags = 4X
IP:   .1.. .... = don't fragment
IP:   ..0. ..... = last fragment
IP:   Fragment offset = 0 bytes
IP:   Time to live = 60
IP:   Protocol = 6 (TCP)
IP:   Header checksum = 8D4E (correct)
IP:   Source address = [15.6.73.68]
IP:   Destination address = [15.6.73.50]
IP:   No options
IP:
TCP:  ----- TCP header -----
TCP:
TCP:  Source port = 46586
TCP:  Destination port = 5696
TCP:  Sequence number = 1108921
TCP:  Acknowledgment number = 346879454
TCP:  Data offset = 20
TCP:  Flags = 18
TCP:  ..0. .... = (No urgent pointer)
TCP:  ...1 .... = Acknowledgment
TCP:  .... 1... = Push
TCP:  .... .0.. = (No reset)
```

```
TCP:  .... ..0. = (No SYN)
TCP:  .... ...0 = (No FIN)
TCP:  Window = 1424
TCP:  Checksum = 0 (No checksum sent)
TCP:  No TCP options
TCP:  [256 byte(s) of data]
TCP:
```

8.10 Troubleshooting Summary

To summarize, here is a checklist to assist with diagnosing twisted pair Ethernet and StarLAN failures:

1. Clean the gold fingers and reseat the Network Interface Card (NIC) in the PC bus.

2. Run the NIC board diagnostics, if available.

3. Check IRQ, DMA Shared Memory, and I/O Base Address for conflicts with other boards. If in doubt, remove all boards but the NIC, and reinsert one board at a time. Visually inspect the NIC for any jumpers that may have fallen off, or any DIP switches not firmly set.

4. Confirm the order of CONFIG.SYS and AUTOEXEC.BAT files, plus any device drivers that are being used.

5. Use the advantage of the star topology to isolate a failure to one hub or concentrator, or multiport repeater, then further to an individual port.

6. Check activity on diagnostic LEDs (if present) on the NIC, hub or concentrator, for proper condition.

7. Check for an unterminated (dangling) cable at the OUT port of the header hub or the last workstation in a StarLAN daisy-chain configuration. Unplug the cable from the OUT port to correct.

8. Look for a break in any StarLAN daisy-chain cabling.

9. Verify pin-to-pin continuity (pin 1 to pin 1, pin 2 to pin 2, etc.) on all cables, and check for any loose crimp connections at the RJ-45 connector.

10. Check for correct power to any hub, concentrator, or multiport repeater; also check fuses.

11. Check for duplicate node addresses with the NIC diagnostic disk or protocol analyzer if software-configurable node addressing has been used.

8.11 References

[8-1] Some of the material in this chapter first appeared in "Troubleshooting StarLAN and Twisted Pair Ethernet," by Mark A. Miller, *LAN Technology Magazine*, Volume 5, Number 9, September 1989.

[8-2] StarLAN Design and Planning Manual, Racal-Interlan, Inc., 1987.

[8-3] Institute of Electrical and Electronics Engineers, Supplements to Carrier Sense Multiple Access with Collision Detection, ANSI IEEE Std 802.3a, b, c, and e – 1989, ISO 8802-3: 1989.

[8-4] StarLAN Network Technical Reference Manual, AT&T Publication 999-300-208, 1986.

[8-5] Institute of Electrical and Electronics Engineers, Twisted Pair Medium Attachment Unit and Baseband Medium, Type 10BASE-T, IEEE Preliminary Draft Standard, April 1989.

[8-6] LattisNet Workgroup Concentrator Installation and Reference Guide, SynOptics Communications, Inc., November 1988.

[8-7] LattisNet Product Description, SynOptics Communications, Inc., July 1988.

[8-8] NI5210-UTP Installation Manual, Racal-Interlan, Document 950-1131-00, March 1988.

[8-9] StarLAN 10 Network Hardware Design Guide, Document 999-120-002, AT&T, 1989.

[8-10] StarLAN 10 Network Hub Unit Installation Guide, Document 999-100-431, AT&T, 1988.

[8-11] Most documentation on ARPANET, TCP/IP, and related protocols are contained in Request for Comment (RFC) papers circulated within the research community, and available from the DDN Network Information Center, SRI International, (415) 859-3695 or (800) 235-3155. Of special interest is RFC-1000, the Request for Comments Reference Guide.

[8-12] A Standard for the Transmission of IP datagrams and ARP Packets over ARCNET Networks, RFC-1051, DDN Network Information Center, March 1988.

[8-13] A Standard for the Transmission of IP Datagrams over IEEE 802 Networks, RFC-948, DDN Network Information Center, February 1988.

[8-14] A Standard for the Transmission of IP Datagrams over Ethernet Networks, RFC-894, DDN Network Information Center, April 1984.

[8-15] Protocol Standard for a NetBIOS Service on a TCP/UDP Transport: Concepts and Methods (RFC-1001), and Detailed Specifications (RFC-1002), DDN Network Information Center, March 1987.

[8-16] Internet Protocol (IP), RFC-791, DDN Network Information Center, September 1981.

[8-17]   Transmission Control Protocol, RFC-793, DDN Network Information Center, September 1981.

[8-18]   Ethernet Network Portable Protocol Analyzer Operation and Reference Manual, Network General Corporation, 1986–1988.

CHAPTER NINE

Keeping the Net Working

To conclude this handbook, we will investigate ways of minimizing network down time. These will include network design and installation procedures in addition to troubleshooting and repair techniques. In summary, here are some tips for keeping your net working (see reference [9-1]).

9.1 Don't Push Network Design Limits

Each network architecture has a variety of fixed parameters associated with its design. For example, IEEE 802.3 10BASE5 networks have a maximum segment length of 500 meters before a repeater; ARCNET networks can have a maximum of 255 nodes. Trying to extend these design limits almost always leads to problems. With Ethernet networks, a bus cable that is too long yields excessive collisions. With ARCNET networks, duplicate addresses cause failures of the reconfiguration algorithm.

In short, don't get creative. If there is a reason that your network architecture is pushing a limit, you may be using the wrong technology or need to add additional components, such as a repeater or bridge. Design limits exist for specific purposes—don't try to get around them.

9.2 Install With Care

By some estimates, somewhere between 70% and 90% of all network failures are related to the hardware elements—the cabling, connectors, cross-connect fields, wall jacks, splices, etc. If this estimate is even somewhat accurate, that would indicate that many network failures can be prevented by careful installation techniques.

Consider where your cables go. Do they run close to the fluorescent lights? Could someone plug a floor polisher or portable arc welder into the same power circuit that feeds the server? What happens if a user moves his or her workstation? Have you considered other user installation issues that could impact the users, such as printer or plotter locations?

All network installations are unique, because of the various choices of topology, cabling, hardware and software components, and operating system. For that reason, it's a good idea to develop action plans for installation that are unique to your network.

Consider four factors in a typical installation plan:

1. Verify the electrical continuity of all wiring, cables, and connectors, and that each plug goes to the appropriate receptacle.

2. Identify the network's functional requirements from a typical user's point of view. In other words, put yourself in the user's shoes and determine the different application programs and peripherals that must be exercised in order to verify that the network is operating properly.

3. Check the operation of all peripherals, including network printers and communication servers.

4. Verify that redundant systems, such as the UPS on the server or power-fail transfer equipment on communication circuits, are operational. Don't wait for the power utility to test these for you during a power outage!

Install with care. Be patient and do it right the first time.

9.3 | Document Your Network

You've probably heard the old saying "a project reaches the point of 95% completion and remains there forever." Since there is a natural tendency to put things off until another day and time, make sure that your network documentation doesn't fall by the wayside. Thorough documentation should cover four areas:

A. Workstation details—indicating each PC's configuration, including:

1. The node name and address, either set by DIP switches or burned into a ROM.
2. CPU type, amount of memory, etc.
3. Other devices (for example, graphics or terminal emulation cards) that are also installed in the workstation.
4. Specific details about each PC add-in card, such as the DMA channel and IRQ line in use, shared memory address, etc.

A convenient way to document these parameters is with an adhesive label on the rear or bottom panel of the PC. Don't forget to update the label when these add-ins are changed.

B. Cabling details—knowing what workstation, server, printer, or peripheral is at the end of each cable. This is especially important if multiple coaxial cables have been run in a common cable tray, or if twisted pair wiring has been used with 66-type punch-down blocks. To summarize, document your cabling—the moment of crisis is no time to wonder where that orange/yellow pair *really* goes.

C. Server details—including which users and peripherals are attached to each server. If a user on your network claims that he or she can't access the server, you must know which server to troubleshoot. Having a network map that details which users are attached to that server will make the fault isolation job much faster. For a quick test of the server, the administrator can go to another workstation attached to the same server and attempt to communicate with it, such as sending an electronic mail message or accessing a file. If this step is successful, the fault most likely lies somewhere in that workstation, not the server.

D. Connectivity devices—to other parts of the network, such as repeaters, bridges, and gateways. Many failures can be isolated to a particular section of the network, such as the cable segment beyond a given repeater, or a gateway to the host computer. Since these devices are often the most complex, it's also a good idea to develop a specific plan for testing and verifying the operation of those devices. We'll look at more detailed troubleshooting plans in section 9.7.

9.4 Understand Your LAN and its Relationship to the OSI Model

The OSI model provides a theoretical framework for computer communication, but can yield some valuable insights into whether a network failure is based in hardware or software.

Most network failures are hardware-related, and thus corresponding to the Physical and Data Link layers of the OSI model. Tools that we would use for these problems would include Volt-Ohm-Milliameters, Time Domain Reflectometers, Optical Power Meters, Break-Out Boxes, etc. The most important tool, however, is the diagnostic disk that accompanies most NICs. These disks can do loop-around tests, read the value of the address ROM, and perform other internal diagnostics of the board. Make sure that you are familiar with the operation of this disk.

At the Network layer and above, software problems will be the culprits. A protocol analyzer, such as the Network General Sniffer, Excelan LANalyzer, Hewlett-Packard 4972 or similar device will be required to diagnose the problem. Again, don't wait until a failure occurs to learn how to use these tools—experiment on a live, functioning network to obtain benchmark measurements of traffic patterns and network utilization for comparison when a failure does occur.

Understanding your LAN also includes being familiar with the LAN's own unique advantages, disadvantages, and potential sources of failure. To quickly review, ARCNET's flexibility in mixing various transmission media: twisted pairs, coaxial, or fiber optics can be used very effectively. Also unique is its requirement for setting the node address manually with DIP switches, therefore giving a greater potential for human-induced network failures.

Token ring networks have many built-in failure-recovery attributes, largely due to the sophistication of the IEEE 802.5 standard. Assembly of the hermaphroditic (genderless) connectors can be difficult for some users, necessitating thorough testing prior to installation.

Ethernet and coaxial IEEE 802.3 networks have the longest history in the LAN marketplace, yielding a multitude of vendors. However, because of the small differences between the Ethernet standard (from DEC, Intel, and Xerox), and the IEEE 802.3 10BASE5 standard, compatibility problems, such as cable and connector pinouts can occur. Make sure that you understand these technical differences.

Finally, StarLAN and twisted pair IEEE 802.3 networks provide simplified failure isolation because of their star topologies, however, reusing existing twisted pair cabling can prove to be a challenge. In some cases, the installation of new twisted pairs is advantageous, thus eliminating any questions regarding the cable length or integrity.

All LAN architectures have their unique characteristics; make sure that you understand the distinctions of *your* network.

9.5 | Predict Network Failures

There are three failure measurements, or metrics, that can be applied to the network and its components that may provide an early warning of a potential disaster:

A. Mean Time Between Failures (MTBF)—a measurement, usually in tens of thousands of hours, of the average (or mean) time that a device should operate properly before a failure occurs. Factors that influence MTBF include the network topology and whether the various elements are connected in series or parallel, plus the reliability of each component that goes into that device. As an example, a PC's motherboard might be rated for an MTBF of 45,000 hours, meaning that a failure about every five years should be expected (for reference, one year equals 8,760 hours).

B. Mean Time to Repair (MTTR)—a measurement, usually less than ten hours, of the average time required to identify, and then repair or replace the failed component. Two factors that affect the MTTR include the complexity of the network and the availability of spare parts. If your organization is providing its own network maintenance, you can significantly improve the MTTR by having service manuals and spare parts readily available. This foresight will eliminate the time required to obtain a replacement part when a failure does occur. For example, a system that has an MTTR of eight hours indicates that one business day is sufficient for fault diagnosis, repair, and retesting.

C. Network availability—a measurement, expressed as a percentage, of the ratio between MTBF and the total time (MTBF plus MTTR):

$$\text{Availability} = \frac{\text{MTBF}}{(\text{MTBF} + \text{MTTR})}$$

Obviously, a very high MTBF and a very low MTTR is optimum, thus yielding a network availability greater than 99%.

To determine the most vulnerable parts of your network, obtain the MTBF and MTTR estimates from the vendors, and consider the effect that the failure of a particular component would have on the entire network. Additional spare parts, training on repair procedures, or redundancy in the design (such as dial backup for communication circuits, or disk duplexing on a server) might be required. Further mathematical details that impact network design can be found in reference [9-2].

9.6 | Don't Overlook Power Protection

Many mysterious network problems, such as servers rebooting and PCs that fail, are often power problems in disguise. These failures can often be identified when a thorough analysis is made of the power feed to the server and other peripherals, and corrective measures are taken. Because of their intermittent occurrence, power and grounding problems can also be the most difficult to track down, often requiring expensive electrical system test equipment. Since many firms do not have the in-house expertise for this work, a call to the local power company, or an electrical contractor, may prove helpful.

In addition to the power survey from a reputable firm, adding a separate power feed (115 VAC, 15 A, or as required) plus a separate ground circuit from the breaker panel to the server can eliminate many problems. Not allowing other appliances (such as fans or copy machines) onto this separate power circuit will also prevent problems. See reference [9-3] for further information.

9.7 | Develop a Troubleshooting Plan

A troubleshooting plan must concentrate on identifying the failed network component. In other words, *determine what doesn't work.*

Here's some guidance for developing your plan:

1. If a user calls with a network problem, consider asking the following questions:

    -   What do you see on the workstation's screen?
    -   Have you made any recent changes to the workstation's hardware or software?
    -   What were you attempting to accomplish when this problem occurred?
    -   What is different this time from the last time that you tried the same procedure?

2. Further isolate the failure to one device using the network-specific techniques we have discussed. For example, isolate an ARCNET failure to a specific hub by disconnecting the individual cable sections, and then isolate further to a particular workstation in a similar manner.

3. When the problem is identified to a particular workstation, server, or connectivity device, have the tools required for further diagnosis and repair. These might include the NIC diagnostic disk, diagnostic software for the PC, cable testing equipment, or a protocol analyzer if a software problem is suspected.

4. Become familiar with diagnostic procedures for each device. Many good troubleshooting hints can be obtained in the hardware installation and operation guides, often listed in the index as "What to do when experiencing difficulty." If no information is contained in the manual, ask the vendor for additional information, such as a maintenance guide, or give some thought to a trou-

bleshooting plan yourself. An excellent example of a methodical process for diagnosing phone-line problems is given in reference [9-4], and could be adapted to many LAN difficulties as well.

5. Consider developing a fault-isolation flowchart unique to your network. Good reference material can be obtained from the hardware and software vendors. Use the model flowchart in Figure 9-1 as a starting point for your network.

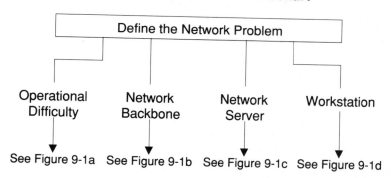

Figure 9-1
Model Fault Isolation Flowchart

Figure 9-1a

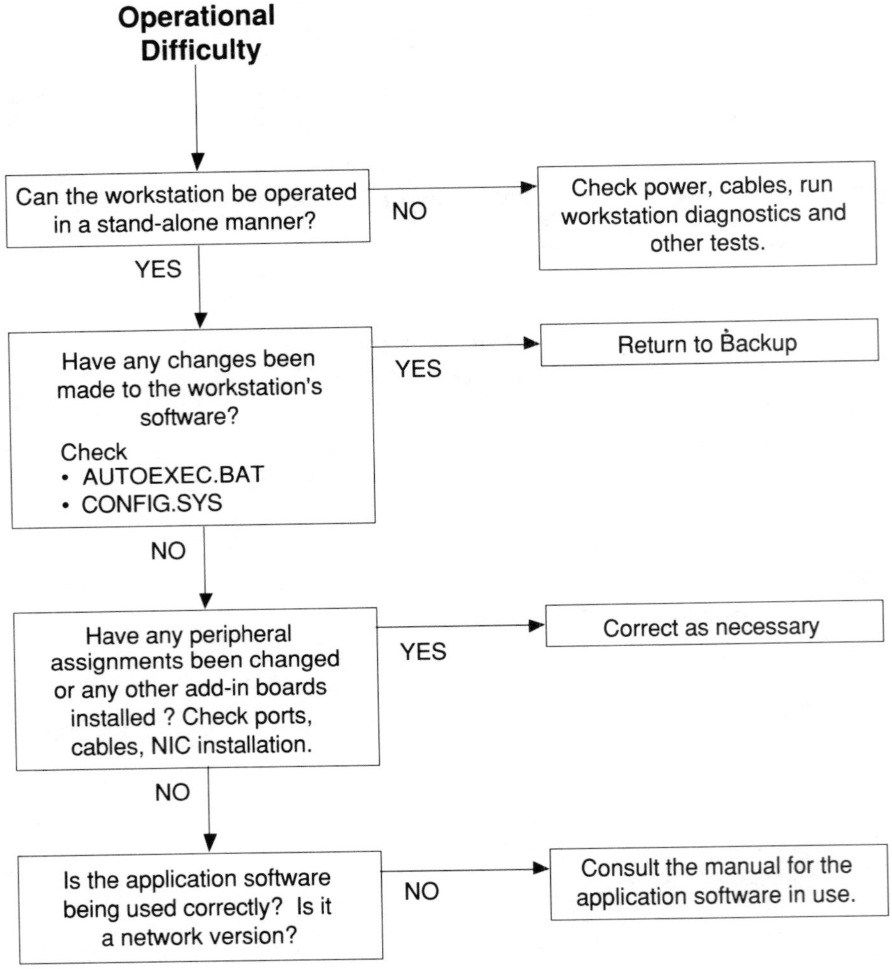

**Operational
Difficulty**

Can the workstation be operated in a stand-alone manner?	NO →	Check power, cables, run workstation diagnostics and other tests.

YES

Have any changes been made to the workstation's software? Check • AUTOEXEC.BAT • CONFIG.SYS	YES →	Return to Backup

NO

Have any peripheral assignments been changed or any other add-in boards installed ? Check ports, cables, NIC installation.	YES →	Correct as necessary

NO

Is the application software being used correctly? Is it a network version?	NO →	Consult the manual for the application software in use.

Figure 9-1b

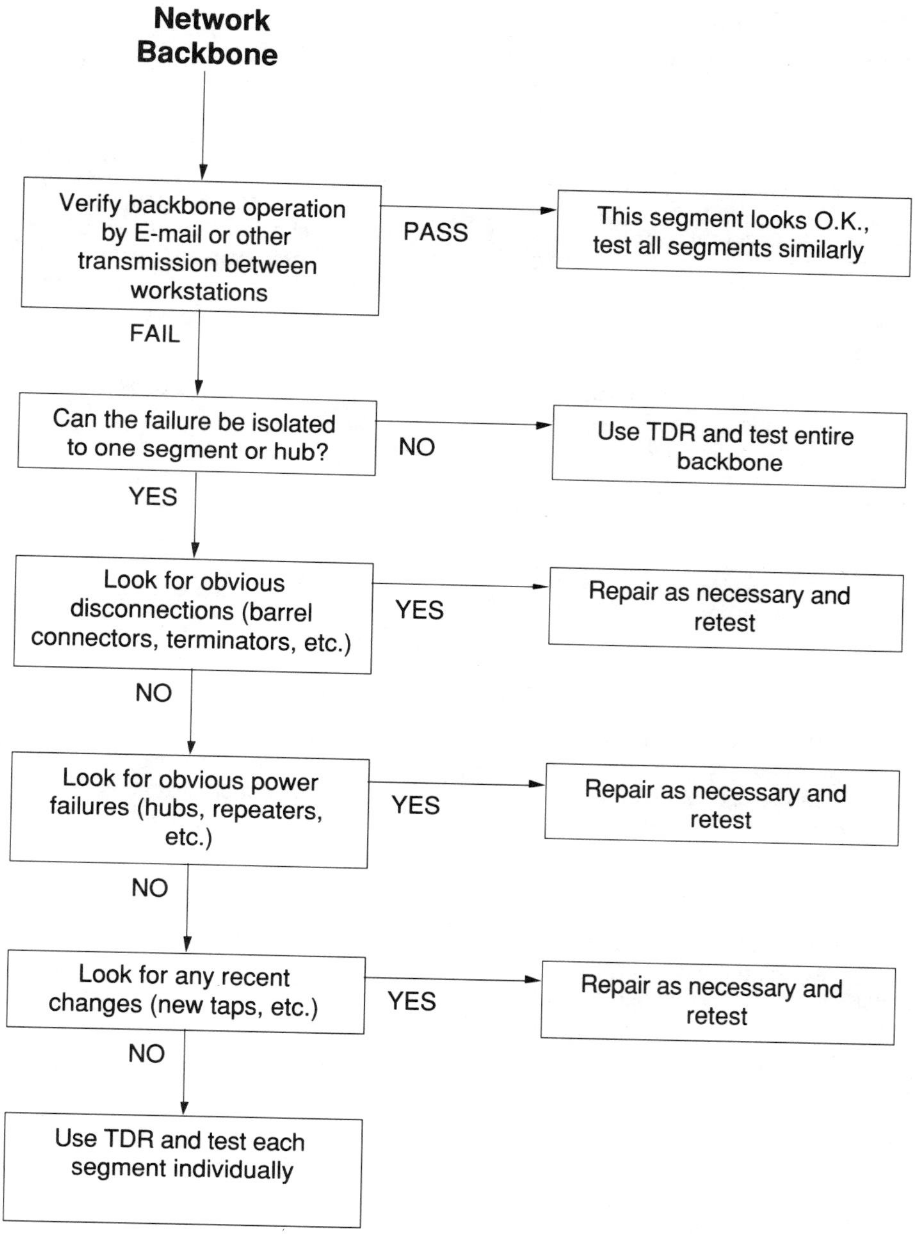

**Network
Backbone**

Verify backbone operation by E-mail or other transmission between workstations	PASS →	This segment looks O.K., test all segments similarly

FAIL

Can the failure be isolated to one segment or hub?	NO →	Use TDR and test entire backbone

YES

Look for obvious disconnections (barrel connectors, terminators, etc.)	YES →	Repair as necessary and retest

NO

Look for obvious power failures (hubs, repeaters, etc.)	YES →	Repair as necessary and retest

NO

Look for any recent changes (new taps, etc.)	YES →	Repair as necessary and retest

NO

Use TDR and test each segment individually

Figure 9-1c

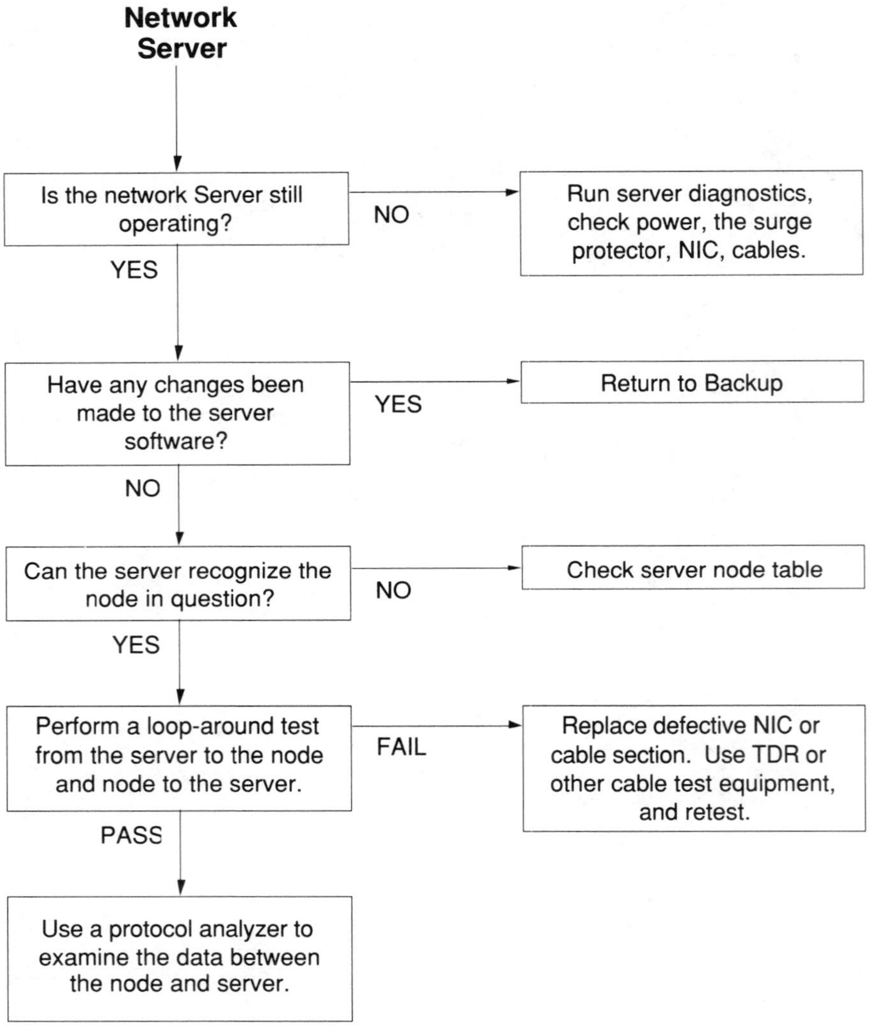

**Network
Server**

Is the network Server still operating?	NO →	Run server diagnostics, check power, the surge protector, NIC, cables.

YES

Have any changes been made to the server software?	YES →	Return to Backup

NO

Can the server recognize the node in question?	NO →	Check server node table

YES

Perform a loop-around test from the server to the node and node to the server.	FAIL →	Replace defective NIC or cable section. Use TDR or other cable test equipment, and retest.

PASS

Use a protocol analyzer to examine the data between the node and server.

Figure 9-1d

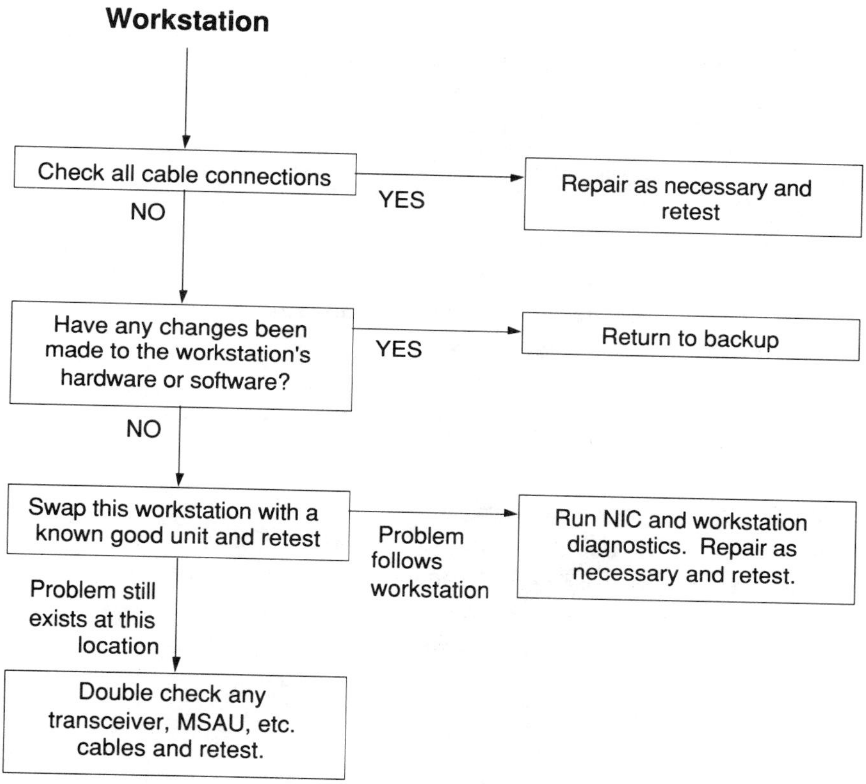

Workstation

```
        │
        ▼
┌─────────────────────────┐
│ Check all cable connections │ ──── YES ────►  ┌──────────────────────┐
└─────────────────────────┘                      │ Repair as necessary and │
        NO                                        │        retest          │
        │                                         └──────────────────────┘
        ▼
┌─────────────────────────┐
│ Have any changes been   │ ──── YES ────►  ┌──────────────────────┐
│ made to the workstation's│                 │   Return to backup    │
│ hardware or software?   │                 └──────────────────────┘
└─────────────────────────┘
        NO
        │
        ▼
┌─────────────────────────┐   Problem      ┌──────────────────────┐
│ Swap this workstation with a│  follows    │ Run NIC and workstation │
│ known good unit and retest  │  workstation│ diagnostics. Repair as  │
└─────────────────────────┘  ──────────►   │ necessary and retest.   │
   Problem still                            └──────────────────────┘
   exists at this
   location
        │
        ▼
┌─────────────────────────┐
│ Double check any        │
│ transceiver, MSAU, etc. │
│ cables and retest.      │
└─────────────────────────┘
```

During the troubleshooting process, make sure that only one hardware or software parameter is changed at a time. Rarely does a network failure result from a combination of two or more failures, therefore making random changes (known as the "shotgun technique") may only make the situation worse. Secondly, make sure that you take some notes during the process—after trying many potential solutions, it's very easy to forget what possible solutions have already been tried.

When the problem has finally been solved, don't forget to document the symptoms, identified problems, and final solutions. Network problems tend to repeat themselves over time, and it's helpful to know what solutions have worked in the past.

9.8   Don't Miss the Obvious

When all the smoke clears, a large number of network difficulties are categorized as "operational difficulties," also known as "cockpit errors." Look for the simple failures: the power cord that is unplugged, the power strip that is turned off, the BNC T-connector that is disconnected at the wrong end, the CONFIG.SYS file that was mysteriously revised, or the CRT that has the brightness turned down. Make a list of some of the typical failures that plague your network, and distribute that list to the network users. By enlisting their help in the troubleshooting process, everyone wins.

9.9   Understand Your Protocols

If 70–90% of network problems are attributed to hardware failures, some portion of the balance must be blamed on software faults. These frustrations usually require a protocol analyzer for resolution. Unfortunately, these expensive ($5,000 to $40,000) tools are only as effective as their human operators. Specific knowledge on the network protocols, such as TCP/IP, DECnet, SDLC, X.25, NetBIOS, or the network operating system is essential. Don't put off this vital part of your education.

9.10   Look Beyond Your LAN

If your LAN is typical of most, it is a subset of your firm's total voice and data communications network. It is wise to resist myopia, and instead look at the big picture. Consider the impact that a failure of the communications lines (which you might not be responsible for) would have on your network. What would happen if the gateway to the host or the public data network failed? If a fire occurred in your office, would your backups be destroyed (along with your data), or have you stored backup disks or tapes in another location? Do your network components have adequate air circulation? Consider these (and possibly other) areas, and do a little network "managing by wandering around."

Finally, remember that there is no substitute for a thorough, working knowledge of the network. The best person to troubleshoot the network is the person who was also involved in the installation, and administers the network on a daily basis.

9.11 References

[9-1]   Some of the material in this chapter originally appeared in "The Well-Tended Network," by Mark A. Miller, *LAN Technology Magazine,* Volume 5, Number 10, October 1989.

[9-2]   Peter M. Haverlock, "The Formula for Network Immortality," *Data Communications,* Volume 17, Number 9, August 1988, pp. 112–116.

[9-3]   Mark Waller, *PC Power Protection,* Howard W. Sams, Indianapolis, IN, 1989.

[9-4]   Jack Douglas, "How to Find Phone-Line Faults and What to do About Them," *Data Communications,* Volume 17, Number 10, September 1988, pp. 179–197.

Limits of Liability
and Disclaimer of Warranty

The Author and Publisher of this book have used their best efforts in preparing the book and the programs contained in it. These efforts include the development, research, and testing of the theories and programs to determine their effectiveness.

The Author and Publisher make no warranty of any kind, expressed or implied, with regard to these programs or the documentation contained in this book. The Author and Publisher shall not be liable in any event for incidental or consequential damages in connection with, or arising out of, the furnishing, performance, or use of these programs.

Index

T

A Library of Technical References
from M&T Books

NetWare User's Guide, Second Edition
by Edward Liebing

Endorsed by Novell, this book informs NetWare users of available services and utilities and describes how to put them to use effectively. This book contains a complete task-oriented reference that introduces users to NetWare and guides them through the basics of NetWare menu-driven and command-line utilities. Each utility is illustrated, thus providing a visual frame of reference. You will find general information about the utilities and for performing particular tasks. The book covers NetWare v2.1 through v2.2. For advanced users, a workstation troubleshooting section describes common problems. Two appendixes cover the services available in each NetWare menu or command-line utility. 520 pp. approx.

Book only　　　　　　　　**Item #235-7**　　　**$29.95**

NetWare Supervisor's Guide
by John T. McCann, Adam T. Ruef, and Steven L. Guengerich

Written for network administrators, consultants, installers, and power users of all versions of NetWare, including NetWare 386. While other books provide information on using NetWare at a workstation level, this definitive reference focuses on how to administer NetWare. Contains numerous examples which address understanding and using NetWare's undocumented commands and utilities, implementing system fault tolerant LANs, refining installation parameters to improve network performance, and more. 510 pp.

Book only　　　　　　　　**Item #111-3**　　　**$29.95**

A Library of Technical References
from M&T Books

LAN Troubleshooting Handbook
by Mark A. Miller, P.E.

This book is specifically for users and administrators who need to identify problems and maintain a LAN that is already installed. Topics include LAN standards, the OSI model, network documentation, LAN test equipment, cable system testing, and more. Addressed are specific issues associated with troubleshooting the four most popular LAN architectures: ARCNET, Token Ring, Ethernet, and StarLAN. Each is closely examined to pinpoint the problems unique to its design and the hardware. Handy checklists to assist in solving each architecture's unique network difficulties are also included. 309 pp.

Book & Disk (MS-DOS)	Item #056-7	$39.95
Book only	Item #054-0	$29.95

Building Local Area Networks with Novell's NetWare, 2nd Edition
by Patrick H. Corrigan and Aisling Guy

From the basic components to complete network installation, here is the practical guide that PC system integrators will need to build and implement PC LANs in this rapidly growing market. The specifics of building and maintaining PC LANs, including hardware configurations, software development, cabling, selection criteria, installation, and on-going management are described in a clear "how-to" manner with numerous illustrations and sample LAN management forms. *Building Local Area Networks* covers Novell's NetWare, Version 2.2, and 3.11 for the 386. Additional topics covered include the OS/2 LAN Manager, Tops, Banyan VINES, internetworking, host computer gateways, and multisystem networks that link PCs, Apples, and mainframes. 635 pp. approx.

Book & Disk (MS-DOS)	Item #239-X	$39.95
Book only	Item #237-3	$29.95

A Library of Technical References from M&T Books

Internetworking
A Guide to Network Communications
LAN to LAN; LAN to WAN
by Mark A. Miller, P.E.

This book addresses all aspects of LAN and WAN (wide-area network) integrations, detailing the hardware, software, and communication products available. In-depth discussions describe the functions, design, and performance of repeaters, bridges, routers, and gateways. Communication facilities such as leased lines, T-1 circuits and access to packed switched public data networks (PSPDNs) are compared, helping LAN managers decide which is most viable for their internetwork. Also examined are the X.25, TCP/IP, and XNS protocols, as well as the internetworking capabilities and interoperability constraints of the most popular networks, including NetWare, LAN Server, 3+Open™, VINES®, and AppleTalk. 425 pp.

Book only   **Item #143-1**   **$34.95**

LAN Primer
An Introduction to Local Area Networks
by Greg Nunemacher

A complete introduction to local area networks (LANs), this book is a must for anyone who needs to know basic LAN principles. It includes a complete overview of LANs, clearly defining what a LAN is, the functions of a LAN, and how LANs fit into the field of telecommunications. The author discusses the specifics of building a LAN, including the required hardware and software, an overview of the types of products available, deciding what products to purchase, and assembling the pieces into a working LAN system. *LAN Primer* also includes case studies that illustrate how LAN principles work. Particular focus is given to Ethernet and Token-Ring. 221 pp.

Book only   **Item #127-X**   **$24.95**

1-800-533-4372 (in CA 1-800-356-2002)

A Library of Technical References
from M&T Books

NetWare for Macintosh User's Guide
by Kelley J. P. Lindberg

NetWare for Macintosh User's Guide is the definitive reference to using Novell's NetWare on Macintosh computers. Whether you are a novice or an advanced user, this comprehensive text provides the information readers need to get the most from their NetWare networks. It includes an overview of network operations and detailed explanations of all NetWare for Macintosh menu and command line utilities. Detailed tutorials cover such tasks as logging in, working with directories and files, and printing over a network. Advanced users will benefit from the information on managing workstation environments and troubleshooting.
280 pp.

Book only   Item #126-1 $29.95

NetWare 386 User's Guide
by Christine Milligan

NetWare 386 User's Guide is a complete guide to using and understanding Novell's NetWare 386. It is an excellent reference for 386. Detailed tutorials cover tasks such as logging in, working with directories and files, and printing over a network. Complete explanations of the basic concepts underlying NetWare 386, along with a summary of the differences between NetWare 286 and 386, are included. Advanced users will benefit from the information on managing workstation environments and the troubleshooting index that fully examines NetWare 386 error messages. 450 pp.

Book only   Item #101-6 $29.95

A Library of Technical References from M&T Books

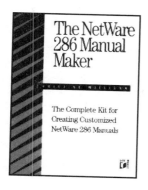

The NetWare Manual Makers
Complete Kits for Creating Customized NetWare Manuals

Developed to meet the tremendous demand for customized manuals, The NetWare Manual Makers enable the NetWare supervisor and administrator to create network training manuals specific to their individual sites. Administrators simply fill in the blanks on the template provided on disk and print the file to create customized manuals and command cards. Included is general "how-to" information on using a network, as well as fill-in-the-blank sections that help administrators explain and document procedures unique to a particular site. The disk files are provided in WordPerfect and ASCII formats. The WordPerfect file creates a manual that looks exactly like the one in the book. The ASCII file can be imported into any desktop publishing or word processing software.

The NetWare 286 Manual Maker
The Complete Kit for Creating Customized NetWare 286 Manuals
by Christine Milligan

Book/Disk   Item #119-9 $49.95   314 pp.

The NetWare 386 Manual Maker
The Complete Kit for Creating Customized NetWare 386 Manuals
by Christine Milligan

Book/Disk   Item #120-2 $49.95   314 pp.

The NetWare for Macintosh Manual Maker
The Complete Kit for Creating Customized NetWare for Macintosh Manuals
by Kelley J. P. Lindberg

Book/Disk   Item #130-X $49.95   314 pp.

A Library of Technical References
from M&T Books

NetWare Programmer's Guide
by John T. McCann

Covered are all aspects of programming in the NetWare environment — from basic planning to complex application debugging. This book offers practical tips and tricks for creating and porting applications to NetWare. NetWare programmers developing simple applications for a single LAN or intricate programs for multi-site internetworked systems will find this book an invaluable reference to have on hand. All source code is available on disk in MS-PC/DOS format. 425 pp.

Book/Disk (MS-DOS)	Item #154-7	$44.95
Book only	Item #152-0	$34.95

Troubleshooting LAN Manager 2
by Michael Day

The ideal reference for network supervisors responsible for the maintenance of a LAN Manager 2 network. *Troubleshooting LAN Manager 2* builds a functional model of LAN Manager from the ground up, beginning with OS/2 and ending with fault tolerance and printer setup. Key components such as data structures, protocols, services, and applications are placed in a troubleshooting context, examining possible problems and providing hands-on solutions. More than basic hints and tips, this book lays a solid foundation upon which you can build a truly outstanding troubleshooting methodology. 337 pp.

Book only	Item #161-X	$34.95

Troubleshooting NetWare for the 286
by Cheryl Snapp

The ideal reference for network supervisors responsible for the installation and maintenance of a NetWare 286 network. Contains a thorough overview of the NetWare 286 operating system plus step-by-step instructions for troubleshooting common and not-so-common problems. Detailed chapters emphasize the information most helpful in maintaining a healthy NetWare 286 LAN, including installation, file server and workstation diagnostics, printing utilities, and network management services. Covers NetWare 286 version 2.2. 350 pp.

Book only	Item #169-5	$34.95

1-800-533-4372 (in CA 1-800-356-2002)

A Library of Technical References
from M&T Books

Running WordPerfect on NetWare
by Greg McMurdie and Joni Taylor

Written by NetWare and WordPerfect experts, this book contains practical information for both system administrators and network WordPerfect users. Administrators will learn how to install, maintain, and troubleshoot WordPerfect on the network. Users will find answers to everyday questions such as how to print over the network, how to handle error messages, and how to use WordPerfect's tutorial on NetWare. 246 pp.

Book only   Item #145-8 $29.95

The Tao of Objects:
A Beginner's Guide to Object-Oriented Programming
by Gary Entsminger

The Tao of Objects is a clearly written, user-friendly guide to object-oriented programming (OOP). Easy-to-understand discussions detail OOP techniques teaching programmers who are new to OOP where and how to use them. Useful programming examples in C++ and Turbo Pascal illustrate the concepts discussed in real-life applications. 249 pp.

Book only   Item #155-5 $26.95

Object-Oriented Programming for Presentation Manager
by William G. Wong

Written for programmers and developers interested in OS/2 Presentation Manager (PM), as well as DOS programmers who are just beginning to explore Object-Oriented Programming and PM. Topics include a thorough overview of Presentation Manager and Object-Oriented Programming, Object-Oriented Programming languages and techniques, developing Presentation Manager applications using C and OOP techniques, and more. 423 pp.

Book/Disk (MS-DOS)   Item #079-6 $39.95
Book only   Item #074-5 $29.95

1-800-533-4372 (in CA 1-800-356-2002)

A Library of Technical References
from M&T Books

Delivering cc:Mail
Installing, Maintaining, and Troubleshooting a cc:Mail System
by Eric Arnum

Delivering cc:Mail teaches administrators how to install, troubleshoot, and maintain cc:Mail, one of the most popular E-mail applications for the PC. In-depth discussions and practical examples show administrators how to establish and maintain the program and database files; how to create and modify the bulletin boards, mail directory, and public mailing lists; and how to diagnose and repair potential problems. Information on using the management tools included with the package plus tips and techniques for creating efficient batch files are also included. All source code is available on disk in MS/PC-DOS format. 450 pp.

Book & Disk	Item #187-3	$39.95
Book only	Item #185-7	$29.95

The Complete Memory Manager
Every PC User's Guide to Faster, More Efficient Computing
by Phillip Robinson

Readers will learn why memory is important, how and when to install more, and how to wring the most out of their memory. Clear, concise instructions teach users how to manage their computer's memory to multiply its speed and ability to run programs simultaneously. Tips and techniques also show users how to conserve memory when working with popular software programs. 437 pp.

Book	Item #102-4	$24.95

1-800-533-4372 (in CA 1-800-356-2002)

A Library of Technical References from M&T Books

Clipper 5: A Developer's Guide
by Joseph D. Booth, Greg Lief, and Craig Yellick

An invaluable guide for all database programmers developing applications for Clipper® 5. Provides a quick introduction to Clipper 5 basics and discusses common programming needs such as designing data files, user interfaces, reports, and more. Advanced topics include networking, debugging, and pop-up programming. Code examples are used throughout the text, providing useful functions that can be applied immediately. All source code is available on disk in MS/PC-DOS format. 1300 pp. approx.

Book & Disk (MS-DOS)	Item #242-X	$44.95
Book only	Item #240-3	$34.95

DOS 5 User's Guide
A Comprehensive Guide for Every PC User
by Dan Gookin

Take control of the MS-DOS® operating system with this complete guide to using the world's most popular operating system. *DOS 5 User's Guide* contains clear, concise explanations of every feature, function, and command of DOS 5.0. Novice PC users will gain a quick start on using DOS, while advanced users will learn savvy tricks and techniques to maneuver their way quickly and easily through the system. Practical discussions and helpful examples teach readers how to edit text files, use directories, create batch files, and much more. Advanced topics include using EDLIN, the DOS text editor; configuring the system; and using the DOS shell. 771 pp.

Book only	Item #188-1	$24.95

ORDER FORM

To Order:

Return this form with your payment to M&T books, 501 Galveston Drive, Redwood City, CA 94063 or **call toll-free 1-800-533-4372 (in California, call 1-800-356-2002).**

ITEM #	DESCRIPTION	DISK	PRICE

Subtotal

CA residents add sales tax ____%

Add $3.75 per item for shipping and handling

TOTAL

NOTE: **FREE SHIPPING** ON ORDERS OF THREE OR MORE BOOKS.

Charge my:
- ❏ **Visa**
- ❏ **MasterCard**
- ❏ **AmExpress**

- ❏ **Check enclosed, payable to M&T Books.**

CARD NO. _____

SIGNATURE _____ EXP. DATE _____

NAME _____

ADDRESS _____

CITY _____

STATE _____ ZIP _____

M&T GUARANTEE: If your are not satisfied with your order for any reason, return it to us within 25 days of receipt for a full refund. Note: Refunds on disks apply only when returned with book within guarantee period. Disks damaged in transit or defective will be promptly replaced, but cannot be exchanged for a disk from a different title.

8027

1-800-533-4372 (in CA 1-800-356-2002)

Order Your
LAN
TROUBLESHOOTING
HANDBOOK
Disk Today!

Collected are a number of practical programs for troubleshooting and monitoring data communications systems. Use this disk to diagnose PC and local area network faults! Included are files that allow the user to change the baud rate of a program, display the RS-232 signals of the COM1 or COM2 ports, provide CPU information, turn a PC into a data scope or data line monitor, conduct a LAN read/write performance test, perform CPU speed and relative performance tests, and much more!

To order, return this postage-paid card with your payment to: **M&T Books**, 501 Galveston Drive, Redwood City, CA 94063. Or, call TOLL-FREE 1-800-533-4372 (In CA 1-800-356-2002). Ask for Item #055-9.

YES! Send me the *LAN Troubleshooting Handbook* programs disk for $20 _____

CA residents add applicable sales tax _____ % _____

TOTAL _____

_____ Check enclosed. Make payable to **M&T Books**.

Charge my: _____ VISA   _____ MasterCard   _____ American Express

Card # _____ Exp. date _____

Signature_____

Name_____

Address_____

City _____ State _____ Zip_____

7054

TransCanada PipeLines

Library